The New Bloom

A review of the first edition:

'This will become the standard work of its kind ... Harry Blamires has written a straightforward, unpretentious 263-page paraphrase, labour of love. Severely restricting flights of interpretation to useful cross-references, he stays close to the text at all times.'

Guardian

Since 1966 readers new to James Joyce have depended upon this essential guide to *Ulysses*. Harry Blamires helps readers to negotiate their way through this formidable, remarkable novel and gain an understanding of it which, without help, it might have taken several readings to achieve.

The New Bloomsday Book is a crystal clear, page-by-page, line-by-line running commentary on the plot of *Ulysses* which illuminates symbolic themes and structures along the way. It is a highly accessible, indispensable guide for anyone reading Joyce's masterpiece for the first time.

To ensure that Blamires's classic work will remain useful to new readers, this third edition contains the page numbering and references to three commonly read editions of *Ulysses*: the Oxford University Press 'World Classics' (1993), the Penguin 'Twentieth-Century Classics' (1992), and the Gabler 'Corrected Text' (1986) editions.

The New Bloomsday Book

A guide through *Ulysses*

Third Edition

Harry Blamires

London and New York

First published 1966 by Methuen & Co Ltd

Second edition first published 1988,
this edition first published 1996
by Routledge
11 New Fetter Lane, London EC4P 4EE

Simultaneously published in the USA and Canada
by Routledge
29 West 35th Street, New York, NY 10001

Reprinted in 1998, 1999

Routledge is an imprint of the Taylor & Francis Group

© 1966, 1988, 1996 Harry Blamires

Typeset in Palatino by Florencetype Ltd,
Stoodleigh, Devon

Printed and bound in Great Britain by
Clays Ltd, St Ives PLC

British Library Cataloguing in Publication Data
A catalogue record for this book is available from the
British Library

Library of Congress Cataloging in Publication Data
Blamires, Harry.
      The new Bloomsday book: a guide through
   Ulysses/Harry Blamires. – 3rd ed.
         p.   cm.
   Includes bibliographical references (p.).
      1. Joyce, James, 1982–1941. Ulysses. I. Title.
PR6019.09U626   1996
823'.912–dc20   95-44440
                                                              CIP

ISBN 0–415–13857–4 (hbk)
ISBN 0–415–13858–2 (pbk)

Contents

References

Numbers cited in the margins and the body of this book refer to current editions of *Ulysses*. Figures in normal type give page numbers in the US Gabler edition of the Corrected Text (1986), italicized figures give page numbers in the current Penguin Twentieth-Century Classics edition of 1992. In order to help readers who are using the Oxford University Press World Classics edition of 1993, a bracketed number in the margin indicates the page reached in that edition. For further help in use of the Oxford edition the Conversion Table relates its paging to that of the Gabler edition.

Conversion table

Gabler		Oxford		Gabler	Oxford		Gabler	Oxford
1	1	3–4		145	168–9		305	355–6
	5	5–6		150	174–5		310	361–2
	10	11–12	**9**	151	176–7	**14**	314	366–7
	15	17–18		155	181		320	373–4
2	20	24–5		160	186–7		325	378–9
	25	30–1		165	192–3		330	384–5
	30	36		170	198–9		335	390–1
3	31	37–8		175	204–5		340	396–7
	35	41–2	**10**	180	210–11		345	401–2
	40	47–8		185	215–16	**15**	350	408–9
4	45	53–4		190	221–2		355	413–14
	50	59		195	227–8		360	419–20
	55	65		200	233–4		365	424–5
5	58	68		205	239–40		370	430–1
	60	70–1	**11**	210	245–6		375	435–6
	65	76–7		215	250–1		380	441–2
	70	82–3		220	256–7		385	446–7
6	72	84–5		225	262–3		390	451–2
	75	87–8		230	268–9		395	457–8
	80	93–4		235	274–5		400	462–3
	85	99–100	**12**	240	280–1		405	468–9
	90	105–6		245	285–6		410	473–4
	95	111		250	291–2		415	478–9
7	96	112–13		255	297–8		420	484–5
	100	116–17		260	303–4		425	489–90
	105	122–3		265	309–10		430	495–6
	110	128–9		270	315–16		435	500
	115	134–5		275	321–2		440	505–6
	120	140–1		280	327		445	510–11
8	124	144–5	**13**	284	331–2		450	515–16
	130	151–2		290	338–9		455	520–1
	135	157		295	343–4		460	525–6
	140	162–3		300	349–50		465	530–1

	Gabler	Oxford		Gabler	Oxford		Gabler	Oxford
	470	536		530	603–4		590	670–1
	475	541–2		535	608–9		595	676
	480	546–7		540	614–15		600	681–2
	485	551–2	**17**	544	619		605	687
	490	557		550	625–6	**18**	608	690–1
	495	562–3		555	631–2		610	692–3
16	501	569–70		560	636–7		615	698–9
	505	573–4		565	642–3		620	704–5
	510	579–80		570	647–8		625	710–11
	515	585–6		575	653–4		630	716–17
	520	591–2		580	658–9		635	722–3
	525	597–8		585	664–5		640	727–8

Note: figures in bold refer to episode numbers

Introductory note

This book arises from two convictions: the first, that *Ulysses* is the major imaginative work in English prose of the present century; the second, that it is high time to extend Joyce's readership. The day ought surely to be not far distant when it will be as unthinkable to neglect *Ulysses* in English Literature courses as it would be to neglect *The Waste Land*. At present many readers are still put off Joyce by the difficulty, or supposed difficulty, of his work. The young student especially, pressed by his teachers to read so much, is tempted to push *Ulysses* aside simply because its reading will demand what seems a disproportionate amount of time. I have therefore tried to provide the kind of guide which will help the new reader to find his way more quickly about Joyce's formidable book. I should like to think that, used alongside the text, *The Bloomsday Book* will enable the reader to get from his first reading of *Ulysses* an understanding which, without my guide, it might have taken him several readings to arrive at.

It is not, of course, possible to work on *Ulysses* for any length of time without making discoveries which, one believes, have something new to add to the literature of Joycean criticism and interpretation. Had I concentrated in my book on such discoveries, developing my own theory of *Ulysses* and pursuing in detail points which exemplify and corroborate it, I might have written a book of some interest to the Joycean specialist but of little interest to others. This was not my aim. It is not my main purpose here to join in the critical conversation carried on among those who already know and love *Ulysses*, valuable as I believe that conversation to be. Rather I wish to interest the student and the general reader whom this specialized critical literature does not touch.

Nevertheless, it would be foolish to pretend that my view of *Ulysses* is exactly the same as the next man's. A reader brings his own interests to a writer as big as Joyce, and Joyce can accommodate them. I myself have been especially interested in the theological patterns of *Ulysses* created by the numerous implicit correspondences and metaphorical overtones, and I have perhaps something new to say in exploring them. But I trust that I have not allowed this interest to become a dominant or disproportionate concern. I would not claim a paramount validity for these theological patterns; only that they exist, alongside other patterns, and demand recognition accordingly.

As I see it, the vital need at present is to stress that *Ulysses* is a great universal masterpiece, not a great freak. Its category is as much the category of *Paradise Lost* (or the *Odyssey*, of course) as that of *Tristram Shandy*. Its apparent eccentricities are superficial by comparison with the depths of its traditionalism. Its experimentation is neither so novel nor so capricious as it seems at first sight. Indeed, the devices of style and technique which startle new readers most, emerge, when studied, as logical extensions of traditional poetic practices as old as *Macbeth* and *Comus* – and older.

I have chosen the method of page-by-page commentary because this seems to me likely to serve best the needs of the student and the general reader whom I have in mind. I deal with matters in the order in which the book itself raises them. Where the text is easy my commentary is naturally brief: where it is difficult my commentary is as full as is compatible with preserving proportion and overall readability. I have purposely allowed my guide to gather depth as it proceeds. That is to say, I have resisted the temptation to pursue straightaway many of the numerous symbolic correspondences which are hinted at in the first three episodes, believing that it is better to allow the reader's interest to be fully engaged before pressing these upon him.

I have followed the now established practice of giving the eighteen episodes of *Ulysses* their Homeric titles. These titles derive from the fact that Joyce based his wanderings of Leopold Bloom in Dublin on 16 June 1904 on the wanderings of Odysseus, but they ought not to deter the reader who is ignorant of Homer. The importance of the Homeric parallel is primarily *structural*: it provided Joyce with a convenient framework, and it provides his critics and readers with a convenient nomenclature.

Finally, it is fair to warn the new reader of Joyce against the mistake which has led even some learned critics astray – that of assuming that a writer cannot be very funny and strangely serious at the same time. What Joyce called the 'jocoserious' is his most characteristic category, a source of simultaneous profundity and fun. Even satire and sympathy can co-exist, as the reader of *A Portrait of the Artist* already knows.

I am grateful to Miss Valerie Dowsett for help in compiling the Index.

1966   H. B.

Preface to the third edition

The main aim of this revision of *The New Bloomsday Book* is to bring its page references into line with current editions of *Ulysses*. At the same time I have taken the opportunity to make some slight alterations and additions here and there.

When my guide was first published thirty years ago (happily on Molly Bloom's birthday) it seemed needful to press upon the reader the stature of Joyce's *Ulysses* as a masterpiece which students of twentieth-century literature could not afford to neglect. What seemed worth saying then is self-evident now. Joyce's book is widely studied in academic courses. Many aids to the understanding of *Ulysses* have consequently become available. Scholars have tracked down allusions, local and historical, literary and musical. One may reasonably ask why my guide has nevertheless kept its usefulness.

The truth is that immediate contact with a vast array of explanatory notes can overwhelm readers who come fresh to Joyce. It is only when they have begun to find their feet in *Ulysses* and to grasp the overall pattern of event and symbol that they can happily relish more detailed exploration of the book's profligate allusiveness. *Ulysses* must not be made to appear more difficult than it is. Joyce's text is a highly organised one, and it only requires a little attention to the network of thematic linkages which undergirds the work to make the new reader feel at home in Joyce's world. That is why I chose the method of page-by-page commentary peppered with cross-reference.

My general emphasis is in line, I hope, with that of Thomas McGreevy, poet and critic, who was close enough to Joyce to be present at his deathbed and to act as his executor.

The splendour of order, to use Saint Thomas's phrase, has not been the dominating characteristic of modern English prose and it is partly because the quality was demonstrated on a vast scale in *Ulysses* that the book marked a literary revolution.

McGreevy went on to stress the epic status of *Ulysses*.

For *Ulysses* is an inferno. As Homer sent his Ulysses wandering through the inferno of Greek mythology and Virgil his Aeneas through one of Roman mythology so Dante himself voyaged through the inferno of the mediaeval Christian imagination and so Mr. Joyce sent his hero through the inferno of modern subjectivity.

McGreevy was writing as one of twelve contributors to a collection of essays on Joyce's Work In Progress (the future *Finnegans Wake*) which Samuel Beckett edited in 1929 under the jocular title, *Our Exagmination Round His Factification for Incamination of Work In Progress*. Joyce personally authenticated this book in a letter to Valery Larbaud: 'What you say about the Exag. is right enough I did stand behind those twelve Marshals more or less directing them what lines of research to follow.'

McGreevy's reference to Dante is noteworthy. Joyce's three-fold design may not closely match Dante's, but the reader of *Ulysses* is spiralled down to the depths of the contemporary inferno in the *Circe* episode and gets many a glimpse of a paradiso in Joyce's favourite episode, *Ithaca*.

The Bloom and Dedalus family trees

THE BLOOMS

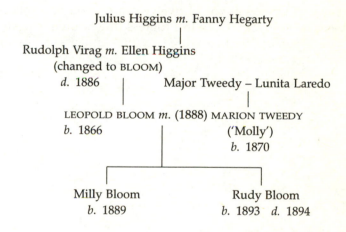

Julius Higgins *m.* Fanny Hegarty

Rudolph Virag *m.* Ellen Higgins
(changed to BLOOM)
d. 1886

Major Tweedy – Lunita Laredo

LEOPOLD BLOOM *m.* (1888) MARION TWEEDY
b. 1866

('Molly')
b. 1870

Milly Bloom
b. 1889

Rudy Bloom
b. 1893   *d.* 1894

THE DEDALUSES

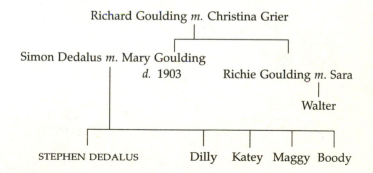

Richard Goulding *m.* Christina Grier

Simon Dedalus *m.* Mary Goulding
d. 1903

Richie Goulding *m.* Sara

Walter

STEPHEN DEDALUS   Dilly   Katey   Maggy   Boody

Part I

Chapter 1

Telemachus

Joyce's symbolism cannot be explained mechanically in terms
of one-for-one parallels, for his correspondences are neither
exclusive nor continuously persistent. Nevertheless certain correspondences recur throughout *Ulysses*, establishing themselves firmly. Thus Leopold Bloom corresponds to Ulysses in the Homeric parallel, and Stephen Dedalus corresponds to Telemachus, Ulysses's son. At the beginning of Homer's *Odyssey* Telemachus finds himself virtually dispossessed by his mother's suitors in his own father's house, and he sets out in search of the lost Ulysses. In Joyce's first episode Stephen Dedalus feels that he is pushed out by his supposed friends from his temporary residence, and leaves it intending not to return. The residence in question is the Martello tower on the beach at Sandycove, for which Stephen pays the rent. Buck Mulligan, a medical student, shares it with him, and they have a resident visitor, Haines, an Englishman from Oxford.

It is morning. The day begins with a parody of the Mass. Buck Mulligan, mimicking a priest approaching the altar, sings the introit and carries his shaving-bowl like the chalice. Stephen watches Mulligan from the staircase as he mockingly blesses his surroundings and offers to an imaginary congregation the 'body and soul and blood and ouns' (wounds) of a female Christ, 'christine', (His 'equine' face and hair like 'pale oak' hint at the treachery of a wooden horse.) The lathered water in the bowl represents the white corpuscles; the three whistles burlesque the sacring bell. Mulligan brings 'Chrysostomos' to Stephen's mind because Mulligan's gold-stopped teeth and his gift of the gab earn him the title which St John Chrysostom's preaching earned him, 'golden-mouthed'. Mulligan's ecclesiastical mummery before

Stephen is a mockery of Stephen's seriousness, his intellectualism,
2   and his former religious fervour.
4   Stephen provides a watchful but weary audience for Mulli-
(4) gan's performance. He complains of the behaviour of their
English guest, Haines, who is subject to hysterical nightmares.
3   Last night Haines raved terrifyingly after dreaming of a black
panther. (Later passages establish the black panther as a symbol
of Bloom, whose Christian name is *Leo*pold. It is a symbol, too,
which carries overtones of divinity. Bloom becomes the lost
'father' whom Stephen discovers.) Mulligan borrows Stephen's
handkerchief, mocks the beauty of the 'snotgreen sea', and
'Algy' Swinburne's description of it as 'the great sweet mother'
5   (in *The Triumph of Time*). The image of the sea as mother introduces a persistent series of linkages between water and
womanhood which relate to an underlying contrast between
barrenness and fertility.
4   Mulligan seriously disapproves of Stephen for having refused
to comfort his mother by praying at her deathbed. (See *A Portrait
of the Artist as a Young Man*.) Because of Stephen's reputation,
Mulligan has been forbidden by his aunt to have contact with
him. Mulligan's rebuke brings back to Stephen the memory of
a dream which he had soon after his mother's death, in which
she appeared to him in her grave clothes. This memory haunts
Stephen intermittently throughout the day and indeed domi-
nates his mind at the moment of crisis in the *Circe* episode,
itself the crisis episode of the book. (See pp. 473–5/681–3.)
At this stage begins the series of hints which establish an
important correspondence between Stephen and Hamlet. As
Hamlet sees his father's ghost on the platform of Elsinore
Castle, so Stephen recalls, here on top of the Martello tower,
the dream of his mother's ghostly reappearance. Mulligan, like
5   Claudius, is a usurper. Mulligan chides Stephen for not casting
his nighted colour off ('He kills his mother but he can't wear
grey trousers'). Claudius-like again, Mulligan fancifully indulges
6   the story that Stephen is mad (has 'general paralysis of the
insane'). He tries to make Stephen see himself as others see
him, holding up a cracked mirror before him; but for Stephen
the mirror is a Shakespearean symbol of art (Drama holds the
'mirror up to nature' in *Hamlet*, and see p. 463/671), and the
6   cracked looking-glass of a servant a symbol of Irish art in
particular. (The metaphor is Oscar Wilde's.) Mulligan talks

of touching Haines for money, then of organizing a ragging of
Haines if he proves troublesome. The memory of how Clive
Kempthorpe was ragged stirs Stephen, who hates violence, to   7
say 'Let him stay'.   7

   Once more Claudius-like, Mulligan tries to probe Stephen's
moodiness, 'What have you against me now?', and Stephen   (8)
refers to an occasion soon after Mrs Dedalus's death when
Mulligan alluded to her callously as 'beastly dead'. Mulligan's   8
response in part parodies Claudius's response to Hamlet. Deaths
occur daily; the only tragic feature in this case was Stephen's
own refusal to humour his mother's dying request. Stephen is
not comforted. He resents Mulligan's insult to himself rather   8
than the insult to his mother. And now, after telling him to stop   9
brooding, Mulligan ironically begins to sing the very song which
Stephen sang for his mother, at her special request, on her
deathbed ('Who goes with Fergus?' by Yeats). This song, too,
recurs to Stephen at later moments of crisis (see pp. 474/681
and 496/702). Here he recalls the deathbed scene, then moments   10
of his mother's life from girlhood, some from her memories   9
handed on to him, others from his own; and these lead to a
fuller and more detailed recall of her ghostly reappearance in
his dream, when the agony of her death and her failure to move
him to pray were re-enacted in grotesque frightfulness (cf. pp.
473–5/681–3). Stephen's rejection of her dying demand that he   11
should go through the motions of Catholic orthodoxy is a focal
act around which cluster his demands for personal freedom.
Indeed, symbolic correspondences give Stephen's act of *disobedience* at his mother's deathbed an archetypal significance. It is
associated with the acts of disobedience by which Lucifer
rebelled against God (p. 42/63: 'Allbright he falls, proud lightning of the intellect . . . etc.'; see also p. 475/682) and by which
Eve rebelled against God (p. 32/46, 'Will you be as gods?').
Thus the Fall of the Angels, by which Satan was cast out from
Heaven, and the Fall of Man, by which Adam and Eve were
cast out of Eden, provide a cosmic background against which
Stephen, exiled from his father's house and from the Martello
tower, seeks independent individual fulfilment as man and as
artist.

   Mulligan calls Stephen down to breakfast and repeats his suggestion that Stephen should touch Haines, who is his admirer,
for money. But this is just the kind of subservience (to English

wealth) which Stephen rejects. Anyway, he reminds Mulligan
(11)   that today is pay-day; whereupon the latter foresees a drink-
10   ing bout at Stephen's expense. Mulligan goes downstairs first,
12   leaving Stephen to meditate on his 'forgotten friendship' and
his forgotten shaving-bowl. Shall he take the bowl down for
him, he wonders, holding it as he used to hold the incense boat
when he acted as server at Mass at Clongowes, thereby once
more, in a different context, assuming the servant's role? ('Server
of a servant' because Catholic Ireland is England's servant and
Mulligan is ultimately the servant of Ireland and convention-
ality.)

13   In the living-room below Mulligan, Haines, and Stephen settle
11   down to breakfast, cooked and served largely, it would seem,
by Mulligan, who continues his ritualistic mummery in the process. The comic story of Mother Grogan establishes a connexion
between making tea and making water, which continues through
the book. The two represent creativity and fertility. The young
14   men carry on a burlesque literary conversation, mockingly
treating Mother Grogan and her story as fit subjects for scholarly research.

15   The milkwoman arrives. Stephen sees her as a symbol of poor,
12   sterile, subjected Ireland, around whom cluster the romantic
phrases of the Celtic revivalists, but whose favour he scorns to
(14)   beg. (She is transfigured into Old Gummy Granny among the
nightmare caricatures of the *Circe* episode, p. 490/696). A true
16   representative of her country, Stephen notes that she has more
respect for Mulligan, the loud-voiced medicine-man, than for
himself, the artist. When Haines tries out his Gaelic on her,
13   she doesn't understand. We may take this as Joyce's comment
on Celtic revivalism.

17   Buck Mulligan pays two shillings to reduce the outstanding
18   milk debt to twopence. Haines speaks of visiting the national
library today. Mulligan proposes a swim first, then teases
Stephen about his reluctance to wash. (Stephen's reluctance to
wash or to bathe is symbolically associated with his rejection
of his own baptism, his failure to commit himself to womanhood, and to engage himself fruitfully in artistic creation. He
has rebelled against his own mother, his mother the Church,
14   his mother country.) When Haines speaks in admiration of
Stephen's sayings and theories, Stephen moodily fobs him off
19   with evasions that smack of Hamlet. This annoys Mulligan,

who claims to have been boosting Stephen to Haines in the hope of touching Haines for money. But Stephen, the artist, refuses to look for support either 'from her or from him', from the milkwoman or from Haines, from poor old Ireland or from wealthy England.

Stephen, Mulligan, and Haines leave the tower, Stephen putting the large key in his pocket. When Haines presses Stephen for his theory of *Hamlet*, whose originality and ingenuity Mulligan has already advertised, Mulligan cries out in mock protest against the thought of tackling so vast a subject without first imbibing the necessary quantity of beer. Mulligan's mockery of Stephen's theory ('He proves by algebra that Hamlet's grandson is Shakespeare's grandfather . . . ') helps to establish what becomes a dominant theme in the book – the exploration of the nature of fatherhood and creativity, human and divine. Haines explicitly compares the tower and cliffs with those of Elsinore. Then, mentioning a theological interpretation of *Hamlet* in terms of the Father–Son relationship, he, too, touches on the theme to be pursued throughout *Ulysses*. Although Mulligan steamrollers this threat of seriousness with his blasphemous comic ballad of Joking Jesus, nevertheless this ballad also explores, in parody, the subject of Christ's paternity and divinity.

Haines attempts to start with Stephen a conventional twentieth-century argument about religious belief, and Stephen, indulging his intellectual superiority, plays with him mentally like a cat with a mouse (or like a Hamlet with a Polonius), meantime brooding on Mulligan's usurpation of the tower and the growing demands of Mulligan's possessiveness. Stephen notes and later recalls (p. 153/238) the green stone twinkling in Haines's silver cigarette case. It suggests an emerald Ireland that is England's pretty ornament, but he accepts a cigarette and, aware that Haines after all means well and kindly by him, he speaks his views more simply and plainly. As an Irishman he is the servant of two masters, the British State and the Roman Church, and of a third, poor old Ireland. Haines tries to be tolerant and sympathetic, and voices the bad conscience of the twentieth-century Englishman. 'It seems history is to blame.'

Images expressing the power and dignity of Roman orthodoxy through the ages occupy Stephen's mind. In particular he sees the apostolic hand putting to flight the great heretics. The

15
20

(18)
21

16
22

23

17

24

25   heretics mentioned – Photius, Arius, and Sabellius – all chal-
18   lenged orthodox teaching on the subject of the consubstantiality
of Father and Son. Each of them brought into question the status
of the Son and his relationship to the Father. (See p. 162/253
for Photius again; p. 171/267 for Sabellius again.) The full significance of this theme in *Ulysses* will emerge gradually. It is
deeply explored in episode 9. At this point the correspondence
between Mulligan and Photius is notable because Photius was
appointed to the Patriarchate of Constantinople when Ignatius
was deposed in 858. This appointment defied papal authority.
Photius was therefore a usurper.

(21)   Stephen and Haines, making their way to the beach, pass two
men on the cliff. One of them, a boatman, speaks of a drowned
man whose body, it is hoped, will be washed up by today's
tide. The image of the drowned man will recur: so, too, the
theme of the body recovered. Down on the beach Stephen and
26   Haines find Mulligan preparing for his bathe. A young man,
already in the water, refers to a friend Bannon who is at
Westmeath and who has found a 'sweet young thing' whom he
calls his 'Photo girl'. This girl turns out to be Milly Bloom,
daughter of Leopold. (See Milly's letter to her father, p. 54/
79–80). An elderly priest finishes his bathe and scrambles out
of the water near by. The young man and Buck Mulligan discuss
one Seymour who has abandoned medicine for the army.

27   Mulligan completes his undressing, gets the tower key from
19   Stephen, borrows twopence in addition, then plunges into the
sea. Haines sits on a stone smoking. Having agreed to meet
Mulligan at The Ship, an inn, at 12.30, Stephen walks away up
the path, the *Liliata rutilantium*, which was recited at his mother's
deathbed (p. 9/11), running through his mind. He glimpses the
28   priest getting dressed after his bathe. His last thoughts are that
he can return tonight neither to the tower nor to his own home.
Mulligan, calling to him from the sea, is the usurper.

'Usurper' is a strong word, and the link it later establishes
between Mulligan and the book's other betrayer, Boylan, eventually adds to its force. Stephen's coming deep rejection of
Mulligan will make sense only if Mulligan's function in this
first episode is fully grasped, and the reader has to be patient
in this respect. Nevertheless, even at this stage, looking back,
we may note that Mulligan's role carries faint diabolical overtones. In his mock mass (his dressing-gown 'sustained gently

behind him in the mild morning air' – like a tail, p. 3/1) he
offers up Irish art (the cracked looking-glass) and Stephen's
intellect (the razor, associated with 'Kinch, the knifeblade',
p. 4/3) at the server of a servant's altar of convention and
compromise. It is as the tempter that he calls Stephen to the
top of the tower, blesses the 'surrounding land and the awaking
mountains', draws Stephen's attention to the world around him
('Look at the sea. What does it care about offences?' p. 8/9),
tries to press Stephen to join him in an attempt to 'Hellenize'
the island (p. 6/6), blames him for not falling down in worship
at his mother's deathbed (p. 5/4), and urges him to exploit his
talents to get money from Haines, the Englishman. The Joycean
can scarcely ignore the hinted scriptural parallels with the temptation of Christ. Stephen resists and, in leaving the tower, takes
up the ashplant (p. 15/20) which later emerges, fitfully, as
symbolic of the Cross (p. 572/*818*).   (23)

Chapter 2

Nestor

20 In Homer Telemachus first seeks news of his lost father from Nestor and hears the story of the siege of Troy. Stephen Dedalus's morning encounter with his headmaster and employer, Mr Deasy, reflects Telemachus's visit to Nestor. There are many references in these first three episodes to the history of the Church, to the history of Europe and of Ireland (in this episode notably), and to the nature and origin of man (episode 3). In the microcosmic patterning by which Joyce shapes his material the first three episodes are the acorn to the oak of the other fifteen.

(24) Stephen is giving a history lesson on Pyrrhus, another hero who suffered from usurpation. In episode 7 Professor MacHugh draws a parallel between the cause of Pyrrhus and the Greeks and that of the Irish nationalists. ('Pyrrhus, misled by an oracle, made a last attempt to retrieve the fortunes of Greece. Loyal to a lost cause', p. 110/*169*.) Pyrrhus is one of a series of heroes referred to in *Ulysses* who were frustrated in trying to lead a chosen people out of bondage. Moses and Parnell are among the others. In Stephen's mind, as he questions his class, are phrases from Blake and elsewhere which speak of the unreality of the past and of the violent destruction to which the temporal process moves. The lesson turns at this point on Pyrrhus's frus-
29 tration, seriously in Stephen's picture of Pyrrhus all but broken
21 by his own victory, comically in his description of a pier as a 'disappointed bridge'. Stephen mocks himself in the thought that this witticism shall be trotted out again for Haines's satisfaction later in the day. In this respect he is an Irish 'jester' at the court of his English 'master'. The disappointed bridge is of course an apt symbol of Stephen's failure to make his escape

from Ireland. It also concretizes the notion of the what-might-   *30*
have-been, the possibilities ousted by time in the progress of
history.

Stephen turns from history to poetry. Talbot begins to read
Milton's *Lycidas*. Stephen is still thinking of the progress of   (26)
history from possibility to actuality, and his mind moves to the
library in Paris where he studied Aristotle on this subject.
(The brief sojourn in Paris was his own attempt to convert the
possibility of escape into an actuality.) The Aristotelian concepts,
'thought of thought' and 'form of forms', seem to promise a   *31*
state of possible intellectual tranquillity and lucidity such as
Joyce attempts to actualize in episode 17. Meantime Talbot is
reading, 'Through the dear might of Him that walked the
waves', and Stephen senses the shadow of Christ on the lives   22
of believers and unbelievers, and the challenge of divided loyal-
ties, to Caesar and to God, which has its special significance
for the Irish. (The image of repeated weaving 'on the church's
looms' associates the church with Penelope.)

It is ten o'clock and time for hockey. Books are put away.
Stephen winds up with a riddle whose answer comes in the   *32*
picture of a fox burying his grandmother under a hollybush.
Later references link Stephen, the hunted artist, with the fox
(p. 159/247). He is fox in cunning subterfuge too, and he has
buried his mother, if not his grandmother. The boy Sargent
shows Stephen his corrected sums. Stephen notes his unkempt   23
unattractiveness, but he is gentle with him, thinking how the   *33*
boy's mother must have loved him despite his ugliness. He
wonders whether perhaps mother love is the only sure reality in
life. (Columbanus was a sixth-century Irish saint who vigorously
pressed the usages of the Celtic Church in Europe. Thus, like
Pyrrhus, he fought for the smaller nation's superior culture. Like
Stephen and Joyce he left Ireland to help civilize the Continent.)
The memory of his own dead mother recurs, the 'poor soul gone
to heaven', and the image of the fox who buried her.

Working out Sargent's sums, Stephen remembers Mulligan's
jibe that he proves his elaborate theory of *Hamlet* quite simply
by algebra, but the sounds of coming hockey from the rooms
and field outside recall him. Sargent completes his task. Stephen,   24
watching him, sees his own past boyhood in his gracelessness.   *34*
But this link between the two of them is superficial compared
to the tyrannical, isolating force of their deep individual

secrecies. Stephen sends him to join the others. He follows him
(29) into the porch where he watches Mr Deasy go out to settle an
 35 altercation among the boys on the field. Then he goes to await
Mr Deasy in his study. There, looking at the room's for ever
unchanging contents, he recalls the occasion of his first visit to
it for interview. He observes appropriate symbols of the
Establishment, civil and ecclesiastical, Mr Deasy so convincingly
represents – the collection of Stuart coins ('base treasure' of
England won from the Irish bog) and the twelve Apostolic
spoons snugly encased in purple plush.

25   Mr Deasy comes in. He pays Stephen his wages, £3 12s., and
 36 gives him good advice about the care of money and the need
to save, quoting Shakespeare's 'Put money in thy purse'.
 37 But Stephen recognizes this as Iago's maxim, not Shakespeare's
– in short, the tempter's maxim. Deasy attributes the success
and power of the English to their prudence with money, their
pride in not getting into debt. Challenged about his own financial position, Stephen remembers ruefully the tale of his own
 26 debts, and his wages begin to look small. Staring at the portrait
 38 of Edward VII over the mantelpiece, Mr Deasy indulges the
tolerant political platitudes of the Unionist. Then he asks
 39 Stephen to take a letter to the Press for publication, relying
on Stephen's acquaintance with Dublin's literary circles. As he
finishes typing it, Stephen studies the pictures of horses round
the walls, recalling Cranly's vain attempts to interest him in
 27 racing and betting. That Stephen stands outside the world of
horse-racing and gambling is notable, for today's Ascot Gold
Cup race later becomes a dominant theme, symbolizing the
masculine pursuit of women and success.

 40   Hockey shouts are heard from the field outside. To Stephen
here is another symbol of life's struggle – the boys' games, his
own remembered school games, the joustings and battles of the
history books. Mr Deasy gives him the letter. It is compounded
of clichés. Stephen runs over them. The stereotyped phrases
develop a case for treatment of the foot-and-mouth disease on
lines followed in Austria.* Deasy insists that it is difficult to get

---

* We later discover that some of these phrases have a bearing on the sexual
relationship between Bloom and Molly. For 'Grain supplies through the narrow
waters of the channel' see p. 144/224, and for 'laissez faire' and the 'imperturbability of the ministry of agriculture' see p. 334/536. The 'foot and mouth
disease' is manifested in the way the Blooms sleep together (p. 606/870).

his view across because of the corruption and intrigue among   *41*
the powers-that-be. It emerges that he (like Haines) puts the   *28*
blame on the Jews. (The anti-semitism helps to give Bloom,
when he appears, the status of an outsider.) Stephen suggests
that merchants, Jew or Gentile, are alike, but Deasy sees the
Jews as sinners against the light, men with darkness in their
eyes and doomed to be wanderers. The image of the dark-eyed
wanderer clearly foreshadows Bloom.

Stephen remembers Jewish merchants on the steps of the Paris   *(34)*
Stock Exchange, then reflects that time scatters all wealth. He   *42*
rejects the tyranny of the past by which men like Deasy appor-
tion blame to Jews. 'History is a nightmare from which I am
trying to escape.' But for Mr Deasy history is a movement
towards the manifestation of God. Stephen, hearing cries from
the boys outside, cryptically identifies God as 'a shout in the
street'. Mr Deasy has nothing to say to this, but moralizes on   *29*
the temptresses of history who have brought great men low –   *43*
Adam, Paris, O'Rourke*, Parnell. He cannot stir Stephen to
political argument even by mention of Parnell. Stephen brings
the conversation back to the letter, which he promises to try to
get into the Press. Then Stephen leaves. Bearer of Mr Deasy's   *44*
letter urging stronger action against the foot-and-mouth disease,
he sees that Mulligan will now be able to mock him as the
'bullockbefriending bard'. Mr Deasy chases after him to deliver   *30*
a final vulgar sally against the Jews. Ireland has a clean sheet
in the matter of persecuting them because, wisely, 'she never
let them in'.   *45*

* Deasy gets his Irish history wrong. Devorgilla was the unfaithful wife of
O'Rourke of Breffni. Her lover, Macmurrough, King of Leinster, drew her from
home when her husband was on a pilgrimage. When O'Rourke sought
vengeance, Macmurrough got English support from Henry II.

Chapter 3

Proteus

31 When Homer's Telemachus visits Menelaus, he learns how Menelaus dealt with Proteus, the slippery god of the sea, whose constantly changing shape enabled him generally to elude all attempts to hold and question him. Menelaus did manage to fix him, and thereby obtained some information about Ulysses's wanderings.

(37)   Stephen Dedalus's struggle is with a Proteus of the intellect. Appropriately he is walking on the mud-flats of Sandymount strand, some nine miles from Dalkey and Mr Deasy's school. His mind is tussling with the problem of the changing face of the world in relation to the reality behind it. The revelation of that reality reaches us under the changing, limited modes of the visible and the audible, within the dimensions of the spatial and the temporal, the one-thing-next-another ('*nebeneinander*') and the one-thing-after-another ('*nacheinander*'). Stephen's starting-point is that things are presented to us under the shifting mode of their visibility. It is the *signatures* of things, rather than their reality, which our minds receive through eyesight. Aristotle, whom Dante calls the Master of those who know ('*maestro di color che sanno*'), put recognition of objects as bodies prior to awareness of colour. Stephen closes his eyes to study what experience is like when the mode of visibility is excluded; then, in the darkness, notes how the mode of audibility asserts itself in the tapping of his stick and of his feet, the crackling and crushing of shells and pebbles and sand beneath them. In these sounds rhythm emerges and pattern is born.

46   Opening his eyes, he sees two midwives coming down the steps from Leahy's Terrace. One of them, Florence, widow of

Patrick MacCabe, carries a bag. Stephen pictures its contents – 32
'a misbirth with a trailing navel-cord, hushed in ruddy wool'.
Hence he reflects on the network of navel-cords linking all
humanity together, back to Eve. (So monks show themselves
bound together in linked membership of the mystical Body   (38)
by their girdles.) The network is like a telephone system linking all men to the central exchange, the navel-less belly of
Eve. Stephen fancifully asks to be put through to Eve, ringing
Edenville 'Aleph, alpha; nought, nought, one'. Stephen's thinking moves from Eve's womb to his own mother's womb and
to the coupling of which he was conceived. 'Made not begotten,'
he thinks, because he lacks the sense of his father's fatherhood
except as a meaningless physical coincidence ('the man with
my voice and my eyes'), and because his mother has now
become a 'ghost-woman' inhabiting his dreams. Thus Stephen
feels his being to have a validity independent of his parents'
personalities. Human parents couple together, but the son's exis-   47
tence is willed externally by the divine Father. Thus sonship is
unheld by a *lex eterna* (an eternal law) transcending human
parenthood. Is that what the orthodox doctrine of the consubstantiality of Father and Son means? Where now is Arius the
heretic to thrash out this argument with?

Stephen remembers his two commitments – to convey Deasy's
letter and to be at The Ship at 12.30. Shall he visit his
Aunt Sara? He hears his father's voice, mockingly commenting
at home on such a visit. (It remains hypothetical.) Simon
Dedalus pours scorn on the family he has married into, and
even mimics cousin Walter Goulding's stammer. (Richie Goulding is the brother of Stephen's mother. Aunt Sara is Richie's
wife. Walter is their son.) Stephen pictures himself being
received at the Goulding cottage, let in by cousin Walter and
welcomed by Uncle Richie. Richie, the broken-down solicitor,   48
lies in bed, orders drinks, sings and praises Ferrando's aria from   33
the first act of Verdi's *Il Trovatore*. The strange family history
recounted in this aria introduces again a mysterious father–son
relationship. Hence the theme, 'Houses of decay'. Stephen recalls   49
pretending at Clongowes school that he had respectable rela-
tives. 'Beauty is not there.' Stephen cannot find what he is
seeking in the company of his own family.

Nor could he find it in intellectual study, as he discovered   (40)
when he forsook the family circle for Marsh's library, where he

read the prophetic books of 'Abbas' Joachim of Fiore. (Joachim, c. 1132–1202, interpreted the whole of history in accordance with the Trinitarian formula. The Age of the Father, BC, and the Age of the Son, AD to 1260, would be succeeded by an Age of the Spirit.) Marsh's library stands in the very cathedral close where Dean Swift lived. Stephen recalls how Swift took refuge in madness, running like a houyhnhnm from the human rabble. Stephen sees himself disillusioned by Mulligan as Swift was by Temple. Then he mocks his own dramatized rebelliousness with 'Come off your perch, bald one, before you get too bald' ('*Descende, calve* . . .') – a suitable rebuke to a tonsured priest too priestly in his rejection of the world. The quotation is from Joachim (see p. 199/312).

Thus, recalling the head of the priest he saw bathing (p. 18/ 26), Stephen pictures himself as the priest he is not to be, amid the endless ritual of the mass – priests here, there, everywhere; elevating the Host, reserving the Host, communicating; up and 34   down, on and off their knees to the tinkle of sanctuary bells. ('Cousin Stephen, you will never be a saint' echoes the remark Johnson attributed to Dryden, 'Cousin Swift, you will never be a poet.') Stephen recalls his early piety, also his early sexuality which clashed with it; then his early ambitions to be a 50   dedicated artist, leaving behind him a series of books, beautiful, profound, mysterious, which scholars in ages to come would treasure and ponder.

He walks on and then stops, realizing that he has gone too 51   far to call on Aunt Sara. He turns and walks towards the Pigeon House. In Léo Taxil's 'La Vie de Jésus' the Virgin Mary attributes her pregnancy to 'le pigeon'. (Mulligan's Joking Jesus said 'my father's a bird'.) The French joke recalls Patrice Egan (the son of Kevin Egan, the Irish nationalist exiled in Paris) and his 35   bright, left-wing, atheistical chatter. (Stephen and he met in the bar MacMahon.) Then Stephen reflects mockingly on his own (42)   assumption of the student role in Paris. From that to the memory of how he arrived in Paris, short of money and just too late to cash a postal order at the post office. He went out in the spirit 52   of an Irish missionary to Europe, a missionary for culture, as did St Columbanus in the sixth century, only to be recalled by a wire bringing news of his mother's end. Amid the jumble of 36   Paris memories that follow, the picture of Kevin Egan stands 53   out, Irish conspirator, sitting in the corner of a Paris café, trying

to enlist Stephen's interest in the cause, and telling him tales of Irish revolutionaries, their plots, disguises, escapes. Now Egan moves between the Paris taverns, sought only by Stephen to whom he gives a message for his son Patrice, but otherwise forgotten.   54
37

Stephen has now come near the sea. He turns to look south in the direction of the Martello tower. It has been usurped by the 'panthersahib' (Haines) and the 'pointer' (Mulligan). He will not return. Like Hamlet he is shut out.   55
(44)

He sits down on a rock, and stares at the carcass of a dog and at the gunwale of a boat sunk in the sand. A living, barking dog approaches, frightens him momentarily, then runs away. He pictures long-past events on the beach – the coming of invaders to possess the land, of whales to be hacked and eaten by his remote ancestors. He examines himself on his own self-exile from the tower. What is he pining for? The theme of Pretenders is explored, men claiming thrones denied to them. He recognizes that Buck Mulligan has courage. Mulligan saved a man from drowning, while Stephen himself is afraid of a yelping cur. The guilt of hypothetical cowardice before the image of the drowning man merges into the guilt of his failure to 'save' his mother, lost in the waters of bitter death.   56
38
57

He is distracted by two cockle-pickers with their dog, and when the dog begins to scrape up the sand, the thought of the fox burying his grandmother recurs. Then the dog, panther-like, reminds him of Haines's dream, and hence of his own dream last night from which Haines's cries awoke him. The images of this dream are a forecast of Stephen's crucial meeting with Bloom today and of Bloom's hospitable reception of him at Eccles Street. In the street of harlots an oriental figure receives him smilingly, offers him melon-fruit, and leads him home over a red carpet to 'You will see who'. The cockle-pickers are now seen to be gipsies, and the woman reminds Stephen of a shawled gipsy girl he saw in the arms of a man one night in Fumbally's Lane (p. 119/183). The couple are presented to the reader in gipsy lingo and Stephen quotes a verse in the same style. They pass him, glancing at his Hamlet hat. (The mixture of languages here reflects the gipsies' wandering and lack of nationality. It adds to the general exploration of flux and change amid which it is difficult to fix pattern and meaning.) His thoughts on the tide and the moon breed some rhythmic   39
58
59
40
60

imaginative phrases ('He comes, pale vampire ...') which seem to Stephen too good to lose. He wants to fix them, get them down, though they are as elusive as Proteus ('Put a pin in that chap, will you?'). He searches his pockets for writing paper while mouthing possible phrases for the poem. He bends over the rock and writes on a piece of paper torn from the end of Deasy's letter.

(48)   Still savouring and rejecting phrases ('Why not endless till the farthest star?'), he suddenly sees himself casting a black shadow and wonders whether anyone is observing it. Next moment he sees his words correspondingly as dark signs on a white field and wonders whether anyone will ever read them.

61   Thus thought moves to Bishop Berkeley's philosophical Idealism, which locates the sense-qualities of things in the human mind, and Stephen experiments, staring fixedly at the scene before him, to decide whether distance is an objectively observed dimension or something imposed on flatness by the observer's mind. Similarly, he suggests that the apparent darkness of the poet's words may be in truth a darkness in the souls of his readers. Our souls, burdened with sin, cling to us as a woman clings to her lover. The image of the ideal beloved emerges, but she is quickly embodied in the real woman, a girl seen in the street on Monday, a girl with stays, suspenders, and darned stockings. (There is much yet to come in *Ulysses* on the relationship between the Ideal and the Real.)

41
62   Stephen lies back, 'hat tilted down on his eyes', looking at the sun. He stares at the shoes he is wearing, Buck Mulligan's cast-offs, hating the feet they have previously shod. But he was delighted when a girl's shoe, tried on in Paris, fitted his small foot.

He relieves himself and the water flows around him. In making water, which runs into the sea, Stephen is involved in the natural flow of life and fertility. The act adds rich overtones to his preceding act of poetic creativity by which a pattern of words pinned down meaning derived from the Protean flux and change of nature. Thus the creative moment may be regarded as the climax of the first three episodes. We have been concerned with the day's beginning, history's beginning, the origin of man, of being itself. We are ready now for the beginning of the book.

63   Meanwhile the tide comes in, and Stephen remembers the drowned man again, sunk like the Edward King of *Lycidas*

beneath the watery floor, and like him due to be raised, though
not by 'the dear might of him that walked the waves', rather
by the tide at one o'clock (p. 18/25). (A more significant raising
up than this is of Stephen himself by the dear might of Leopold
Bloom, in episode 15.) He pictures the corpse's rising and the
business of hooking it in. He muses on the corpse, Hamlet-like   42
on the process by which drowned man feeds the fish and moves
through barnacle and goose to featherbed. Thought moves from
sea death as a mild, inviting death, to Christ, who died thirsting.   (50)

It clouds over, and the thought of possible storm and lightning to come leads to that of Lucifer and the 'lightning of his
intellect'. The Luciferean role of the rebellious artist is a dominant image in the *Portrait of the Artist* and casts its shadow over
Ulysses (see p. 475/682). Quickly we are back again with death
by drowning in the echoing of Ophelia's lines ('my cockle hat
and shoon').

Logical consequentiality disintegrates, and thoughts shift
rapidly – the day, the coming midsummer's day, Tennyson's
Queen of the May, Drumont's description of Queen Victoria
(p. 36/53), 'old hag with the yellow teeth' (as quoted by Egan),   64
and the state of his own teeth.

He seeks in vain the handkerchief Buck Mulligan borrowed.
He picks his nose, and lays the results on a rock. He turns in
response to a prophetic intuition ('Behind. Perhaps there is
someone') which clearly foreshadows a silent encounter with
Bloom later in the morning (p. 178/279, 'About to pass through
the doorway, feeling one behind, he stood aside').What he sees
therefore has a heavy symbolic value. It is a three-master at sea,
its masts, like three crosses on the horizon, forecasting crucifixion.

Part II

Chapter 4

Calypso

In Homer the goddess Calypso holds Odysseus in amorous 45
captivity for seven years until she is ordered by the gods to 65
release him. Here Leopold Bloom takes his morning departure
from the wife to whom he is likewise bound in amorous
captivity.

Leopold Bloom is in the kitchen of his home, 7 Eccles Street, (53)
preparing his wife's breakfast on a tray. (She is still in bed.) It
is eight o'clock, The cat cries 'Mkgnao' and Mr Bloom studies
her, then bends down to pet her. He gives her some milk and 66
as he watches her lapping it up his own appetite is whetted. 46
What shall he have for breakfast? He decides on a pork kidney
from Dlugacz's, the butcher's. He steals upstairs, halts outside 67
the bedroom door, quietly tells his wife that he is going out for
a few minutes and asks whether she wants anything special for
breakfast. He is answered by a sleepy, soft grunt, 'Mn'. Marion
Bloom (known as 'Molly') turns over on the bed and Bloom
hears the brass quoits of the bedstead jingle. (The jingling will
remain hereafter, in Bloom's mind and in the reader's, linked
with Molly's varied bed-life.) Bloom thinks he must get the bed
attended to. Like Molly herself, it has come all the way from
Gibraltar, bought, he believes, at a sale of the Governor's furniture by Major Tweedy, Molly's father. (He is wrong about this.
Molly has deceived him, p. 635/918). The major's clipped military talk echoes in Bloom's mind – 'Yes, sir. At Plevna that was.
I rose from the ranks . . . .' The major was apparently a shrewd
businessman too. He made a corner in stamps.

Bloom takes his hat and looks inside it to check that his
secret white slip of paper is safely there, tucked in the leather
headband. (He is going to need it later this morning. It bears

his false name, 'Henry Flower'.) He feels in his pocket too. The potato he always carries as a talisman is safe, but his latch-key is missing – left in another pair of trousers. He decides (55) not to risk disturbing his wife by getting it now (so we have two keyless heroes). He pulls the door gently to, and goes out.

It is warm, and Bloom foresees discomfort, for he has a funeral 68 to attend this morning and cannot wear his light suit. In his 47 sunny summer-morning mood Bloom indulges a daydream of setting out in the east and travelling to a strange, walled oriental city with its turbanned crowds, carpet shops, its pedlars and mosques, its rich night sky and the damsel with her dulcimer. But Bloom has enough common sense to recollect that the dream east of books misrepresents the real thing. (The dichotomy between real and ideal is with us again.) He debunks his own sentimentality, recalling how Arthur Griffith mocked the rising sun in the headpiece over the *Freeman* leader. (The phrase 'home-rule sun rising up in the northwest' is to recur, and appears to gather symbolic overtones; see p. 134/*208*.)

69   Bloom approaches Larry O'Rourke's, and catches sight of Larry in the shop. Bloom is an advertising agent and knows Larry as a 'cute old codger' who can't be canvassed. He pictures how cleverly Simon Dedalus mimicks him. Shall he stop and have a word with him about Paddy Dignam's funeral? Instead, he looks through the doorway and passes the time of day. 48 Where, he wonders, do these grocers get their money? They come up from the country as 'curates' (barmen), then suddenly blossom out with their own businesses. He calculates what is 70 to be made from the sale of drink. Next moment he passes St Joseph's school and hears the children reciting their alphabet and their geography.

Halting at Dlugacz's, the butcher's, he studies the sausages and polonies in the window, then goes in. The girl standing (57) before him at the counter is the servant from the house of his next-door neighbour, name of Woods. She orders sausages, while Bloom studies her hands and hips. Neighbour Woods has an oldish wife, he reflects, and this girl he keeps about the house has young blood. He has seen her vigorously whacking carpets on the clothes-line, and the image of her swinging skirts is to recur to him intermittently throughout the day. As he waits, Bloom takes up a page from the pile of cut newspapers on the

counter. He studies an advertisement of a model farm on the
lakeshore of Tiberias and a picture of the cattle.   71

The girl is served and goes out. Bloom gives his order quickly;   49
he would like to catch her up and follow her home, taking pleasure in the movement of her hips. He pays for the kidney.   (58)
Dlugacz, the Hungarian Jew, seems to ask with his eyes for the   72
recognition of a compatriot; but Bloom does not respond.
'No: better not: another time.' By the time he gets out of the
shop the girl has disappeared. But he still has the page of
newspaper and reads it as he walks. Another advertisement
('Agendath Netaim' – Hebrew for 'Plantations Association')
from a German company planning to plant citrus groves in
Israel (ruled by the Turks), stirs his dreams of the fruit-laden
east. His admission that the advertisement 'has an idea behind
it' is an understatement. Possession of melonfields in the
Promised Land is symbolically connected with happy marriage
('Your name entered for life as owner in the book of the union').
Bloom's moment of marital satisfaction tonight is to register this
('He kissed the yellow smellow melons of her rump', p.
604/867). The company's address corroborates the symbolism.
'34' (Molly's age) is located in 'Bleibtreustrasse' (Stay true street)
and 'W 15' (established as 'double-you' by a pun on p. 624/899)
gives us Milly's age. (Stephen too has dreamed of being offered
a melon by a stranger met in 'the street of harlots', pp. 39/58–9
and 179/279.)

Bloom's thought moves, by way of a pun to poor Citron and
Mastiansky, Jewish friends of Bloom in earlier days, from whom
his apostasy seems to have cut him off (p. 405/617). Meantime
a man passes whom he vaguely knows but cannot identify: he   73
is on the point of greeting him, but he passes Bloom without
noticing. A watering-cart, too, passes by.   50

A cloud slowly covers the sun, and Jewish images of a greyer
tint succeed; the desert, the dead sea, the plagues, the cities of
the plain, the desolation of a captive, then a scattered people.
At the same time an old hag crossing the street with a naggin
bottle strengthens the sense of barrenness, bringing the image
of an old woman's shrivelled and shrunken genitals. Replacing the rich dreams of the east, this is a sudden reminder of
a hidden horror lurking at the heart of the physical world, and
ready to leap into human consciousness. But Bloom casts off
the chill, attributing it to 'morning mouth'. He turns his attention

74 to the houses around him and the pleasing breakfast to come.
Sunlight returns and a golden-haired girl runs past.

Back home, Bloom finds the morning mail on the floor of the
hall – a letter to himself from Milly, his daughter, a letter and
a card for his wife. Sadly he notes the handwriting on the letter
to Molly: it is Boylan's (Molly's lover). He goes into the bedroom
and gives his wife her mail. Molly, glancing at the envelope,
puts the letter under the pillow. The card is evidently from
51 Milly, acknowledging receipt of a parcel. Bloom returns to the
75 kitchen to boil the tea and cook the kidney. He takes a quick
first look at Milly's letter, and a few words catch his eye –
'Thanks: new tam . . .', etc. The tea is made. His own cup, a
birthday gift from Milly, brings back memories of her girlhood.
76 Bloom takes the breakfast tray into the bedroom. As Molly
(61) shifts, the bed brasses jingle again, appropriately accompanying
the sensuous images of her 'large soft bubs' and her body-
52 warmth. Seeing that Molly has opened her own letter in his
absence (and the recollection of the torn envelope peeping from
under the pillow is to torment him several times today), Bloom
asks who it is from. 'Boylan,' she says. 'He's bringing the pro-
gramme.' Molly, professionally known as Marion Tweedy, is
a concert singer, and Boylan is to act as her impresario on a
coming tour. She is to sing *Là ci darem*, the duet from *Don
Giovanni*, with J. C. Doyle, and *Love's Old Sweet Song*. (These
songs are to be much in Bloom's mind and hers today.)
77 Munching, Molly points silently but requestingly. Bloom picks
up her underwear. 'No: that book.' Bloom discovers the book
under the bed. Molly finds the place she wants. The word
'metempsychosis' has baffled her. Bloom explains it – 'the trans-
migration of souls', thereby introducing explicitly the theme of
reincarnation implicitly present in the reproduction of Ulysses's
adventures in Leopold Bloom's. Molly, we learn later, pronounces the word 'Met him pike hoses'. Here she protests,
'O rocks', at her husband's incomprehensible explanation of the
word. Bloom looks farther in Molly's book, *Ruby: the Pride of
the Ring*, a cheap erotic novel with a sadistic flavour. A lurid illus-
78 tration of 'the monster Maffei', horsewhip in hand and naked
53 circus-girl at his feet, reminds Bloom of circus cruelty to animals,
of a sickening trapeze act, then of death, then of Dignam.

Molly asks Bloom to get her another novel by Paul de Kock.
The name is significant ('Poldy Cock'). Molly calls her husband

'Poldy'. So doing she de-lionizes him, knocking the 'Leo' out
of his name. Joyce has fun with such word-games. Molly's first
uttered word in the book was 'Mn'. This feminine Yes/No, interpreted by Bloom as a negative, is to be transformed into 'Yes',
her last word in the book. Sort out Leo and put him back inside
Mn and the answer is a melon. Bloom explains the theory of
reincarnation, glancing meantime at the nude study, 'Bath of
the Nymph', over the bed. The nymph is to have her say in
the nightmare projection of Bloom's inner life in the *Circe*
episode (pp. 444 ff./655 ff.). Molly smells something burning,
and Bloom rushes off to rescue the kidney.   79

He eats his breakfast in the kitchen and now reads Milly's   54
letter carefully. Milly is learning photography at Mullingar. She 80
mentions the young student, Bannon, referred to by the young
man bathing (p. 18/26).

Milly was fifteen yesterday, 15 June. Bloom recalls her being
born, the midwife, then his son Rudy who didn't live and who
would now have been eleven. Various memories of Milly's girlhood recur, mingling with a slight apprehension about what her 81
reference to the 'young student', Bannon, might mean in her
now opening sex life. The fact that Bannon sings Boylan's song, 55
'*Those lovely seaside girls*', classifies him mentally for Bloom and (65)
for the reader. (Like mother, like daughter.) Images tumble after
each other through Bloom's mind – the seaside girls, the letter
from Boylan stuffed under Molly's pillow, Boylan's jaunty, swag-
gering, self-assured air as, hands in pockets, he confidently sets
foot in Bloom's home as a 'friend of the family', Milly's sexual
awakening, Molly's past . . .

Bloom promises himself a trip to see Milly. The cat mews.   82
Nature calls him to the lavatory, and he finds an old number
of *Titbits* to take with him. He goes through the garden, mentally
planning improvements to it, enters the outside closet and settles 56
down on the seat with *Titbits*. The lines running through Bloom's 83
mind, 'The maid was in the garden' (p. 55/82) and 'The king
was in his countinghouse', link up significantly with other lines
from '*Sing a song of sixpence*' (see p. 61/91). As he eases himself,
he looks at the prize story, 'Matcham's Masterstroke', for which
a Mr Philip Beaufoy has won three and a half guineas. The
masterstroke (the lion's stroke) by which Matcham (Match'em?
cf. p. 306/487, 'As God made them He matched them') wins   84
his 'laughing witch' distantly forecasts Bloom's final triumph.

('Hand in hand' is a key phrase in another epic, *Paradise Lost*.) So Beaufoy's masterpiece is itself a capsulated epic, in its diminutive simplicity fit food for babes – a tit bit, in fact. Bloom wishes he could emulate Beaufoy. He recalls his own efforts to write – when he used to put down on his cuffs Molly's conversation as she dressed. Remembered fragments are quoted. And Molly, dressing, stays in his mind, especially dressing on a

57   memorable morning after a dance at which she first met 'Blazes'
85   Boylan. We may note that, after his evacuation, Bloom tears a piece off Beaufoy's creative work in order to wipe himself. Stephen tore the edge off Deasy's effusion in order to do his creative work (p. 40/60).

When he leaves the closet, studying his smart black trousers, Bloom turns his mind to the funeral. The church bells ring. An episode which begins with morning sunlight ends with images of the passing hours, with church bells, and with the thought

(67)   of death. 'Poor Dignam!'

Chapter 5

The Lotus Eaters

In the *Odyssey* the followers of Ulysses are given the lotus to 58
eat when they land among the lotus-eaters. The effect of the
drug is to reduce men to inertia, to make them forgetful of their
homes and desirous only of remaining where they are. Ulysses
has to drag them back aboard against their will till the effect
of the fruit wears off.

Bloom is walking in the city. Fragments of what he sees and (68)
of what he thinks about what he sees, are recorded in a loosely 86
moving sequence that expresses the idle, receptive, restful mood
of this episode – a mood of drugged surrender to the impression of the moment.

Halting before the window of the Belfast and Oriental Tea
Company in Westland Row, Bloom furtively transfers the card
from behind the headband of the hat to his waistcoat pocket.
Meantime the Tea Company's window brings on another
oriental reverie of sun-drenched ease. The image of the dead 87
sea induces in Bloom a series of reflections about the nature of 59
weight and gravity. But he is too somnolent in mood, and too
much possessed with another interest, to follow through his
scientific calculations.

He crosses the road and rolls his newspaper into a baton.
Lightly swung at his side, it is the Ulyssean sword of the modern
advertising agent. Finding the Westland Row Post Office empty,
he goes in and hands his false visiting card to the postmistress,
who then gives him a letter addressed to his pseudonym, 'Henry 88
Flower'. As he pockets it, a recruiting poster showing soldiers
on parade catches his eye. He recalls (among other things) his
father-in-law, Major Tweedy; but uniforms are not for Bloom –
except the masonic dress.

60   Out in the street he meets M'Coy, whose chatter is only an
annoying distraction, for his mind is on the envelope crumpled
between his fingers in his pocket. He can feel that it contains
something, but cannot make out what. Not hair; not a photo-
89   graph; perhaps a badge. Bored with M'Coy, Bloom gazes across
(70)   the road at a little scene enacted before the door of the Grosvenor
Hotel. A porter is hoisting a valise on to a cab; a man searches
his pockets for change; a woman stands waiting, about to start
on her journey. She is stylishly dressed, haughty in bearing and,
as M'Coy chatters about Dignam's death, Bloom's attention is
90   held by her hand, her hair, her skin; then by her high boots
61   and well-turned foot. He is just preparing to enjoy the sight of
her silk-stockinged leg as she climbs into the cab, when a tram
91   passes and obscures the view. Bloom feels 'locked out of it';
and he is soon to experience even more disappointing frustrations near the goal.

Bloom idly unrolls the newspaper (*Freeman*) he is carrying,
and his eye falls on an advertisement which is to come back to
his mind several times during the day. *'What is home without
Plumtree's Potted Meat? Incomplete. With it an abode of bliss.'* (Its
symbolic overtones will emerge later.) M'Coy, whose wife has
had pretensions as a singer, mentions that she is on the point
of getting a concert engagement. Bloom recognizes this opening
gambit to a trick by which M'Coy has already benefited at his
friends' expense. (See the story 'Grace' in *Dubliners*. 'Mr M'Coy
had recently made a crusade in search of valises and port-
manteaus to enable Mrs M'Coy to fulfil imaginary engagements
in the country.') He deflects the talk to his own wife's coming
tour, whilst picturing her still in bed at home, the significant
torn edge of Boylan's envelope portending one more recurrence
of *'Love's Old Sweet Song'*. The remembered jingle, 'Queen was
in her bedroom eating bread' misquotes another line ('bedroom'
should be 'parlour') from *'Sing a song of sixpence'*, which was
earlier in Bloom's mind (p. 56/*83*). The verse acquires symbolic
overtones as the study of Molly gathers significance (see
92   pp. 122/*188* and 561/*802*). Bloom's talk of the coming tour
('There's a committee formed. Part shares and part profits.')
62   has ironic appropriateness to the way Boylan and he 'share'
Molly. M'Coy takes his leave, asking Bloom to add his name
to the list of mourners at Dignam's funeral. Bloom congratulates himself on not falling for M'Coy's valise gambit, and

mentally rejects M'Coy's attempts to put the two wives on the same level.

Among advertisement hoardings Bloom sees an announce-   93
ment that Mrs Bandmann Palmer is to play *Leah* tonight. Bloom
has seen this play and would like to see it again. Last night,
he recalls, Mrs Palmer played Hamlet as a male impersonator.
The idea is toyed with that Hamlet was perhaps a woman in
disguise. The theory would at least explain Ophelia's suicide.
The thought of suicide converges with the memory of his
father's enthusiasm for the theatre in general and for a scene   (73)
from *Leah* in particular, and Bloom recalls the old man's way
of quoting it. (Leopold Bloom's father, Rudolph Virag, came
from Hungary and settled in Ireland. 'Virag', in Hungarian,
means 'Flower' – hence Leopold's choice of pseudonym.
Rudolph anglicized the family name as 'Bloom'. He died by his
own hand. See p. 84/127.) Then he remembers the tragedy of
his father's death.

Bloom's reflections on the cab-horses with their 'long noses   63
stuck in nosebags' and 'stumps of black guttapercha wagging   94
limp between their haunches' reinforce the other images of
drugged receptivity and impotence which constitute the main
correspondence with the Lotus Eaters. (One should note that
Bloom's affair with Martha Clifford, now to be explored, is an
inactive experiment in mental self-indulgence. Bloom seems to
have no intention of translating paper-talk into act.)

Eventually Bloom finds quietness and solitude in Cumberland
Street. He opens the letter 'within the newspaper'. It contains a
yellow flower. Bloom reads the letter, and the reader gets the
first picture of Martha, his pen-pal. Martha is anxious to meet   95
her correspondent, and it appears that in an earlier letter she   64
suggested that they might meet some Sunday after rosary, but   96
Bloom is loath to commit himself to the 'usual love-scrimmage'
and the furtive difficulties that ensue – 'running round corners'
to avoid recognition in the street. (We learn later that this
pen-friendship started when Bloom inserted an advertisement in
the *Irish Times* reading, 'Wanted smart lady typist to aid gentleman in literary work', and selected Martha from among the
applicants. See p. 131/202.) He puts Martha's flower in his heart
pocket: the pin which held the flower he throws away. (He is not
going to prick himself in this relationship. He will have the rose
without the thorn. There are too many pins among a woman's

underclothes. It is safer to love at a distance.) The doggerel about
Mary losing the pin of her drawers brings together for the first
time the names Martha and Mary, names of our Lord's two
admirers, and Bloom's if we equate Molly–Marion with Mary.
65   Bloom recalls a picture of our Lord sitting in the house at Bethany
with the two women, and another day-dream of oriental peace
succeeds. (Bloom's letter from Martha is the nourishment of an
inert, 'ideal' passion. Molly's letter from Boylan is the mechanism
of an all too 'real' and active one.)

97   Prudently Bloom tears Martha's envelope to bits and scatters
them. Thus 'Henry Flower' is destroyed. A cheque could be
(76)   destroyed as easily. Bloom remembers a story that Lord Iveagh
of Guinness's once cashed a cheque for a million pounds
(he remembers the family's misfortunes too – the disease of
Iveagh's brother, Lord Ardilaun), and he calculates how much
porter you have to sell to make a million on the sales.

98   He goes into All Hallows' Church. A notice announces a
sermon by the Rev. John Conmee, SJ, on St Peter Claver and the
African mission. Images of conversion follow – and of the Faith
66   as a drug for natives. Inside a service is in progress: a priest is
99   communicating women at the altar rails: the rite, the Latin, the
Host, like so much else in this chapter, are seen as stupefying
drugs. Blooms sits in a corner reflecting on the cosy togetherness
which Catholic practice induces. The priest puts the chalice away.
100   Linked references to pins in clothes, thorns in roses, and the nails
of the Cross begin to form a thematic thread of imagery relative
to the minor and major pricks and pains of life. In his ignorance
Bloom thinks that INRI (abbreviated Latin superscription on the
Cross, 'Jesus of Nazareth, the King of the Jews') means
'Iron nails ran in' and IHS ('Jesus the Saviour of Men') means 'I
have suffered'. He recalls refusing to meet Martha 'one Sunday
after rosary'. Images of communion wine and of Guinness's
67   porter (the two drugs of Dubliners) are juxtaposed.

Bloom wonders who is organist now at All Hallows: he recalls
101   'Old Glynn' who played when Molly sang in Rossini's *Stabat*
(79)   *Mater* at the church in Gardiner Street. (See pp. 540/770 and
616/886.) From this thoughts run to other sacred music, including 'seven last words'. (The recurring title prefigures the book's
conclusion: 'yes I said yes I will Yes'.)

The priest comes forward and prays in English, thereby, in
102   Bloom's eyes, throwing his congregation 'a bone'. An outsider,

Bloom admires the efficiency of the Roman Catholic organiza- *68*
tion, the effectiveness of its psychological devices like Confession, and the competence of its financial administration.

The service ends: Bloom stands up, notices that two buttons *103*
of his waistcoat are open, and fastens them. He goes out, finds
it is 10.15, and remembers that he has to call for some face
lotion for Molly. He has forgotten the recipe (like the latch-key
it is in the 'other trousers'), but he relies on the chemist's being *69*
able to check up on the previous prescription. The chemist
searches back page after page while Bloom surveys the bottles *104*
and drugs and potions which seem to make his shop the focus
of the lotus-eating world. Images of perfume, skin-lotion, soap,
baths, massage, succeed one another in Bloom's mind as the
chemist locates the recipe. Bloom promises to call back for the
lotion 'later in the day'. (In fact, he forgets to do so.) Meantime *105*
he purchases a cake of lemony-scented soap. *(82)*

Outside again, newspaper baton under his armpit and a cake *70*
of soap clenched in his left hand, Joyce's epic hero is equipped
with the shield as well as the sword of modern man. He bumps
into Bantam Lyons, who borrows his newspaper. Lyons wants
to check on a horse due to run today in the Ascot Gold Cup *106*
race. Bloom has finished with the paper, says Lyons can
keep it, repeats that he was just going to 'throw it away'. The
repetition of this phrase proves unfortunate. Bantam Lyons
wrongly assumes that Bloom is giving him a betting tip, for
Throwaway is the name of a runner. This misunderstanding is
to cost Bloom dearly later in the day. He himself has, of course,
the prudent attitude to gambling which one would expect of
him.

Bloom moves on towards the baths and greets Hornblower, *107*
the porter, at the college lodge. In the 'heavenly' warm weather *71*
he looks forward to enjoying a clean, cool bath. He foresees
his own body reclined in the great bowl of the bath, like the
divine body in the chalice, like the naked body in the womb.
(See p. 552/789–90 ff., for the justification for reading into this
passage a correspondence with the Annunciation and the
Incarnation.)

Chapter 6

Hades

72
(84)
Bloom's attendance at Glasnevin Cemetery for Paddy Dignam's funeral parallels Odysseus's visit to Hades in Homer.

108
We are outside the Dignam home, No. 9 Newbridge Avenue, Sandymount. Martin Cunningham, Mr Power, Simon Dedalus, and Leopold Bloom enter the same cab to be transported to the cemetery. Bloom sees an old woman peeping at them through a window, and dwells for a moment on woman's role in bringing us into the world and tending our corpses at the end, on the image of Molly and Mrs Fleming – her daily help – making the bed, and on the trimming of a corpse's hair and nails. As he settles down in the cab, Bloom finds himself sitting on something hard and remembers that it is the cake of soap in his hip pocket.

109
73
The carriages move off and the journey begins. Pedestrians bare their heads as the procession goes by. Bloom sees Stephen Dedalus 'clad in mourning, a wide hat' (Hamlet-like still), and points him out to Simon, who asks whether 'that Mulligan cad' is with him, 'his fidus Achates'. Bloom says not. Simon assumes that Stephen is staying with the Gouldings, and the mention of the family brings to Bloom images of Richie Goulding's wild

110
career as a card and of the price he is now paying physically. As so often, Bloom's commercial interests and his shrewdness emerge here in his reflections on the pills Richie Goulding takes. 'All breadcrumbs they are. About six hundred per cent profit.' Simon Dedalus gives vent to a tirade against Buck Mulligan, who is ruining his son. Bloom does not like Simon's temper, but feels he is right to be 'full of his son'. If only his own son had lived. He recalls little Rudy's boyhood, then the occasion of Rudy's conception, then Molly's pregnancy, lastly

Molly's self-reproduction in Milly, with her maturing interest in   74
a 'young student' as revealed in this morning's letter to 'Dearest   111
Papli'.

The occupants of the cab find it a tight fit: they sway simultaneously as it rocks along. It is not clean either: there are
crumbs on the seat. They stop at the Grand Canal, the second   112
of the waterways which correspond to the rivers of Hades
(cf. 'Dodder bridge', p. 73/109). Looking out, Blooms sees the
gasworks, recalls that the smell from the gasworks is said to
cure whooping cough, then dwells on the diseases of children.   75
The sight of the Dogs' home converges with this train of
ideas and Bloom's mind once more returns to his dead father,
whose last wish was that Leopold should be good to his old
dog Athos.

The conversation turns to last night's revels with Tom Kernan   113
and Paddy Leonard, then to Dan Dawson's speech in this
morning's paper. (See pp. 102–4/157–61.) Bloom is about to look   (88)
up the speech when Simon (oddly 'conformist' in many ways)
checks him. 'Later on, please.' Bloom's eye travels down the
edge of the obituary column with its list of names, its pious
requests and sentimental verses.

Soon they are passing the 'hazard' (cab-stand) and the feeding   76
horses (now reduced to two) which Bloom passed on foot only   114
an hour ago. A tramway pointsman comes into view, then the
concert rooms, St Mark's, the railway bridge, the Queen's theatre
with its bills announcing future programmes. Now a queer coincidence occurs. 'He's coming in the afternoon. Her songs,' Bloom
thinks. 'He' is Blazes Boylan, whom Bloom never refers to by
name, such is his dislike of the man, his wish to keep him at
a distance, mentally and physically. At that moment Martin
Cunningham and Mr Power greet someone outside. Simon asks   115
who it is. Blazes Boylan, Mr Power said. There he is airing his
quiff. The jaunty figure and the 'white disc of a straw hat' flash
by as quickly as that. Bloom's response is intensely moving, a
miracle of Joycean economy and pathos. 'Just that moment
I was thinking,' and the compressed implicit emotion breaks
out as he nervously studies his finger-nails and wonders what
it is that 'they' and 'she' see in Boylan, the 'worst man in Dublin'.
(The emphasis on the 'nails' of his hands suggests that here is
Bloom's private crucifixion.) So his mind turns, after its
customary centripetal fashion, to that centre which, like the leg

of Donne's compasses, it constantly yearns and leans after –
Molly, her shoulders, hips, plump buttocks.

Mr Power questions Bloom politely about his wife's coming
77 concert tour, eliciting that Bloom will not be going with her,
having an engagement in County Clare. Mr Power's smilingly
116 courteous reference to Molly as 'Madame' lingers in Bloom's
(90) mind as they pass Farrell's statue of Smith O'Brien (an MP who
agitated for repeal of the Union), then on the south end of
O'Connell Bridge. Bloom sees O'Callaghan, former solicitor,
struck off the rolls for some misdemeanour and now reduced
to selling bootlaces at the roadside, his old silk hat a pathetic
relic of his former status. 'Madame', Bloom reflects, is now
presumably up and about. Mrs Fleming, the cleaner, has arrived.
Molly is doing her hair and humming 'Vorrei e non vorrei' from
Don Giovanni. ('Vorrei e non vorrei' – 'I would like to and I
wouldn't like to' – smacks of Molly's ambiguous initial 'Mn'.)
The word 'Madame' and the accompanying smile have established a sympathetic feeling for Mr Power in Bloom, who
ponders whether the story is true that Power keeps another
woman as well as his wife – though not, strictly speaking, as
117 his mistress. They pass 'under the huge-cloaked Liberator's
form' – the statue of Daniel O'Connell on the north end of
O'Connell Bridge – so the carriage has now crossed the third
waterway, the river Liffey.

The sight of Reuben J. Dodd, money-lender, introduces
78 another father–son theme into the conversation, and we hear
how Dodd's son, destined for the Isle of Man by his father in
order to get him away from a female attachment, jumped off
118 the quay into the Liffey and was saved from drowning on the
end of a boatman's pole. (Here we have a less grave version of
the theme of the drowning or drowned man raised up.) The
joke is that Reuben senior gave the boatman a two-shilling tip
for saving his son's life. 'One and eightpence too much,' Mr
Dedalus observes, and the company smother their unseemly
laughter, meantime passing Nelson's column and the plum-
seller who is offering plums at eight a penny. The laughter
provokes a counter-balancing outburst of sentiment for poor
119 Paddy. His death is attributed to heart trouble by Martin
79 Cunningham; by Bloom, silently, to too much drink. Mr Power
laments the suddenness of his death, but Bloom thinks sudden
death the best kind of death.

A tiny coffin flashes by, followed by a single mourning coach – a more rushed, huddled funeral than Dignam's, the funeral of an illegitimate child (the white horses and their white plumes give this away). 'In the midst of life,' Martin Cunningham *120* observes, and death remains the central preoccupation. Mr Power, ignorant of Bloom's personal tragedy, pronounces suicide the 'greatest disgrace to have in the family'. Martin Cunningham steps in sympathetically and tactfully to smother this conversation, avoiding Bloom's eyes. Bloom reflects on the Irish Catholic mercilessness towards suicide and infanticide; also on *(93)* Martin Cunningham's touching sympathy and friendliness, the *80* more moving because he knows something of Cunningham's own family worries – the drunken wife at home who pawns his furniture behind his back. Cunningham becomes, in the Joycean imagery, the suffering Sisyphus of the Dublin Hades, for ever struggling to make a fresh start. (See *Dubliners*: 'Grace', for more about Mr Cunningham and Mr Power.)

Bloom sees that Cunningham reads his own personal tragedy *121* correspondingly, and his thoughts revert to the inquest on his father, to the hotel room at Ennis in which his father's body was found, to the evidence of the 'Boots' who made the discovery, to the letter of explanation left by Rudolph senior to his son. Phrases from it linger with him. 'No more pain. Wake no more. Nobody owns.'

The cab gathers speed along Blessington Street, then turns into Berkeley Street. A street organ is heard playing a music-hall tune, '*Has anyone here seen Kelly*?' They pass Eccles Street, where the Blooms live; then Our Lady's Hospice for the *122* Dying, where Mrs Riordan (Dante of the *Portrait*) spent her last days.

The carriage is held up by a drove of cattle and a flock of sheep, apparently *en route* for Liverpool and England's dinner *81* tables. Mr Bloom, ever practical, ingenious, and businesslike, regrets the lack of a corporation tramline to transport cattle across the city to the docks. He also recommends the Milan practice of running municipal funeral trams. Mr Dedalus pictures a funeral cortège complete with pullman car and saloon *123* dining-room, while Martin Cunningham, agreeing, recalls how a hearse capsized round Dunphy's and upset the coffin in the road, spilling the corpse. The spilt corpse of Dignam is imaged in Bloom's mind as they themselves round Dunphy's corner.

Bloom as ever ponders the relevant scientific problems. Does a
124 corpse bleed?
82   They reach Crossguns Bridge and cross the Royal Canal, the
        fourth of the waterways. Waterways run through Athlone,
        Mullingar (where Milly is now living), and Moyvalley. Bloom
(96) toys with the idea of a walking tour on the towpath to see
        Milly, perhaps dropping in on her by surprise. They pass the
125 stonecutter's yard of Thos. H. Dennany, monumental mason,
        then an old tramp emptying dirt and stones out of his boot.
        'After life's journey,' Bloom thinks, and the images of death and
        gloom accumulate. Mr Power points out the house where Childs
        was murdered, now shuttered, tenantless, desolate. Bloom, still
83   pondering a possible visit to Milly, decides that it would be
126 unwise to go without warning her in advance. 'Must be careful
        about women. Catch them once with their pants down. Never
        forgive you after.'
        The white stones and statuary of Prospect Cemetery come
        into view. The procession halts. Stepping out of the coach, Bloom
        deftly transfers the uncomfortable slab of soap from hip pocket
        to inner handkerchief pocket. His thoughts are dominated by
        the subject of death – the stereotyped pomps and practices
127 surrounding it, the frequency of it. The mourners from the
        pathetic funeral of the illegitimate child come out of the gates
        as Bloom's party waits for Dignam's coffin to be lifted from the
        hearse. Joyce's terse, economic glimpses of the child's mourners
        are unidealized yet charged with compassion – 'woman and a
        girl. Lean-jawed harpy, hard woman at a bargain, her bonnet
        awry. Girl's face stained with dirt and tears, holding the
        woman's arm, looking up at her for a sign to cry.' And behind
        this little group lies another mystery of paternity.
84   Dignam's coffin is shouldered and the mourners follow it
        through the gates, Corny Kelleher (the undertaker) and the boy
        coming up behind with the wreaths. Martin Cunningham seizes
        the opportunity to warn Mr Power of his indiscretion in
        discussing suicide before Bloom. (It is characteristic of the diffi-
        culties encountered by the reader in his first reading of *Ulysses*
        that this is the first clear statement that Bloom's father poisoned
        himself. Thus the sentence enables us to make sense of much
        that has already passed through Bloom's mind. See pp. 62/93
        and 80/121.) From suicide and sonlessness Bloom's image
        gathers overtones of life-denial and sterility.

As the mourners follow the coffin there is some quiet conver- *128*
sation between Bloom and Kernan about the deceased's widow
and children, between Simon Dedalus and Ned Lambert about
Cork (Simon's birthplace). Meantime Bloom ponders the lot of
widowhood, the strange mourning of Queen Victoria, who
ought to have been looking forward to her son not backward
to her dead consort. 'Her son was the substance. Something
new to hope for not like the past she wanted back, waiting.'

Ned Lambert speaks of a whip round for the youngsters to *129*
which John Henry Menton has promised a pound. The *85*
son–father relationship is still in Bloom's mind as he watches
Dignam's boy with the wreath. Again into a single economical *(99)*
phrase – 'All he might have done' – is compressed a world of
emotion centring on the failure of communication between
father and son, and the sense of inadequacy and hopelessness
with which the son must watch his father's last unconscious-
ness, last halting attempts to communicate. They enter the
chapel and kneel. 'A server bearing a brass bucket with some- *130*
thing in it comes out through a door.' Here, as in the visit to
All Hallows, the religious ceremonies are seen through the eyes
of Bloom who neither understands them nor has the appropriate vocabulary. Fr Coffey – 'bully about the muzzle . . . like
a sheep . . . like a poisoned pup . . . eyes of a toad' – is no
doubt, as Stuart Gilbert points out, a kind of Cerberus seen
comically.

We are now in the depths. The ultimate horrors of the Joycean
underworld have that touch of humour, even of farcicality,
which distinguishes his work. From the swollen figure of Fr
Coffey Bloom's mind moves to the inflating power of bad gas
and the grim need to burn off the accumulated gas from the *131*
coffins in the vaults of St Werburgh's. With this, the main theme *86*
in Bloom's mind is the monotonous repetitiousness of Fr
Coffey's grim duties, 'every mortal day a fresh batch' of corpses
to deal with.

The grave-diggers come in and take the coffin out, placing it
on a cart, which they shove towards the grave. The mourners
follow again. They pass the memorial to Daniel O'Connell whose *132*
last wish was that his heart should be buried in Rome and his
body in Glasnevin. Simon Dedalus points to his wife's grave,
breaks down, and weeps. 'I'll soon be stretched beside her. Let
Him take me whenever He likes.' Tom Kernan, who comes of

133 Protestant stock (see *Dubliners*: 'Grace'), criticizes Fr Coffey's
 87 performance. He prefers the simplicity and solemnity of the
vernacular Anglican Prayer Book, quoting, '*I am the Resurrection
and the Life*', but Bloom is preoccupied with something less dignified, that breaking-down of the heart's pumping system which
constitutes death. He is concerned with the physical finality of
(102) death: the idea of a general resurrection on the last day – 'every
fellow mousing around for his liver and his lights and the rest
of his traps' – does not move him.

Corny Kelleher, the undertaker, seeks commendation for the
134 smoothness of the proceedings. John Henry Menton asks who
Bloom is and is astonished to learn that he is the husband of
Marion Tweedy. Menton recalls Marion in her prime, and indeed
we learn later that he is to be numbered among her suitors (p.
 88 601/*863*). Ned Lambert tells us that Bloom has been a traveller
for blotting-paper with Wisdom Hely's.

The mourners are formally greeted by John O'Connell, the
135 cemetery caretaker. His joke about the two drunks who came
to see the grave of Terence Mulcahy and criticized the statue
of the Saviour over it as being a bad likeness of the deceased,
is seen by Martin Cunningham and Hynes as a professional
gambit to take the mourners' minds off their grief. Bloom sees
136 O'Connell as the keeper of the cemetery keys and is reminded
of the Keyes advertisement which he has to deal with today.
The mourners are following the coffin to the graveside now,
and Bloom's thoughts run out centrifugally from the figure of
 89 O'Connell. What must it be like to be the wife of a cemetery-
keeper? How does a cemetery-keeper persuade a girl to come
and share his lot? And so to the fascination of sexual activity
in graveyards; the enormous number of corpses O'Connell must
137 have dealt with; the cemeteries packed with corpses, trim with
flowers; the richly manured soil that corpses produce; soil
swirling with maggots (hence to Boylan's song 'Your head it
simply swurls ... Those pretty little seaside girls'); the cheerfulness of O'Connell; the humour of death; the grave-diggers
 90 in *Hamlet*; and so on.
138 The grave is reached. There is a brief business interchange
between Corny Kelleher, the undertaker, and O'Connell, who
pockets the official burial papers. The mourners take up their
positions around the grave. Bloom notices a mysterious
stranger. 'Now who is that lankylooking galoot over there in

the macintosh? Now who is he I'd like to know?' So would the
reader, for MacIntosh remains a teasing mystery throughout.

Business-minded Bloom reflects on the waste of wood as the   *139*
coffin is prepared for its descent. He also notes that there are
twelve of them round the grave. 'The chap in the macintosh is   (106)
thirteen. Death's number.' The grave-diggers ease the coffin
down into the grave, then clamber out. In the pause which   91
follows, Bloom ponders the strangeness of human identity, 'If
we were all suddenly somebody else,' then a donkey brays in
the distance and, as the son stares into the black hole after the
coffin, Bloom dwells on the restfulness of death accomplished   *140*
and the unpleasantness of the actual moment of death as it
approaches; the dying man's loathness to believe that it really
is his turn; the whispers around him in the darkened room; the
trembling and delirium and the crowding memories of the past;
then the moment of expiry; Edgardo gasping out his last aria
in the final scene of Donizetti's *Lucia di Lammermoor* (a tragedy
rooted in a doom-laden father–son relationship); and then the
speed with which the dead are forgotten.

The last prayer for the repose of Dignam's soul is said.
Bloom's crude, street-corner version of what it amounts to –
'Hope you're well and not in hell' – shows his remoteness from
the prevailing Catholic mind of the Dubliners. A second later
his mind is on the plot reserved for his own burial, where
Mamma and little Rudy already lie. As the grave-diggers begin
to throw earth on the coffin, the familiar apprehension strikes
Bloom. Suppose Dignam were not really dead. Ought there not
to be surer safeguards against the possible blunder of burying   *141*
a man alive? One by one, the mourners put on their hats.
O'Connell moves off. Joyce stresses his Homeric ancestry in the
idiom of classical translation. 'Quietly, sure of his ground, he
traversed the dismal fields.'

Hynes, the reporter, jotting down the names of the mourners,   92
checks up on Bloom's Christian name. 'L,' Bloom stresses, with
odd irony in view of the fact that when the printed list of
mourners does emerge the 'L' is lost from his surname 'Boom'
(p. 529/*751*). Faithfully, Bloom asks for M'Coy's name to be
added to the list. We learn, partly from the talk, and partly from
what passes in Bloom's mind, that Charlie M'Coy used to work
on the *Freeman* himself; that he got the sack for levanting with
the cash of a few ads, and that he works now in the morgue.

Hynes, like Bloom, like the reader, wants to know who MacIntosh is.

142   The grave is filled up with clay. The wreaths are laid on it. The grave-diggers withdraw from it. One coils the coffin band ('His navelcord' – and the image recurs which Stephen indulged on p. 32/46). The mourners move away, Hynes proposing that they go round by 'the chief's grave' – Parnell's.

143   The earthy, calculating, anti-sentimental side of Bloom asserts
93   itself in his walk past the monument-littered graves. The monuments are wasteful of good money; the language of the inscriptions is unreal ('Pray for the repose of ... Who departed this life ... The great physician called home'); the idiom of Catholic and Protestant piety alike leaves him unmoved; he is
144   more touched by the sight of a bird tamely perched on a poplar
(109) branch, looking as though it were stuffed, reminding him of the pathos of dead animals, and how little Milly once buried a dead bird in a large kitchen matchbox and decorated the grave with a daisy chain. A statue of the Sacred Heart likewise calls out in him nothing but the misunderstanding of an alien: the sheer number of the graves, however, draws out the reflections common to us all – the impossibility of remembering, vividly remembering, the innumerable dead. One can remember faces only with the help of photographs. Bloom toys comically (and prophetically) with the thought of immortalizing one's friends' voices on records in a similar way, and putting poor old great-grandfather on the gramophone after Sunday dinner.

94   The rattle of pebbles halts him. He peers down into a
145   stone crypt and sees an obese grey rat wriggling under the plinth. Mentally he sees the rat making a meal of a corpse, and the last cluster of death images is flung before us in the mind of Bloom – corpse as bad meat; cheese as corpse of milk; the cleaner way of cremation; the quicklime pits used during the Plague; death by lethal chamber; burial by water; the moment of drowning at which you 'See your whole life in a flash'. The sequence reaches a fanciful climax in the idea of hungry rats and flies waiting the news of the arrival of a new corpse.

      Then Bloom goes through the gates. 'Back to the world again.
146   Enough of this place.' The last images of corpse-hunting and ghosts fade away. Martha's mis-typed letter comes back to mind ('I do not like that other world,' she wrote – meaning 'word',

p. 63/*94*). 'No more do I,' Bloom thinks. 'Plenty to see and hear and feel yet.'

Martin Cunningham comes towards him, talking with Menton. Bloom knows Menton, as a solicitor, and as a man with whom he once had a misunderstanding in a game of bowls; but he does not know him as his wife's former admirer (p. 87/*134*.), and there is irony, humour, and pathos in his memory of the incident at bowls – 'Why he took such a rooted dislike to me. Hate at first sight. Molly and Floey Dillon linked under the lilac-tree, laughing. Fellow always like that, mortified if women are by.' (For further details of this memorable gathering in the garden of Matthew Dillon's house at Roundtown in 1887, see pp. 344/*552*; 556/*795*; and 637/*921*.) Bloom tries to be politely helpful when, seeing that Menton has got a dinge in his hat, he tactfully draws attention to it. But his courtesy is snubbed. Menton stares at him in silence. Cunningham comes to the rescue, himself pointing to the dented hat. Reluctantly Menton responds with a terse (and not to be forgotten), 'Thank you.' Bloom accepts the snub philosophically. 'Thank you. How grand we are this morning.' 95 (111) 147

The rebuff is symptomatic of what Bloom's practical experience tends to be. His day-dreams take him to the fruitful east: his thoughts dwell often on simple, homely satisfactions: his reflections before the Tea Company's window established tea, a symbol of creativity, among a cluster of associations of desired human warmth and harmony ('choice blend, finest quality, family tea. Rather warm.' p. 58/*86*). But this was inert musing. Bloom's actual journey so far has brought him slowly from the bed of potential feminine fertility to the cemetery, from contemplating bubs at the bed-side to contemplating maggots at the grave-side. Later, in *The Sirens* episode, there is to be a counterbalancing journey across Dublin, rapid and cocksure, made by Boylan to the bed which Bloom has vacated.

Chapter 7

Aeolus

96 In Homer Aeolus helps Ulysses on his way by giving him the winds unfavourable to his voyage tied up in a bag. As they are nearing home, Ulysses's followers open the bag out of curiosity; the winds are released; and they are blown back off their course. When Ulysses makes a second application to Aeolus for help, he is rebuked and dismissed. The correspondence here between the Homeric guardian of the winds and Myles Crawford, the editor of the daily newspaper, is apt and amusing. Bloom comes to Crawford hoping to do a little deal, goes off thinking he has it all but clinched, returns to find Crawford in a changed mood, and is rebuffed.

Appropriately, the theme of frustration, and more particularly of frustration experienced just at the moment when the goal is in sight, recurs throughout the episode. As so often in Joyce, the theme is present on the universal scale and on the individual scale, nationally in the destinies of the Jewish and the Irish nations, personally and in miniature in the day's business frustration of Bloom. That individual man's day-by-day disappointments or successes are on a par with the large-scale disappointments or successes of epic heroes or nations, is one of Joyce's most telling emphases. Joyce is not playing a clever little game when he parallels a Stephen with a Hamlet, a Bloom with an Odysseus, or even a Bloom with Christ; rather he is giving to human experience at the commonplace level a weight and a universality which the greatest literature gives to it – and which the religious dimension also gives to it.

The atmospheric correspondence between Joyce and Homer is interesting. As in *The Lotus-Eaters* episode a drugged sun-drenched atmosphere prevailed, enriched by images of eating, perfume, and flowers, and by allusions to the inert and the impotent, so here there is a background throbbing with noise, haste, and bustle. The clanging, ringing trams in the street set the tone. The printing presses, with their ceaseless Sllt Sllt, the shouting newsboys, and (in a different sense) the screaming headlines, all help to create the feel of restlessness. In the corporeal scheme of correspondences, as explained by Stuart Gilbert (*James Joyce's Ulysses*), this episode represents the lungs, for ever pumping air in and out. There is 'gas' everywhere, not least the gas of inflated rhetoric and hectoring, wordy conversation. The rush of words, of rumour, of news, let loose daily from this pulsing, hectic organ, is pumped into the life of Dublin as newsboys are exhaled on to the streets. (112)

The trams start their noisy journeys before Nelson's Pillar, the mail-cars load in North Princes' Street, the draymen roll barrels across the pavements. Meantime Bloom is in the offices of the *Weekly Freeman and National Press* and the *Freeman's Journal and National Press*. Red Murray supplies him with a clipping from a past edition. It is apparently the advertisement for Alexander Keyes. Bloom is to take it round to the *Telegraph* office (in the same building, for the papers are under common ownership) in order to carry out his commission. He decides to go through the printing works. Red Murray is willing to arrange to insert a paragraph puffing the Keyes firm in the *Freeman*. *148* *97*

Murray and Bloom pause to watch the stately figure of William Brayden, owner of the press, enter the offices and solemnly mount the staircase. Murray thinks Brayden's bearded face is like Our Lord's, and Bloom's mind turns back to the picture of Christ talking in the dusk to Mary and Martha of Bethany. Bloom imagines a facial resemblance to Mario, the operatic tenor. The image of a Jesus-faced Mario with rougy cheeks, doublet, and spindle legs, his hand on his heart, singing the aria '*M'appari*' in Flotow's *Martha*, sets up a number of Joycean correspondences. Simon Dedalus is to sing this aria in the Ormond bar (p. 225/352). A 'Martha' is the object of one of Bloom's 'ideal' passions. The lines from the aria, '*Come thou lost one, Come thou dear one*', not only point forward to Bloom's cathartic response to Simon Dedalus's singing (pp. 226–7/355-6), they also hark back to the resurrection theme – and more especially the raising of Lazarus, Martha's brother ('Come forth Lazarus', p. 87/133). The inter-relation of symbolic themes *149* is impressive; but there is a lapse of verisimilitude, in that the tenor Mario retired from the stage in 1867, and Bloom, who was born in 1866, could scarcely have memories of his performances.

150   Bloom makes his way to the office of Councillor Nannetti,
98   the *Freeman's* business manager. Here he finds Hynes, who has
(114)   evidently come to hand in his copy covering the Dignam funeral (see p. 529/751). Bloom waits his turn patiently, reflecting on the fact that Nannetti has never seen his 'real country', Italy, but has asserted his Irish nationality and become a member of the Dublin City Council. There is a hint of pathos here. Nannetti,
151   the Italian (like Cuprani too, the printer) is accepted by Dublin: Bloom, the Jew, as this episode shows, is but tolerated. Bloom, waiting and always ready to allow his mind to play on the business aspect of things, runs cursorily over the various features of the weekly paper which appeal to the public, and we have a capsulated account of a typical edition, from official gazette and estate advertisements to tots page and pictures of bathing girls.

Hynes is wise enough to call Nannetti 'councillor', which Bloom notes, mentally prophesying that he may well become
99   Lord Mayor. As Hynes moves off, Bloom helpfully suggests to him that he'd better hurry if he wants to catch the cashier. This
152   is apparently the third time that Bloom has 'tactfully' reminded Hynes that he owes him three shillings. This instance of Bloom's effort at tact, taken alongside his attempt to be courteously helpful over the dinge in Menton's hat (p. 95/146) suggests an alien's blundering, though well-meaning, sociability, out of key with the spontaneous and engaging frankness of the Dubliners.

Bloom puts his cutting of the Keyes advertisement before Nannetti, explaining the idea for the symbol of the crossed keys. Nannetti, accustomed to working in the midst of ceaseless racket, never wastes words, and his silence leaves Bloom unsure
153   how his approach is being received. He is anxious to make the proposal clear to Nannetti, but anxious, too, not to appear to be trying to 'teach him his own business'. This unsureness of Bloom, trivial in a sense, is yet one with the lostness of a Ulysses far from home, a Moses brought up in an alien land, a Stephen Dedalus, artist, at loggerheads with the culture that has reared him. Bloom insecure, Bloom snubbed, is all this – and more.

He is a man lost and rootless in a world too limited to satisfy him. And, as later correspondences indicate, he is the prophet coming to his own and finding that his own receive him not.

Nannetti agrees that the suggested advertisement can be produced and asks for the design of the keys symbol. Bloom promises to get this: it has already been used in an advertisement in a Kilkenny paper. (He goes later to the National Library (116) in order to find a copy.) Bloom presses his request for a little paragraph calling attention to Keyes's business in return for renewal of the advertisement. Nannetti agrees to this if Keyes will make it a three months' renewal, thus presenting Bloom with new obstacles to be surmounted. The successful achievement of this little business commission has now become Bloom's major commercial quest of the day. By deft symbolic touches Joyce relates it to Bloom's other more personal hungers, and indeed to every man's pursuit of success and security. The key is throughout the instrument of entry which ends exclusion and alienation. Thus the emphasis on the two keys, crossed in a circle, has overtones of the climatic meeting between keyless Stephen and Bloom. Alexander Keyes, as 'tea, wine and spirit merchant' is himself a miniature Trinity of creativity, redemption, and comfort. References to the house of keys, the 'innuendo of Home Rule', 'licensed premises' (cf. 'Your name entered for 100 life as owner in the book of the union' in the Agendath Netaim advertisement, p. 49/72), and 'longfelt want' together constitute a reminder of Bloom's hunger for married happiness and security in a home that has lately been over much visited by a tourist 'from the Isle of Man'.

A typesetter brings a sheet of proofs to be checked. Bloom watches Nannetti checking the spelling. Not for the first time, 154 not for the last time, he is now being ignored and feels it. Hence his thoughts return to the moment when he muffed his attempt to ingratiate himself with Menton over the dinge in his hat (p. 95/146). He realizes that he ought to have said something light-hearted 'about an old hat or something', oiling the move with humour or banter in the Irish way. Nannetti gives back the checked proof and asks for the archbishop's letter to the *Freeman* which is to be printed in the *Telegraph* too (thus enlightening the reader about the point of the archbishop's phone call referred to on p. 97/149). Bloom makes a parting remark to Nannetti ('Then I'll get the design . . .'), but it receives no reply. 155

101   He ponders the difficulty of getting a three months' renewal from Keyes. It will be necessary for him to rub in the advantages of advertising in August, the month of the horse show, and the tourist season.

Bloom walks through the caseroom, passing Old Monks, the day-father. The sight of a typesetter reading the type backwards reminds him of his father reading the Hebrew script from right (118)   to left in his hagadah book, and so of the Passover (Pessach) and all the rituals associated with it. Bloom, who is suffering too much in the way of neglectful 'passovers', is no more comfortable at home with Jewish orthodoxy than he is with 156   Catholicism. He decides against taking a tram out to visit Keyes, with the danger that he might find him out. Instead, he will phone him. The number 2844 he remembers as being like the number of Citron's house, 28.

Dabbing his nose with his handkerchief, he receives a citron-lemon smell from the soap in his pocket: he restores the soap to its original place in his hip pocket. The scent sets his mind 102   on its familiar centripetal course to Molly. 'What perfume does your wife use?' The question in Martha's letter recurs to him time after time. But what is not said here is, as often, more moving than what is said. 'I could go home still: tram; something I forgot. Just to see before: dressing. No.' There would be no time to go home before visiting the library, making the excuse that he has forgotten something, and having the pleasure of seeing Molly before she dresses to receive Boylan. There is pain as well as pleasure in the hypothetical anticipation.

As Bloom approaches the *Evening Telegraph* office a sudden screech of laughter greets him, and he recognizes Ned Lambert's voice. He enters the office softly, unobtrusively. He wants to use the phone to ring up Keyes and get authorization for a three months' renewal of the advertisement.

In the office are Professor MacHugh, Simon Dedalus, and Ned Lambert. Of Bloom's entry MacHugh murmurs, 'The ghost walks,' giving Bloom the status of ghost-father to Stephen's 157   Hamlet; while Simon Dedalus's oath, 'Agonising Christ,' seems to provide another apt commentary on Bloom, the despised and rejected Hebrew trying to be one of their fellowship. (Agonizing Bloom will eventually imprint his own 'heartburn' on an arse, p. 604/*867*, and if now he is received before an 'empty fire-place', he will then have lit the fire in the home with 'one ignited

lucifer match', p. 547/*781*.) Ned Lambert is mockingly reading
a flowery patriotic speech made last night by Dan Dawson and
printed in the *Freeman*. Dedalus and MacHugh both find it
intolerable. To Bloom, too, the speech is 'highfalutin' stuff'.   *158*

   J. J. O'Molloy comes in, and the opening door hits Bloom,   103
reminding him (and the reader) that there is little enough room
for him in this office. In Bloom's thoughts we learn something
of O'Molloy – that he used to be the 'cleverest fellow at the
junior bar', but has declined and suffers from money troubles.   (120)
In this episode, so packed with images of frustration and disap-   *159*
pointment, he is one more might-have-been, a man of promise
who gambled, accumulated debts, and went downhill. Just now
he is seeking Myles Crawford – and a loan.

   Ned Lambert continues to recite bits of the flowery rhetoric   104
of Dan Dawson to the jeers of Dedalus and MacHugh. Dedalus's
cry, 'shite and onions!' contributes to the establishment of a   *160*
thematic association between empty rhetoric, farts, and faeces.
Remember what Bloom did with 'Matcham's Masterstroke',
p. 57/*85*. (And see p. 239/*376*.) Bloom, a more gentle soul than
any of them, reflects that Doughy Daw's rhetoric, crude as it
may look in print, goes down well with a living audience. The
reference to 'What Wetherup said' introduces one of the little
mysteries of *Ulysses*, Wetherup's significance (if he has any) and
identity being as teasing as MacIntosh's. (See p. 539/*768*, for
another of Wetherup's platitudinous apophthegms.)

   Myles Crawford, the editor, bursts into the room. He has a   *161*
'scarlet beaked face', a 'comb of feathery hair', and a harsh
voice. The pressman is the cock who crows out betrayals.
(See p. 233/*367* and cf. 'Weathercocks', p. 103/*159*.) He and
MacHugh exchange virulent abuse at the bantering level – and
once again one feels how remote and alien Bloom's smooth
politeness is from the virile intimacies of shared obscenity and
blasphemy by which the Dubliners give voice to their mutual   105
friendship. And the cryptic references to past Irish military
achievements, like the asides about Crawford's alcoholism
('incipient jigs'), exclude Bloom from the ethos of their companionship. Simon Dedalus and Ned Lambert go off for a drink.
Bloom, 'seeing the coast clear' (an Odyssean image), threads his   *162*
way through, explaining to Mr Crawford that he wants to
'phone about an ad'. He receives no reply, but a moment later
we hear him calling the number.

Lenehan comes in with pages of the *Sports* edition. He offers
Sceptre as a tip for today's Ascot Gold Cup race. The newsboys
106   waiting for the Racing Special have created a minor fracas
163   outside, the door bursts open, and a wind blows Lenehan's
Sports pages about the floor. MacHugh deals roughly with the
offending boys. Joyce's headline, 'SPOT THE WINNER', invites
us to consider in advance the symbolic significance of the Gold
Cup race. The cup is to emerge as a symbol of feminine sexuality.
Lenehan's tip, and Boylan's bet, *Sceptre*, with its powerful
(123)   phallic overtones, does not after all achieve the cup. The
despised dark horse, the outsider, beats his flashier rivals to it
– the ignored Bloom, now on the phone. We overhear his conversation and gather that he has found Keyes out – at the auction
rooms, whither he must pursue him. Hurrying back from the
inner office, he collides with Lenehan. Lenehan's apology,
'Pardon, monsieur,' is polite, but its tone of mock dignity sets
Bloom apart as one who demands special treatment.

164   Bloom explains that he is going to Dillon's Auction Rooms
107   in Bachelor's Walk in search of Keyes. Crawford dismisses him
with mock solemnity. Professor MacHugh and Lenehan watch
him through the windows as the capering newsboys follow him,
165   aping his walk. Lenehan himself caricatures the performance,
mazurkaing across the floor. Crawford suggests following
Lambert and Dedalus who have gone for a drink; and there is
a significant moment, for the reader, as Myles Crawford walks
'jerkily back into the office behind, parting the vent of his jacket,
jingling his keys in his back pocket'. They jingle too as he locks
his desk drawer. The convergence of jingle and keys – the one
a symbol of Molly's bed-life with Boylan, from which Bloom is
excluded, and the other a symbol of Bloom's more general exclusions from home, from Dublin's life, from successful commercial
activity, is momentous. And here the reader needs to know that
Bloom and his wife Molly have not had full sexual intercourse
since the birth (and death, eleven days later) of their son Rudy
over ten years ago (p. 605/*869*). Thus Bloom's separation from
Molly is in important respects no shorter than Odysseus's separation from Penelope, and today's wanderings, which eventually
lead him back to her, compress within their mental range a lostness and a longing no less pathetic than Odysseus's own.

166   Myles Crawford comes back into the room, theatrically
108   lamenting the powerlessness of Ireland before the *imperium*

romanum of Britain. Professor MacHugh disparages English civilization as being, like the Roman, a matter of sanitation rather than of culture. The English have covered their lands with water-closets. The Irish ancestry were 'partial to the running stream' – a life-giving symbol in the 'Waste Land' of contemporary Dublin, as Mother Grogan, and later Molly herself, testify. Meanwhile Lenehan tries to announce his new riddle, but is frustrated, not for the first time, not for the last time. 167

Mr O'Madden Burke comes in, followed by Stephen Dedalus. Stephen hands Mr Deasy's letter to Crawford, who remarks that a piece has been torn off it. A verse from the poem which Stephen wrote on the torn-off slip (p. 40/60) passes through Stephen's mind, reducing to their final form some of the jumbled phrases we heard as he composed on the seashore ('Mouth to my mouth' in the lyric counterpoints the 'Foot and mouth' theme.) Stephen explains that the letter is not his but Mr Garrett Deasy's. Crawford, recalling how Mrs Deasy, 'the bloodiest old tartar God ever made', once threw the soup at a waiter in a hotel, sheds new light, for Stephen and for the reader, on Deasy's claim that 'a woman brought sin into the world' (p. 29/42–3). 109 / 168 / (127)

Professor MacHugh compares the role of the Irish with that of the Greeks. His lot is to teach the language (Latin) of the vulgar civilization which dominated Greek culture and to speak the language of the materialistic civilization (English) which swamps Irish spirituality. The Irish, subject to a civilization based on cash and water-closets, are the true heirs of European catholic chivalry and Greek intellect. Pyrrhus, like contemporary Irish revolutionaries, tried to retrieve the fortunes of his country (Greece). We recall that Stephen gave a lesson on Pyrrhus (p. 20/29) and perhaps that Dedalus had a son called Pyrrhus. There is mock mourning for frustrated Pyrrhus, and Stephen's mind turns again to his mother 'beastly dead'. 169 / 110 / 170

Crawford agrees to publish the letter. Lenehan at last gets his riddle out; the opera that resembles a railway line is *The Rose of Castille*. The pun recurs later. The company mutually compliment one another as a little gathering representative of all the talents. MacHugh notes sarcastically that Bloom, representative of 'the gentle art of advertisement', is missing; Burke that Madam Bloom, 'the vocal muse', is also missing. Lenehan's cough and at first mystifying joke – 'I caught a cold in the park. The gate was open' – is explained only when we discover that 111 / 171

Lenehan himself has had his bit of fun with Molly Bloom in the past (pp. 192–3/300–1).

Crawford asks Stephen to write something for him. 'You can do it. I see it in your face,' he says, and Stephen's thoughts flash back to a memorable day at Clongowes school recorded in *A Portrait of the Artist*. Stephen had broken his glasses and been exempted from writing by Fr Arnall. But Fr Dolan treated his excuse as a trick and caned him for it. 'Why are you not writing like the others?' he asked. 'Lazy little schemer, I see schemer in your face.'

(130)   No less interesting than this flashback to Joyce's earlier work is the appeal which Crawford immediately afterwards makes to Stephen the writer. 'Give them something with a bite in it. Put us all into it, damn its soul. Father Son and Holy Ghost and Jakes M'Carthy.' This, of course, is exactly what Joyce has done in *Ulysses*; put them all into it, the Persons of the Trinity and the riff-raff of Dublin too. The headline above – YOU CAN DO IT – is richly meaningful, for a trinitarian correspondence emerges in which Bloom is Father, Stephen Son, and Molly the Comforter. Not that this scheme is fixed, for Joyce's symbolism shifts, and Bloom is intermittently Elijah, Moses, and Jesus, while Molly is intermittently Eve, the Virgin Mary, and the Church as the Mystical Bride.

172   In asserting Stephen's power to 'paralyse Europe' with his pen, Crawford recalls proudly how Ignatius Gallaher, former
112   pressman with the *Freeman*, brought off 'the smartest piece of journalism ever known'. It was in 1882, immediately after the Phoenix Park murders. The *New York World* cabled for news. Gallaher wired back details of the murderers' movements by referring New York to an advertisement in the *Weekly Freeman* of 17 March and basing a code upon it. There are several references in *Ulysses* to the 'Invincibles', the gang who murdered the Chief Secretary and Under-Secretary in Phoenix Park on 6 May 1882 – 1881 in the text here. The actual murderers were executed. Others involved received prison sentences. We learn here that one Skin-the-Goat, or Fitzharris, now keeps a cabman's shelter at Butt Bridge. This is the shelter which Bloom and Stephen visit in episode 16 (see pp. 508/715–6 and 514/726). We also learn that another of the gang, Gumley, is now a corporation night-watchman. He, too, appears in episode 16. (For more of Gumley, see pp. 264/418; 503/708; and 522/739). It is

during the full spate of Crawford's excitement in recounting   *173*
this triumph of journalism that the phone bell rings. MacHugh
answers it. It is Bloom, unintentionally blundering once more   *113*
against the ironies rigged against him. 'Tell him to go to hell,'
Myles Crawford says, in understandable irritation. That these
Irishmen are too excitedly romanticizing their own past suffer-
ings to pay attention to the needs of the living stranger in their
midst is one of Joyce's telling ironies.

Crawford's use of the word 'history' reminds Stephen of the
aphorism he framed for Mr Deasy this morning, 'History is a   *174*
nightmare from which I am trying to awake' (p. 28/42), here
reversed, 'from which you will never awake', while Crawford's
reference to Dick Adams sets Lenehan, the flippant punster and   *(132)*
quipster, reciting hackneyed palindromes – 'Madam, I'm Adam.'
(See Stuart Gilbert* for a detailed account of how this chapter
comprises 'a veritable thesaurus of rhetorical devices and might,
indeed, be adopted as a textbook for students of the art of
rhetoric'.) Meantime MacHugh's voice is heard on the phone
replying to Bloom that Crawford is still here and that Bloom
had better come across himself.

Returning, MacHugh takes up the conversation about the
'Invincibles'. It appears that Lady Dudley, wife of the Lord
Lieutenant, has bought a postcard view of Dublin at a street
stall outside the viceregal lodge, only to discover that the card
is a commemoration card celebrating the memory of one of the
Phoenix Park murderers. The hawkers have found themselves
in the dock. Hence to Crawford's view of the contemporary   *175*
Dublin law-courts, which is like his view of the contemporary
Press. Both Press and Bar have deteriorated. There are none to
match the great pleaders of the past, Whiteside, Isaac Butt,
O'Hagan. Crawford's mouth twitches with excitement. Stephen's
mind goes back to his poem, the image of the kissed mouth,   *114*
then to the search for rhymes, which suddenly are concretized,
men in couples, girls in threes. Rhyming phrases from Dante
float through Stephen's thoughts. Thus, while Myles Crawford
and J. J. O'Molloy continue to lament the decay of literary talent
in the service of Press and Law, Stephen is preoccupied with
the thought of literary talent more vocationally exercised in the
work of the poet. In this mood, like Joyce himself, he feels called

---

* *James Joyce's Ulysses*, A study by Stuart Gilbert, Faber and Faber Ltd.

to resist the pressures upon him to exploit his talent profitably in Ireland.

176 O'Molloy cites Seymour Bushe, KC, as an exception to Crawford's generalization about the decay of eloquence. He claims that Bushe uttered one of the most polished periods he ever listened to during the Childs fratricide case. Mention of this case brings Stephen once more mentally face to face with Hamlet's Ghost. The Ghost's line, '*And in the porches of mine ear*

115 *did pour*', teases Stephen. How could old Hamlet, poisoned in his sleep, know how the poisoning was accomplished? When

177 O'Molloy actually recites Seymour Bushe's sentence, it turns out to be a very flowery piece of rhetoric, and Stephen, pressed to say that he likes it, 'his blood wooed by grace of language and

(135) gesture', silently blushes.

178 O'Molloy mentions a conversation with Professor Magennis in which the professor spoke of Stephen. He asks Stephen what he thinks of the 'hermetic crowd', A. E. and company, who are

116 dabbling in theosophy. Stephen, egocentric as ever, is intensely curious to know what Professor Magennis said of him, but represses the desire to ask. Meanwhile Professor MacHugh continues the conversation about oratory, claiming that the finest display of it he ever heard was an impromptu speech by John F. Taylor. MacHugh describes how the college historical society was debating a paper advocating the revival of the Irish tongue

179 at a time when the nationalist movement was new and weak, and Mr Justice Fitzgibbon, the present Lord Justice of Appeal, had poured scorn on it. Taylor, who had come there from a

180 sick-bed, compared Fitzgibbon's case to that of an Egyptian high
117 priest trying to persuade the youthful Moses to accept submission to the culture, religion, and language of Egypt, arguing that the Jews were a poor nomad tribe, the Egyptians the masters of a mighty and wealthy empire.

As Taylor's moving sentences, implicitly comparing captive Israel to captive Ireland, are quoted, even Stephen is touched by the solemn dignity of the words. It is a moment of sharp temptation for him – the temptation to compromise and come to terms. The temptation is symbolized in the quotation from *Cymbeline*, '*And let our crooked smokes*', which is part of the English king's speech at the end of the play, when he accepts graciously the authority of Rome which he is anyway not powerful enough to reject. The speech is worth greater attention than at first sight seems justifiable, because it is quoted again at the end of episode 9 (p. 179/280). It speaks of the Roman and British ensigns waving 'friendly together', of advantageous compromise peaceably accepted. The contexts in which this speech is remembered mark out a parallel between Ireland's temptation to submit to the power of England and Stephen's temptation to put himself, as man and writer, wholly at the service of Ireland, its culture, and its cause. So far as the temptation to Stephen the writer is concerned, it is notable that the *Cymbeline* speech comes from an aged Shakespeare resting at the end of a sometimes tempestuous life, his work done. Stephen's is yet to do. He must defend himself in advance against the seduction of rhetoric. 'Noble words coming. Look out. Could you try your hand at it yourself?'

It is St Augustine, another much tempted soul, who comes (136) to Stephen's rescue. A sentence from the *Confessions* swims into his mind. 'It was revealed to me . . .' This sentence marks for St Augustine a crucial moment of conquest, when the long intellectual struggle over the question of God's omnipotence and goodness, man's freedom and the presence of evil, is at last closed in the realization that evil is not a reality in its own right but a deprivation of good. This realization marks the moment of intellectual victory which precedes the decisive act of conversion. Joyce's correspondences here are powerful and subtle. 'Those things' – the Irish homeland, the Irish tradition, culture, revolution – are indeed good. It is *because* they are good that they can be corrupted. It is also because they are not the *supremely* and *absolutely* good that they can be corrupted. It is right to be drawn by them. It is also right to resist their attractiveness; though resistance is costly. Vocation always is. 'Ah curse you!' It is with a curse upon the costliness of his own vocation to cut himself off from what draws him so sweetly, so profitably, that Stephen is to face the demands of exile and self-dedication. Meantime MacHugh completes the magnificent *181* quotation from John F. Taylor, mocking England's invitation to Ireland to accept submission to superior power and wealth, and showing how Moses's rejection of the easy way brought him and his people ultimately out of bondage into consecrated nationhood.

O'Molloy points out that Moses died 'without having entered 118 the land of promise', linking Moses's disappointments with the frustrations of Irish revolutionaries and with the frustrations today of Bloom the canvasser. Stephen's reflection is that political oratory (literary talent exploited in a cause) is ephemeral, 'gone with the wind'. The vast crowds who gathered at the mass meetings to listen to the great revolutionary O'Connell provided only 'miles of ears of porches' into which the poison of propaganda was poured. The oratory of the tribune and the

182   statesman is 'dead noise'. (And note that, in Stephen's eyes, Moses, after being child and man, finished up as a lifeless 'effigy . . . stonebearded'. The phrases recall those of the Seymour Bushe speech quoted by O'Molloy on p. 115/*177*, where the Moses of Michelangelo is a 'stony effigy in frozen music'. Thus images accumulate which equate the noisy oratory of the Irish movement with the paralysis of art. The nightmare of history holds these sentimental, backward-looking revolutionaries in its grip. Stephen knows that he must escape it.)

(138)   Stephen now proposes an adjournment to a pub. Lenehan, the incorrigible japester, voices the general agreement in his forced music-hall pseudo-rhetoric. Crawford has to go back in

183   search of his keys (now 'blasted'). Amid the windy banter, the opening and closing of doors, the marching feet and yelling

119   voices of newsboys, Stephen sums up his position in one of Joyce's telling, economical lines, 'Dublin. I have much, much to learn.' The attachment to Dublin and the rejection of Dublin are felt by the reader, and the simple humility of Stephen's admission gives the flavour of conversion to it. It is perhaps another Augustinian moment.

Stephen's vision, which he now recounts, is a parable. It concerns two old ladies from Fumbally's Lane, the place whose mention brings back to Stephen's mind a memorable incident (already referred to on p. 39/*59*, 'A shefiend's whiteness under her rancid rags. Fumbally's Lane that night: the tanyard smells'), when he saw a couple making love in the darkness, caught a glimpse of a gipsy face under a shawl, and heard the excited whisper, 'Quicker, darlint' – an incident which amounts to one more instance of frustration when fulfilment is in sight. The two old ladies are Anne Kearns and Florence MacCabe. Though they are called 'vestal virgins' here, no doubt for the purpose of making a correspondence with the parable of the Wise and Foolish Virgins, on her last appearance (p. 31/*46*) Florence MacCabe, the midwife, was described as 'Mrs Florence

MacCabe, relict of the late Patk. MacCabe, deeply lamented, of Bride Street'.* The two women want to see the views of Dublin from the top of Nelson's Pillar. (It will be remembered that Lady Dudley's pursuit of a postcard view of Dublin came to a frustrating end when she found she had purchased a revolutionary commemorative card, p. 113/174.) They save up their money in a 'red tin letterbox moneybox' (very much a symbol of the British imperium – see THE WEARER OF THE CROWN section,   *184* p. 96/147). They buy brawn, bread, and 'four and twenty ripe plums' to make a picnic, and then climb up the winding staircase of Nelson's column.

Stephen's parable is interrupted at this point. MacHugh   120 wonders what is keeping Myles Crawford, who went back for   (140) his keys. Crawford now emerges behind them, talking with   *185* J. J. O'Molloy who, as we learn, has been trying to touch him for a loan.

Bloom appears at a moment of maximum inconvenience, when newsboys are rushing out with the racing special, when Crawford and his companions are just setting off for a drink, when Stephen is in the midst of recounting his parable to MacHugh, and when Crawford is engaged in a deeply personal interchange with O'Molloy. Bloom's news is that Alexander Keyes is trying to strike a businessman's bargain with the newspaper, offering to give a renewal of his advertisement for two months (instead of the three asked for) and demanding in return a paragraph calling attention to his business in the *Telegraph*. Bloom is rudely rebuffed by Crawford, who gives him an obscene retort to convey to Keyes. Bloom sums up the   *186* situation in some respects and shows an odd interest in Stephen's welfare, but he does not quite know how seriously to take Crawford's hilarious rebuff. The invitation to kiss the editor's arse is the nearest Bloom gets to commercial success this morning. It is comically congruous with what he achieves later in re-establishing physical contact with Molly (p. 604/*867*). Moreover Crawford's 'KMA', like Molly's 'Mn', was pre-echoed

---

* Here the two women are said to have lived fifty and fifty-three years in Fumbally's Lane; but we cannot therefore assume that two different Florence MacCabes were intended by Joyce, for 'Bride Street', the address given on p. 31/46, was Joyce's own emendation of 'Blackpitts' in an earlier MS, and Fumbally's Lane is 'off Blackpitts'. See Robert M. Adams: *Surface and Symbol*, p. 148 (Oxford University Press, 1962).

in the cat's 'Mkgnao' which greeted Bloom this morning (p. 45/65).

121   As it becomes clear that O'Molloy has been trying to borrow money from Crawford and has been reluctantly refused, he, too, joins the ranks of the disappointed and frustrated (swelling ranks now – Bloom, Moses, Lady Dudley, Pyrrhus, the gipsy girl, Stephen's virgins).

187   Stephen continues his parable. The ladies eat their bread and brawn, approach the railings, but are afraid the pillar will fall, find it makes them giddy to look down, and so do not enjoy the view they promised themselves. Instead, they settle down and peer up at the 'statue of the onehandled adulterer' Nelson. This gives them a crick in their neck. Thus they can enjoy neither looking down at the city of Dublin, nor up at the figure representative of Britain's defective and immoral power. One by one,

122
188   they eat the plums, spitting out the stones so that they fall on the city below. The twenty-four plumstones spat out by the ladies match the 'four and twenty blackbirds baked in a pie' celebrated in the unquoted line from 'Sing a song of sixpence', and the twenty-four suitors of Molly Bloom (p. 602/863).

MacHugh says that Stephen reminds him of Antisthenes who took the palm of beauty from Helen of Troy and gave it to

(142)   Penelope. Stephen is reminded of Sir Philip Sidney's Stella, Penelope Rich. The reader is reminded that Joyce does indeed give the palm of beauty to Penelope in the shape of Molly Bloom. The association made here between the two virgins and Molly Bloom (through Penelope) is important, for it gives us the key by which to interpret Stephen's parable when he narrates it a second time towards the end of Ulysses (see p. 561/802).

Meanwhile there is a sudden failure of a different kind as a short circuit puts Dublin's city tramways temporarily out of action. Dublin becomes a paralysed city in another sense.

189   We may note that Stephen calls his parable 'A Pisgah Sight of Palestine or the Parable of the Plums'. The phrase 'Pisgah view' is used of 'any vision or hope of which a man will not

123   see the realization' (Oxford Dictionary of the Christian Church). The theme of Moses disappointed thus recurs. The theme of the foolish virgins who came too late and missed the bridegroom reinforces it. Myles Crawford, looking up at Nelson's statue, presses home the sexual element in the parable. The one-handled adulterer has excited the old maids frustratingly, and they spit

out the plum-stones. Both Nelson's column and the plum-tree have phallic significance. (Home is incomplete without Plum-tree's potted meat, when the meat is not put into the pot through sexual intercourse, as Bloom knows well.) The final 'note' of the episode, the sexual frustration of spinsterhood, corroborates the prevailing mood of this episode's study in disappointment.   (143)

Chapter 8

The Lestrygonians

124
190 The Homeric basis is the episode of the Lestrygonians, whose cannibalistic habits put Odysseus's followers in peril. Odysseus-like, Bloom is repelled by the eating habits in The Burton and withdraws from a horrifying exhibition of stomach-churning crudity.

(144) It is one o'clock and Bloom wanders about Dublin's streets, the thought of food much in mind. He passes Graham Lemon's sweet-shop, where a girl assistant is shovelling up sweets for a christian brother. He is presumably purchasing them for some school treat. The notice 'Lozenge and comfit manufacturer to His Majesty the King' reminds Bloom of the national anthem and of a silly jingle.

A young YMCA man gives Bloom a throwaway. Looking at it, Bloom reads the letters 'Bloo' and at first almost expects an 'm' to follow them; but the phrase is 'Blood of the Lamb'. The leaflet is advertising a meeting to be addressed by a high-pressure American evangelist, Dr John Alexander Dowie, 'restorer of the church in Zion'. A slogan reads, 'Elijah is coming. Is coming! Is coming!! Is coming!!!' Bloom reflects on the profits to be made from mass evangelism and from commercializing religion. Recalling how a Birmingham firm put a luminous crucifix on the market, he remembers the bluey silver glow of a bit of codfish (Godfish) left in the larder one night.

191 He catches sight of Stephen's sister, Dilly Dedalus, outside Dillon's auctioneers, and thinks compassionately how a home 'always breaks up when the mother goes'. His fear that the Dedalus family are suffering from poverty and neglect has emerged before on sight of Stephen in the *Freeman* office (p. 120/*186*). The Dedaluses had fifteen children, a 'birth every

year almost'. This intolerable strain on the home's finances
Bloom blames on the rigorous anti-contraceptive pressures from
the RC priests – who, he thinks, do themselves pretty well in
the way of food and comforts. Bloom's concern for Dilly's   125
poverty-stricken dress and underfed look is both genuine and   (145)
touching.

He crosses O'Connell bridge, under which a brewery barge
sails out with stout for England. Looking down on the dirty
water, he remembers the story of Reuben J. Dodd's son   192
and Simon Dedalus's droll joke that two shillings was one and
eightpence too much to pay for his rescue (his 'redemption',
we might say, p. 78/*118*). Rolling up his throwaway, he flings
it down between the flapping gulls – 'Elijah is coming'
approaching the water at thirty-two feet per second. The gulls
are not 'such damn fools' as to mistake the paper ball for food.
They 'live by their wits' and are not easily taken in. (It is implied
that human gulls are more likely to mistake this prophet for
the true Elijah and his word for the living food, the bread
of life.)

An old apple-woman calls, 'Two apples a penny.' Bloom buys
two Banbury cakes from her stall, breaks them up, and throws
them in the Liffey. The gulls swoop swiftly and silently on the
fragments, and they are gone. (Real food, this.) Bloom has cast   *193*
his bread upon the waters. Reflections on the diet of fish and   126
the taste of swan meat follow.

An anchored rowboat holds an advertisement in view of
passers-by on the bridge, '*Kino's 11/– Trousers*'. Bloom's professional eye approves this advertising gimmick. Advertising in
unlikely places can be effective. The memory of posters in
urinals, on which quack doctors offer treatment for VD introduces a horrible, unutterable thought which Bloom thrusts from
himself. 'If he . . . O! Eh? No . . . No . . .' One may interpret, 'If   *194*
Boylan had VD . . .' The possible consequences are too terrible
to contemplate. 'Think no more about that.'

Passing the ballast office, Bloom notes the timeball, recalls a
book by Sir Robert Ball, the astronomer, and ponders the word
'parallax'; his problem word, like Molly's 'metempsychosis'. The
two words refer to two different kinds of change with which
Ulysses is concerned; the change which converts an Odysseus
into a Leopold Bloom, and the change which converts the
reader's view of Boylan as seen through Bloom's eyes to that

as seen through Molly's eyes. 'O rocks!' was Molly's mocking exclamation when Bloom tried to explain 'metempsychosis' to her (p. 52/77). Molly, Bloom concludes, is right in her scorn of big words. She has her own wisdom, even wit. 'She used to say Ben Dollard had a base-barreltone voice.' This witticism of (147)   Molly's is dissected and every ambiguity explored. Bloom shows us that there is more in it than appears at first sight; shows us thereby how wide awake we need to be when reading *Ulysses*. 'It all works out.' Ben Dollard, by the way, is listed on p. 602/*863*, among Molly's past admirers. The number of the past admirers who are mentioned in this episode (most of them entering into the mind of Bloom at one point or another) is so large that it can scarcely be accidental.

127   A file of sandwich-board-men moves towards him, advertising Wisdom Hely's, with the letters HELY'S in scarlet on their tall white hats. To Bloom this is a poor way to earn a living, 195   'three bob a day': it is also an ineffective way of advertising. (Bloom used to work for Wisdom Hely, stationer. His varying professional connexion with paper is symbolic. He has virtually earned Molly's daily bread wrapped in paper. He recalls how he tried to persuade Hely to send round a transparent show-cart with 'two smart girls inside, writing letters'. There is some psychology in this appeal to curiosity and to sex interest, as Bloom explains. But Hely rejected the idea. Hely's advertising notions were on the same level as the howler which Bloom quotes here and elsewhere – when Plumtree's Potted Meat was advertised immediately under the obituaries, 'cold meat department'. The examples Bloom cites of Hely's advertising gambits are certainly depressing. ('You can't lick 'em. What? Our envelopes', etc.) Bloom feels well out of the Hely business. He had a difficult job collecting payments from convents they supplied. The memory of a sweet-faced carmelite nun, disturbed by him at her devotions on the occasion of such a visit, lingers with him.

He crosses Westmoreland Street, trying to date the past accu-196   rately, and the reader begins to get a clearer picture. Bloom got the job in Hely's the year he and Molly married. Rudy, their son, died ten years ago, in 1894 (and since that time he and Molly have not had full sexual intercourse: he has been a wanderer). The party Bloom recalls here seems to have been especially memorable. Val Dillon, the lord mayor, is later listed among Molly's suitors and, if Alderman Robert O'Reilly is 'Maggot O'Reilly', then so is he. Professor Goodwin, also at the Glencree Dinner, is a third (pp. 601–2/*863*.) We learn later that Lenehan was present too. (For his memory of the occasion see p. 192/*300* and for Molly's recollection of it see p. 617/*887–8*.) Bloom, recalling Molly at this party, 'just beginning to plump   128 it out well' in her beautifully fitting elephant-grey dress, looks back on these days as especially happy. Milly was still a kiddy.   (148) He sees her soaped all over on her tubbing night.

The stream of life image recurs. Bloom tries, but fails, to remember the name ('Pen something') of a 'priestly looking chap' who was always squinting in when he passed their snug little room in Lombard Street West. The name he cannot recall is 'Penrose' (p. 149/*231*).

Bartell d'Arcy, the tenor, another of Molly's past admirers, figures in Bloom's recollections too. He used to see Molly home   197 after practising with her. The song he gave her, '*Winds that blow from the south*', echoes Stephen's poem, written on the rocks (p. 109/*168*). It is characteristic of Joyce's pathos and irony that Bloom's touching, nostalgic memories here of Molly the young wife, in the home and in the street, in the kitchen and in the bedroom, should be so entangled with his recollections of the men who admired her too intimately.

His recollections are interrupted. He meets an old flame, Mrs Breen, wife of Denis Breen, who has become feeble-minded. Bloom and Mrs Breen exchange greetings and formal inquiries.   198 When Bloom, approaching the subject tactfully, asks after her   129 husband, Mrs Breen declares him a 'caution to rattlesnakes'. Even now he is looking into the law of libel; and Mrs Breen dives into her handbag to show Bloom the latest. Inhaling the   199 smells and vapours of Harrison's café, Bloom watches her rummaging among the contents of her bag – hatpin, money, medicine bottles, pastilles. The new moon last night must have made Denis especially bad, Mrs Breen says, for he woke her up complaining of a nightmare in which he saw the Ace of Spades walking up the stairs. (Like the black panther of Haines's nightmare, p. 4/*3* and the oriental stranger of Stephen's dream, p. 39/*59*, the Ace of Spades, walking up the stairs, matches the wandering, intruding, dark-suited Bloom.) Then she finds what she is seeking, and hands Bloom a folded postcard which bears the cryptic message 'U.p.'. Outraged by receipt of this card,   130

200   which implies that he is mad and done for, Denis is now seeing the solicitor (Menton), bent on an action for damages.

Bloom notes Mrs Breen's dowdiness, her shabby gentility, her ageing features. The smell of soup from Harrison's assails his nose as he tries to identify the fading woman before him as Josie Powell, with whom he evidently carried on a mild flirtation prior to his wooing of Molly – and in particular at a memorable party at Dolphin's Barn. (See pp. 309/492 and 612/879.)

(151)   Bloom asks after Mrs Beaufoy, changing the subject quickly – too quickly, for in his haste he gets the wrong name: he means Mrs Purefoy: 'Beaufoy' is the name of the man who won the competition in *Titbits* with the story which he read this morning in the outside water-closet. (Did he remember to pull the chain?) Mrs Breen tells him that Mina Purefoy is in the maternity hospital in Holles Street, where she has lain in labour now for three days. (Thus the confused pair, Beaufoy and Mrs Purefoy, are both involved in creative labour.)

201   Mr Bloom gently touches Mrs Breen's arm so that she moves out of the way to let an eccentric Dubliner pass, Cashel Boyle
131   O'Connor Fitzmaurice Tisdall Farrell, who strides staring along the curbstones, going round all the lamp-posts on the outside. Mrs Breen spots her husband now and goes after him. Bloom watches the two near-lunatics, Denis Breen shuffling along with two great tomes hugged to his ribs, Farrell with dangling stick,
202   umbrella, and dustcoat, looping round the lamp-posts. The movement of both, like Bloom's roaming, interrupted course in this episode, like the sentences themselves, has that quality which Joyce called 'peristaltic' – appropriate imitative of the successive muscular contractions which drive matter along the alimentary canal.

Bloom imagines that the postcard to Denis Breen must have been the work of Alf Bergan or Richie Goulding – and sent for a lark.

He passes the offices of the *Irish Times* and now for the first time we learn the full story of his pen-friendship with Martha. He thinks there might be other answers lying there now which he would like to deal with – answers, that is, to an advertisement he inserted in the paper, reading 'Wanted smart young lady typist to aid gentleman in literary work'. He decides not to bother at present. He has already waded through forty-four answers. Sentences from Martha's letter this morning float through his mind ('I called you naughty boy ...', p. 63/94). Then he recalls the reply he received from another interested party, one Lizzie Twigg, who wrote, 'My literary efforts have had the good fortune to meet with the approval of the eminent poet A. E. (Mr Geo. Russell).' It appears that Bloom thought this lady *too* interested in literature for his purposes. (In fact she published verses in the *United Irishman*.) 'No time to do her hair drinking sloppy tea with a book of poetry.'

Bloom reflects on the success of the *Irish Times*, with its small ads and its 'toady news' of society activities. It now owns the *Irish Field* too, with its coverage of the smart set's hunting. Bloom, in some respects a rather feminine man, has something of an obsession about masculine women (as will emerge powerfully in the *Circe* episode, p. 381 ff./593 ff.) Here he dwells on the toughness of the hunting women who ride astride like men and toss off their brandy neat. The woman he watched outside the Grosvenor Hotel this morning comes back to mind – and the spite of the tram-driver who denied him his view of her as she mounted the cab (p. 61/90) – then a Mrs Miriam Dandrade, from whom he purchased her old wraps and underwear in the Shelbourne Hotel; so tough and unselfconscious was she that she handed him her underclothes as impersonally as if he were a clotheshorse. He saw this lady again when Stubbs the park ranger worked him admission to a Viceregal garden party on a Press ticket.

His mind turns to poor Mrs Purefoy and to her Methodist husband, methodical in his highly disciplined eating habits, methodical in presenting his wife annually with an offspring. Bloom's disapproval of the large family and his pity for the mother's ceaseless round of breast-feeding, year after year, all hours of the night, is in line with his thoughts on the Dedalus family (p. 125/191), his ten-year absence from coition with Molly, his fruitless emission in episode 13, his indulgence of the passive cerebral relationship with Martha, his identification (in *The Lotus Eaters*) with symbols of inertia and drugged impotence. Moreover, it is in line with the thoughts which follow here on the long-drawn-out labour of Mrs Purefoy; for though these thoughts are important as expressing Bloom's compassion and hatred of suffering, they also reflect a rejection of the crudely animal process of birth – the laborious clumsy progress of the

203
(153)

132

204

baby 'groping for the way out' – which is in tune with the rejection, later in this episode, of the crude processes of carnivorous mastication in the Burton restaurant (p. 139/215).

Bloom thinks it is time the powers-that-be gave their minds to doing something about the pain of childbirth instead of 'gassing about the what was it the pensive bosom of the silver effulgence'. (This sentence, sentimental 'flap-doodle', incorporates remembered phrases from the speech of Dan Dawson which Bloom heard Ned Lambert reading in the *Freeman* office, p. 102/157.) He calculates the cost and benefits of a welfare system, based on taxation, which would not only ensure painless childbirth but would also settle a small invested sum on each child to encourage the saving habit. (Socialistic, welfare-minded Bloom is to come comically into his own in the

(154)   wish-fulfilment fantasies of the *Circe* episode, p. 399/610 ff.) He
133   recalls the comic sight of Molly and Mrs Moisel together when
205   both were pregnant; and it is the difficulties and inconveniences of human fruitfulness which are still dominant in his mind, the hazards of midwifery (old Mrs Thornton got her hand crushed in delivering the massive-headed son of Tom Walls) and the ill-requited lot of doctors ('People knocking them up at all hours' and then keeping them waiting months for their fee).

A flock of pigeons flies by, recently well fed, and now excreting on people below. 'Must be thrilling from the air,' Bloom thinks. He sees a squad of policemen going on duty, fresh from their lunch, with 'food-heated faces'. This is the best time to tackle a policeman, when a punch in the pudding-stuffed stomach will be effective. A second squad of policemen marches off duty, bound for the station and 'their troughs' of soup.

The statue of Tom Moore, erected over a public urinal, strikes Bloom as peculiarly appropriate if only because of Moore's famous song, *'The Meeting of the Waters'* (*'There is not in the wide world a valley so sweet/As that vale in whose bosom the bright waters meet'*). Bloom sympathetically laments the lack of public conveniences for women. (Apparently Edwardian public plumbing had not yet made its full impact on Dublin.) Women are driven to such expedients as running into cake-shops, pretending they want to adjust their hats. (For Julia Morkan see *Dubliners*, 'The Dead'.)

206   Gazing after the uniformed policemen, Bloom reflects that the police can be pretty brutal if a man resists arrest. Nor can he

blame them, considering what they have to put up with from young trouble-makers. He once got himself mixed up with a pro-Boer student demonstration when Joseph Chamberlain came to Dublin to receive an honorary degree at Trinity College. On that occasion a mounted policeman was unhorsed and 'cracked his skull on the cobblestones'. It was on the same occasion that Bloom got to know young Dixon, now a doctor at Holles Street hospital where Mrs Purefoy is lying. Bloom reflects philosoph- 134
ically that these rebellious young students quickly change into respectable servants of the establishment they have challenged. They are the 'Butter exchange band': they know which side their bread is buttered.

'Never know who you're talking to.' Bloom thinks Corny Kelleher has the look of a 'Harvey Duff' (the disguised police agent in Dion Boucicault's play, *The Shaughraun*). He reflects on the dangers due to the fact that today's revolutionary may be tomorrow's civil servant, that an apparent rebel in the nation-alist cause may be a paid spy of the government, like the man Carey who 'blew the gaff on the invincibles', the gang that brought off the Phoenix Park murders. A plain-clothes man 207
will flirt with a servant-girl, then question her about a young gentleman in her household. A 'hot-blooded young student', flirting with the servant-girl, will imprudently let slip a hint of his mysterious revolutionary activities. 'There are great times coming, Mary.' Thus the game is lost. Bloom admires the safeguards against betrayals of this kind designed by the revo- (156)
lutionary James Stephens, who organized men in closed circles of ten so that no one could possibly betray more than his own group. The movement would execute a betrayer, by firing-squad if he stayed in, by a knife in the back if he left. After reflection on the revolutionary's need for mob-appeal, political and nutri-tional thoughts converge. The use of lavish hospitality to win people over to a political cause is dwelt upon. 208

A heavy cloud slowly hides the sun, the 'Home Rule sun', and Trinity's face is shadowed. (When the face of the Son is hidden, then the Trinity's front is surly. The rising of the Son, Stephen – for Rudy – in the northwest of Dublin, 7, Eccles Street, is to restore Home Rule to the Bloom household. The Son–Sun pun is important at many points. See p. 521/737, 'washed in the blood of the sun'.) Bloom is correspondingly depressed by the thought of the futile repetitive sameness of things, people 135 being born, people dying, houses changing hands, civilizations rising and decaying. The low point of depression is marked by Bloom's thought, 'No-one is anything.' (As his sense of insecurity before the mystery of death at the funeral was marked by the thought, 'If we were all suddenly somebody else,' p. 91/*139*.) Bloom's sense of the unreality of things, his quest for identity, his pursuit of repose, his questioning uncertainty before the fact of fluidity and change (metempsychosis) and of unstable relative viewpoints (parallax) universalize him.

209   The sun reappears and Bloom sees Parnell's brother, John Howard Parnell, passing, a woebegone figure in Bloom's eyes, and the member of an odd family. 'All a bit touched.' A couple pass him from behind and he picks up a fragment of the man's intellectual conversation ('Of the twoheaded Octopus . . .').

210   Bloom recognizes A. E. (George Russell) with a young woman,
136   perhaps the very Lizzie Twigg who answered his own adver-
(158)   tisement and claimed the friendship of the poet (p. 131/*202*). Bloom's reflections on the sentimental vegetarianism, dreamy symbolism, and careless dress sense of these 'literary etherial people' are scornful.

211   The window of Yeates and Son, with its display of field glasses, reminds him of his deficient old binoculars and he wonders about replacing them by buying a pair at the railway lost-property office. He experiments, trying to see a little watch that is located on the bank roof opposite for testing glasses by, and trying to blot out the sun with the tip of his little finger.
137   He wonders whether he could develop his frustrated scientific interest in astronomy by going out to the observatory at Dunsink
212   and getting an interview with Professor Joly. It would have to be done tactfully by establishing some family connexion with the man. It would be useless, he reflects comically, to barge in and blurt out the question which is really on his mind – 'What's parallax?' He would be shown the door.

The day-dream of intercourse with the great scientist fades. He will 'never know anything about it'. The sense of futility recurs; of the cosmic pattern by which gas solidifies into worlds, then worlds cool and die into moons. Mrs Breen said there must be a new moon, he recalls. Perhaps there is. The full moon was a fortnight last Sunday when he and Boylan (unnamed) were walking down by the Tolka with Molly between them, the two lovers humming the lines of a love-duet to each other, their

elbows, arms, and fingers touching and conversing too. He
forcibly puts a stop to this detestable train of thought and
concentrates on his immediate surroundings. He sees Bob Doran
(the victim of Mrs Mooney and her husband-hunting daughter
Polly in 'The Boarding House' in *Dubliners*) on his annual
drinking spree, 'sloping into the Empire', and recalls past shows   *213*
there seen in happier days. Looking back, he builds up his biog-
raphy for us more clearly. He was twenty-eight and Molly
twenty-three when they left Lombard Street West and the change
came. Molly ended their full marital relationship with the plea
that she 'could never like it again' after their son Rudy's death.
The frustration mood throws back again the inviting phrases
from Martha's letter ('Are you not happy in your home, you
poor little naughty boy?', p. 63/*94*).

He wanders down Grafton Street, looking in the fashion store
windows, and remembers his threat to buy a pincushion in   *138*
defence against Molly's habit of leaving pins and needles about   (*160*)
the house, in curtains and the like. He inspects a graze on his   *214*
arm produced by an encounter with one of Molly's stray pins.
Perhaps he could buy her a pincushion for her birthday, 8
September. (Since 8 September is the Feast of another Nativity,
that of the Virgin Mary, we may assume a symbolical connexion
here.) There follows a convergence of sensuous images in
Bloom's mind – the silk underwear and stockings in the shop
windows, jewellery, fruits, and spices of the east, the advertisement of Agendath Netaim, the planter's company working
in Turkey which he read about in the pork butcher's shop this
morning (p. 49/*72*), and the warm human plumpness which he
hungers for as he hungers for food. The pressure of this double
hunger drives him, day-dreaming of bodies yielding to one
another, into the Burton restaurant, where a powerful anti-
climax turns urgent desire into revulsion. For, as he opens the   *215*
door, the stink grips him and the sight of swilling, wolfing men
repels him. Suddenly he sees human eating for the crude animal
thing that it is, as food is shouted for, torn, rammed, chewed,   *139*
munched, amid reek and smoke and stickiness. He backs out   *216*
from this Lestrygonian horror, determined to get a light snack
at Davy Byrne's instead. ('Not here, Don't see him.' indicates
the obsessive anxiety not to run into Boylan.)

He indulges a nightmare vision of communal eating in some
future communistic world where people of all ranks and stations

140
217
queue up with tommycans and take turns with the 'incorporated drinking cup'. People would still quarrel, seeking the best for themselves, and children fight for the scrapings of the pot.

Momentarily, after his painful experience in the Burton, Bloom begins to feel that there is something in vegetarianism after all. Things from the earth have a fine flavour. Animals suffer in the cause of human carnivorism. Bloom sees mentally the calves in the slaughterhouse, the blood and bones of the butcher's shop.

218
He enters Davy Byrne's. Nosey Flynn, a regular, greets him from his nook. (Flynn is one of the drinkers in Davy Byrne's with whom Farrington goes on the spree in 'Counterparts' in *Dubliners*.) Bloom orders a glass of burgundy and spends a moment wondering what to eat. In that moment there is a quick sequence of thought – sardines on the shelves before him; shall he have a sandwich? potted meat; Plumtree's absurd advertisement inserted under the obituary notices; cannibalism; its

(163)
141
stimulating effect on human potency; hence a new aptness in the latter half of Plumtree's ad (*With* the potted meat the home is 'an abode of bliss'); doubt about what there is in the potted meat anyway; Jewish food regulations, hygienic in essence though religious in appearance; connexion between eating and religion as evidenced in Christmas feasting followed by hangovers. After this tangled excursion into an area of thinking where the dominant theme still seems to be marked by the conjoint symbols of Potted Meat and Coffined Dignam ('Dignam's potted meat'), it is perhaps not surprising that Bloom decides to order a cheese sandwich. He would like a cool salad too, were it avail-

219
able, to complete the cleansing vegetarian menu.

Nosey Flynn asks after Mrs Bloom. Is she doing any singing? Bloom thinks Flynn knows as much about music as my coachman, but his instinct as an advertiser leads him to give polite information about his wife's coming tour, nevertheless. Meanwhile Bloom, as he is served by the barman, is mentally preoccupied in trying to remember the exact lines of a sexually cannibalistic limerick about the Reverend MacTrigger. Gradually he puts the thing together. The cannibal celebrated in the lines, by consuming the genitals of the Reverend MacTrigger, achieved a potency which gave his wives the time of their lives. Thus eating potted meat turned one more home into an abode of bliss.

Flynn keeps the talk going. He has heard already of Molly's coming tour. 'Isn't Blazes Boylan mixed up in it?' A shock of embarrassment and envy hits Bloom, and his eyes rest on the 'bilious clock' whose hands, now at two, will inexorably move to four, bringing Blazes to Molly at his home. The restless yearning *220* for his wife rises again. He controls himself and answers Flynn coolly. Blazes Boylan is 'the organiser in point of fact'. Flynn, *142* Bloom assumes, is not trying to get at him, is not implying anything against Molly. He hasn't the brains for suspicion or innuendo. Scratching himself, he chats admiringly of Boylan's activities as a boxing impresario.

Flynn asks Davy Byrne for a tip for the Ascot Gold Cup, but Byrne is not a gambling man. Bloom, refreshed with wine and food, begins to relish his physical surroundings, the quietness *221* of the bar, the curve of the counter. Flynn repeats the racing news, mentioning that Lenehan is tipping *Sceptre* (and Lenehan is another of Molly's past admirers). Bloom has little use for *143* Flynn, and decides that it would be pointless to warn him against Lenehan's tip. A fool and his money are soon parted one way or another. He watches the dew-drop moving down *(166)* Flynn's nose, and considers the lot of a woman kissed by a cold-nosed man. Perhaps she might like it. He recalls a scene from the later days of Mrs Riordan, when Molly fondled her *222* cold-nosed Skye terrier in the City Arms Hotel.

The sandwich and the wine, carefully savoured, satisfy Bloom, and he dwells now, objectively and without hunger, on the food before him and other odd things that people eat. In a packed passage his thoughts touch on an enormous number of questions, images, and recollections. Instinct guides you to certain foods (as the roundness of fruit attracts you), but warns you off others (as the gaudy colour of poisonous berries repels you). The idea of rich, tempting, luscious foods recalls the familiar 'orange groves' and the address 'Bleibtreustrasse' of the firm whose advertisement he took from Dlugacz's (p. 49/72). But how did the human race ever come to taste the superficially unattractive foods like oysters? The connexion between certain subtly flavoured, highly valued foods and garbage and corruption is touched on. Then the episode reaches a climax in a *223* concentrated series of images dealing with expensive foods, banquets, rare dishes, high life, waiters, and half-naked ladies in evening dress.

144

And into this dream of rich food and sex intrudes the symbolic reminder of Molly and (I take it) himself (or Boylan?) in the two buzzing flies stuck on the window-pane.

224   The taste of the burgundy warms Bloom to a vivid recapturing of the day (to be frequently recalled) when he and Molly lay on Howth Hill, overlooking the bay. Molly was still young and tender, and when he kissed her she pushed from her mouth to his the 'seedcake warm and chewed'. The remembered incident adds significance to the reference in Mr Deasy's letter to 'Grain supplies through the narrow waters of the channel' (p. 27/40). Molly too recalls the occasion with delight (p. 643/831). The contrast, for Bloom, between his lot then, when Molly gave herself to him so fervently, and now, when she awaits the appointment with Boylan, is pressed home with powerful Joycean economy. 'Me. And me now.' And the symbolic flies, stuck, still buzz.

It is significant that Bloom, frustrated thus, turns from thoughts of living sexuality to the 'frozen music' of sculpture.
225   He determines to visit the naked goddesses of the museum, who can neither care nor speak. Joyce thus fixes another aspect of 'paralysis'. But more important is the recurring ideal–real
(168)   dichotomy. Bloom contrasts the crudity of the actual – women who put you in your place, and tanner lunches on boiled mutton and ale – with the ideal – divine ambrosial banquets in the company of immortal goddesses. The real alimentary system
145   'stuffing food in one hole and out behind' is in sharp contrast to the ideal. Or is it? Bloom asks himself. Perhaps the sculptured goddesses have their holes behind too. 'Never looked. I'll look today.' His investigation need not be made too obviously. He can let something fall and bend down to pick it up, at the same time checking up on the anal details of the statues.

The call of Nature takes him to the yard: reality's call.

Davy Byrne asks Flynn who Bloom is, and learns that he canvasses for the *Freeman*. Byrne, but not Flynn, has noticed his mourning clothes, but has been too tactful to raise the subject.
226   Flynn assumes that Bloom cannot live as he does on his earnings from canvassing. Bloom is a freemason. 'They give him a
146   leg up.' Byrne and Flynn agree that Bloom is temperate, 'God almighty couldn't make him drunk', and prudent. Flynn thinks
227   'he's not too bad ... He's been known to put his hand down too to help a fellow.' But Bloom's reputation for canniness is

shown in the assurance Flynn gives that you could never get
him to sign his name to anything.

Paddy Leonard, Bantam Lyons, and Tom Rochford come in.
Paddy stands the drinks, but Bantam Lyons has a stoneginger
while Tom Rochford asks for a glass of water and spills his
indigestion powder into it. Bloom passes through on the way   *228*
out. Bantam Lyons tells his companions, wrongly, that Bloom   *147*
gave him his tip for the Gold Cup race. (This mistake, from
which trouble arises for Bloom later on, derives from Lyon's
misunderstanding of Bloom on p. 70/*106*.)

Bloom continues his walk. A ravenous terrier, choking up a   *(171)*
cud and lapping it afresh, touches both his obsession with food *229*
and his sense of humour. 'Returned with thanks having fully
digested the contents.' (The jargon of the business world is never
far from Bloom's mind. Frequently Joyce's humour depends
upon the convergence of such jargon either with the crude
actualities of physical life – as here – or with the mind's richer
and more romantic thoughts.) Cheerfully Bloom hums an aria
from Mozart's *Don Giovanni*, referring to the supper at which
symbols of love and death meet, his eyes traversing the lavatory seats displayed in William Miller's, the plumber's, so that
in one more context thoughts of sex, feasting, alimentation, and
death converge.

Bloom calculates what he is likely to make out of the adver-   *230*
tising deals he is involved in at present. A quick computation
suggests he may be able to buy 'one of those silk petticoats for
Molly'. From Molly's underwear the mind would travel on its
familiar course to the imminent meeting between Molly and
Boylan, but Bloom drives it back forcefully. 'Today. Today. Not
think.' He prefers to indulge the daydream of an English tour   *148*
with Molly when the coming trip is over. A moment later,
passing the Reverend Thomas Connellan's book-store and
noting the anti-Catholic propaganda, Bloom dwells appropriately on one more connexion between food and religion – the
practice of bribing converts with food in time of famine.

Bloom sees a blind stripling and charitably helps him across
the road. The impulse is that of the compassionate Jesus–Bloom,   *231*
and also of the outsider–Bloom, hungry for companionship and
sympathetic towards a fellow-outsider. He tries to help without
being condescending; and the stripling's hand 'like a child's
hand' becomes momentarily the hand of the son he has lost,

the son he is seeking, the son he finds in Stephen. Watching
him as he taps his way along the curbstone, Bloom wonders at
149   the sensitivities of the blind; then suddenly the man's 'blood-
less pious face like a fellow going in to be a priest' gives him
the name which he could not remember earlier in the episode,
'Penrose' (p. 128/196). Penrose was the 'priestylooking chap'
who used to stare in their window at Molly when they lived
in Lombard Street West. (He is listed among the suitors on
232   p. 601/863.) There follows more about the compensating sensitivities of the blind; how quickly they can read with their fingers;
how strong their sense of smell must be. How strange it must
be, Bloom reflects, to make love to a woman you cannot see.
Can you feel the differences of colour in the different textures
of hair and skin? He remembers the need to answer Martha
(with whom he is having a love-affair which is not only sight-
less but touchless and soundless too). He thinks of sending her
a postal order for two shillings.

Bloom experiments to find out what the perception of a blind
person must be like, first feeling the skin of his cheek, then
putting his hand inside his clothes to feel the smoothness of his
belly. At this point Bloom's thinking touches Stephen's, who
was much concerned with the 'ineluctable modality' of the
visible at the beginning of episode 3 and made the experiment
of closing his eyes to see what experience was like when the
(174)   mode of visibility was excluded (p. 31/45). In spite of the intel-
lectualized surface of the thinking, Stephen's essential concern
then was what Bloom's is now.

The blind man has turned into Frederick Street. Bloom pities
233   his lot and the injustice represented by innate physical defects
and by great accidental disasters. The thought of cosmic injustice throws up again the theme of reincarnation. Meantime
Bloom sees Sir Frederick Falkiner, the judge, going into the
freemasons' hall, pictures him and his cronies enjoying their
150   expensive wines, admires him for his fairness, his way of
resisting the insatiable hunger of the police for charges, his
toughness with money-lenders like R. J. Dodd.

He sees a placard advertising the Mirus bazaar in aid of funds
for Mercer's hospital, the hospital for which Handel's *Messiah*
was first performed, and wonders about going to it. Immediately
after this hint at the Messiah–Bloom correspondence, there is a
234   moving little crisis. No name is named; but the symbols flashed

before the reader – 'Straw hat in sunlight. Tan shoes' – unmistakably present Blazes Boylan. Bloom's shock at the sight of him, his uncertainty, then his conviction and his agitation, are all vividly compressed, and Joyce's prose strikes like a hammer. 'Is it? Almost certain. Won't look. Wine in my face. Why did I? Too heady. Yes, it is. The walk. Not see. Not see. Get on.'

He strides towards the museum gate, heart thudding, breath (175) fluttering, and seeks a refuge from the warm, living flesh which betrays him in the cool cream curves of stone. Hasty hands go into and out of his pockets, so that agitation is veiled in an apparent search for something. Searching, the hand comes to rest eventually on the cake of soap in his hip pocket. At that moment he reaches the safety of the museum gate. The soap, an artificial chemical product, serves as a talismanic reminder of the disinfected, hygienic civilization in which Bloom puts his trust. It counterbalances Stephen's ashplant, with its richly natural and traditional associations. Indeed it has assumed the status of a Homeric shield, as Bloom's rolled-up newspaper, the weapon of modernity, seemingly became a Homeric sword (see pp. 59/87 and 70/105). We recall that it was soapy water, the life-blood of our civilization, which Mulligan offered up in the chalice of his shaving-bowl at the beginning of the day and the book (p. 3/1). (175)

Chapter 9

Scylla and Charybdis

151 In the Homeric parody Ulysses–Bloom passes unnoticed
235 between the whirlpool Charybdis and the many-headed
monster Scylla, who stretches out her six necks to snatch
up victims from passing ships. Here Scylla and Charybdis
are but metaphors. The twin dangers are not physical but
oratorical. The menace is created by a wordy encounter
between Stephen Dedalus and a group of talkative scholars in
the National Library. Whirlpool images occur several times,
associated with the swirling deeps of Platonist metaphysics
in which Russell and the librarians are whirled. By contrast
rapiered Stephen, weaponed with logic on his Aristotelian
rock (Kinch, the knife-blade), continually sticks his neck out to
snatch bitingly at the statements of the others, taking on all-
comers at once.

(176) It is two o'clock. Stephen is in the director's office of the
National Library. Present with him are A. E. (George Russell),
the poet, John Eglinton, and Lyster. ('John Eglinton' was the
pseudonym used by the essayist, William K. Magee.) Lyster, the
Quaker librarian, is praising Goethe's observations on *Hamlet*
in his novel *Wilhelm Meister*. He sees Hamlet as 'the beautiful
ineffectual dreamer who comes to grief against hard facts'. He
is called away by an attendant.

Youthful Stephen sneers at Lyster's critical platitude. Eglinton,
giving tit for tat 'with elder's gall', mocks the foolish clever talk
236 of Stephen and his companions. Stephen sees that his youth-
152 ful follies are being held as hostages, to be trotted out when
he tries to be clever at other people's expense. Nevertheless, he
seems to be determined to persist in his role of debunking
critical theorists by out-theorizing them.

Russell decries the kind of critical speculation which would identify Hamlet with an actual person. Russell is a platonist, and for him the function of a work of art is to reveal to us the formless spiritual reality hidden behind our world. Stephen, trained by the Jesuits, confronts Plato with Aristotle. He has no use for the esoteric metaphysics which Russell and his group have embraced. Difficult as his allusions are at this point, it is plain that he rejects the gnostic strain found in theosophy and freemasonry, with all their high-sounding jargon, because of its vagueness and unrelatedness to real life. 'The life esoteric is not for ordinary person.'

*237
(178)*

Mr Best, another librarian, enters just as Stephen is claiming that Hamlet's musings on the after-life, like Plato's, are shallow by comparison with Aristotle. Eglinton rejects the comparison angrily. Mentally Stephen prepares for dialectical battle. In the Aristotelian armoury of exact definition are the weapons for dealing with the vagueness of the pseudo-Platonists, worshipping their 'streams of tendency'. Not for him to creep away from this 'vegetable world' as though it were an unreal shadow. He will hold on to the living present, the immediate here and now 'through which all future plunges to the past'. The existence of the book we are reading is evidence that Stephen's thinking is close to Joyce's own here.

*153
238*

Best speaks of Haines, the English student we met in episode 1, staying at the Martello tower with Stephen and Mulligan. Haines has become enthusiastic about Hyde's *Lovesongs of Connacht*. Stephen, a little penitent about the guest whose baccy he smoked and yet whom he treated so rudely, nevertheless rejects Haines's sentimental ('We feel in England') interests in the emerald isle. Russell claims that it is from the love-songs of peasants rather than from the sophisticated literature of academies that truly revolutionary movements arise. His mention of Mallarmé reminds Best of Mallarmé's description of a French provincial performance of *Hamlet*. Though Stephen seems to share the view of the others that the French, 'an excellent people', are nevertheless not at their best with Shakespeare, he shows sympathy here with Mallarmé's view that *Hamlet* is a 'sumptuous and stagnant exaggeration of murder'. By the end of the play nine deaths have paid for old Hamlet's murder. He compares the slaughter of the last act with the arm-chair bloodthirstiness of Swinburne.

*239

154

240*

John Eglinton induces Stephen to air his own theory about *Hamlet* which Buck Mulligan prayed to be spared in episode 1 (p. 15/21, 'He proves by algebra that Hamlet's grandson is Shakespeare's grandfather and that he himself is the ghost of his own father'). Stephen obliges. He defines a ghost as 'one who has faded into impalpability through death, through (180) absence, through change of manners'. In this sense, the Shakespeare who returns to Stratford after his sojourn in London is a ghost, and the Stephen (or Joyce) who returns to Dublin from Paris is a ghost. Likewise Bloom, long sexually impalpable in relation to Molly, is a ghost in his own home.

155 Stephen pictures a performance of *Hamlet* by Shakespeare's
241 company at the Globe theatre. In act one the Ghost enters 'in the castoff mail of a court buck' (as Stephen wears the cast-off shoes of Buck Mulligan). Shakespeare, as the Ghost, speaks to Richard Burbage who takes the part of Hamlet. He also, as ghost–father, speaks to the son of his body, Hamnet Shakespeare. (Hamnet Shakespeare died in 1596 at the age of eleven and a half. The appearance of Rudy Bloom in episode 15 is as 'a fairy boy of eleven', p. 497/702. That would be Rudy's age had he lived until now.) Shakespeare, identifying himself with the murdered father, tells Hamnet that he is the dispossessed son, that his mother Ann is the guilty queen.

Russell protests against this use of literature as a means of conjectural prying into the lives of the writers who produce it.
242 The literature itself is what matters. Best supports him silently. Thus challenged, Stephen reminds himself that Russell lent him a pound (he said a guinea on p. 26/37) when he was hard up; moreover, that he spent it on a whore (Georgina Johnson) instead of on the food it was given to buy. Examining himself remorsefully, he admits that he has no intention of paying the money
156 back yet, and Mr Deasy's advice of this morning comes back to mind (the proudest boast of the Englishman – 'I paid my way'). Stephen undergoes a continuing mental conflict here between self-condemnation and self-excuse. Deasy, he tells himself, is an Ulsterman whose advice is therefore apparently not to be taken too seriously. Moreover, since the debt is five months old and molecules change continuously, it can be argued that the 'I' of today is a totally different person from the 'I' who borrowed the pound. 'Buzz. Buzz.' He quotes Hamlet, rejecting the ingratiating nonsense of Polonius. There is a stable 'I' preserved by

memory under the everchanging 'I's: the 'I' who sinned and prayed and fasted in the adolescent religious phase recorded in *Portrait of the Artist*; the 'I' whom as a child Father Conmee saved from unjust punishment at Clongowes. There are four 'I's of which different and even contradictory propositions might be posed according to the classification of formal logic (A – affirmative universal proposition, E – negative universal proposition, I – affirmative particular proposition, O – negative particular proposition), A.E.I.O. Stephen adds the fifth vowel to produce the execrable pun A. E. (Russell) I.O.U. (money).

  Eglinton repeats the traditional critical estimate of Ann Hathaway, that she was of no significance in the life of Shakespeare the writer. Stephen replies that she was his first mistress, the mother of his children, and the presider over his deathbed: and the image of his own mother's deathbed recurs. Eglinton's view is that Shakespeare 'made a mistake' in marrying Ann Hathaway and then got out of it as best he could by leaving Stratford for London. Stephen's view is that 'a man of genius makes no mistakes': he wills his own errors and then learns from them. Eglinton denies that a man can learn anything from a shrewish wife and cites the case of Socrates's Xanthippe. The threatened digression on Socrates is forestalled by Mr Best, who brings them back to Ann Hathaway.

  Stephen argues that Shakespeare was seduced by Ann Hathaway. The evidence is there in *Venus and Adonis* and in *The Taming of the Shrew* ('poor Wat', 'the cry of hounds', 'the studded bridle' and 'her blue windows' – eyes – are phrases from *Venus and Adonis*). Shakespeare's less masterful heroines are the idealized creations of a boy's mind. His actual experience of love was that of an eighteen-year-old boy taken by a determined woman of twenty-six. ('And my turn? When?' Stephen asks himself, wondering when he himself will be taken thus by a woman. 'Come!' He is ready for it.)

  Russell rises and announces that he must go. Eglinton asks whether he will be at Moore's (George Moore's) party tonight, but A. E. has a prior engagement. As A. E. speaks of 'our meeting', Stephen's mind turns again scornfully to the jargon and ritual of the theosophists. Their vague creed engulfs them like the whirlpool Charybdis. Lyster, still playing up to the great man, asks about the coming anthology of younger poets' verses which A. E. is editing. There follows a conversation to which

243
(182)

244

157

245

158
246

Stephen compels himself to listen. It is packed with chatter about Dublin's literary life – A. E.'s new anthology and the poets who are to figure in it; the latest gossip about Yeats, George Moore, James Stephens, Synge, and the Gaelic League. The reader is moved by the exclusion of Stephen Dedalus – uninvited to George Moore's party, not asked to contribute to A. E.'s anthology, shut out from a share in this chatter of literary celebrities. Stephen feels his exclusions keenly. 'Cordelia. *Cordoglio.*

(185)   Lir's loneliest daughter.' (*Cordoglio* is Italian for 'affliction'. One of Moore's *Irish Melodies*, 'Silent, O Moyle', celebrates 'Lir's lonely daughter', Fionnuala, who was transformed into a swan and compelled to wander over Irish lakes and rivers until the coming of Christianity and the first mass-bell should signal her release.) Before the literary conversation ends, Stephen manages to insert one literary request – that for Mr Deasy's letter to be

247   recommended to the editor of the *Homestead*. A. E. graciously promises. (The irony here is powerful. That Stephen Dedalus, the self-appointed artist *in propria persona*, should be limited to the function of foisting bullock-befriending correspondence on to 'The pig's paper' is farcically pointed.) Lyster, returning from seeing the great A. E. out, turns back to Stephen with devastating politeness for a further instalment of his 'most illuminating' views. Does he think that Ann Hathaway was not faithful to the poet?

159   Stephen's reply is a crisp one. Where there is a reconciliation – such as is reflected in Shakespeare's later plays – there must have been first a sundering. In his own mind he sees Shakespeare as a 'Christfox' running away to hide from the hue and cry of sexual pursuit. The image is a complex one. Lyster is a Quaker, so that the image of a Christlike Fox in leather trews (George Fox, founder of the Society of Friends) is fused with that of the double hunt in *Venus and Adonis* (the hunting of the fox and the sexual pursuit of a young man by a seductress). The Christlike George Fox forsook the comforts of home life to walk lonely in the chase, and women of all ranks and kinds were won to him. So Shakespeare. Meantime Ann, his wife, aged back in Stratford. (There is a recurring correspondence between Stephen and a fox arising out of the riddle about the fox burying his grandmother; see p. 22/32.)

As the door is closed on the librarian's room, Stephen becomes

248   aware of the unreality of the scholarly thinking pursued here –

the hypotheses of the what-might-have-been. It is a coffined, mummyfied thinking that books hold, though once they were alive in men's brains. The librarians continue to talk at their platitudinous level, Eglinton saying that Shakespeare is an enigma, Best that *Hamlet* is a deeply personal document, (186) Eglinton again that Shakespeare identified himself with Hamlet the prince.

Stephen rises to the bait. Just as the molecular structure of 249 our bodies is for ever changing, so the artist's images have a changing symbolic content. (This is notably true of *Ulysses*. Bloom is God the Father in some contexts, God the suffering Son in others. He is also, from time to time, Ulysses, Moses, Elijah, Hamlet's Ghost, etc.) Just as the mole remains on the breast (cf. Imogen in *Cymbeline*) though the body's tissues are 160 always being renewed, so the image of the unliving son may look forth through the ghost of the unquiet father. (Note that Rudy is the unliving son looking forth through the ghost of unquiet father Bloom.) Past, present, and future meet at moments of intense imaginative vision. 'He is in my father. I am in his son.' These sentences carry significant ambiguities which anticipate correspondences that reach their fullest expression in the *Circe* episode and thereafter.

Stephen argues that the true nature of the personal agony 250 reflected in Shakespeare's tragic plays can be understood only by considering the nature of the joy which relieves the agony in the last plays of reconciliation. (One notes here that Stephen's own true need will be revealed only when the thing which relieves it is encountered – Bloom.) In that sense the future alone can fully reveal the present. (Eglinton regards Stephen's fanciful biographical interpretation as a pursuit of the bypaths of apocrypha. Established critical interpretation moves, by contrast, on the high roads, dull perhaps by comparison, but leading somewhere.) Thus in *Pericles* and *The Winter's Tale* the fulfilment of 161 joy occurs when the lost daughter is found. A man is unlikely to love a daughter whose resemblance is to a mother he has hated; but the lost daughter in these plays is the image of her mother, dearly loved by the husband who now recovers his child. No equation therefore can be made between Perdita–Marina and a daughter of Ann Hathaway. Rather Perdita–Marina is Elizabeth Hall, Shakespeare's only and loved grandchild, the daughter of his elder daughter Susanna.

251   Lyster continues the stereotyped phrase-turning of conventional literary criticism, felicitous but moribund, while Stephen tries to prove that Shakespeare lost his sexual self-confidence (188) when Ann Hathaway seduced him between the acres of the rye, and that no attempt to play the philandering Don Giovanni could restore it. He was wounded too deeply. Stephen implicitly draws an imaginative correspondence between Adonis, *252* wounded and killed by the tusk of the boar he himself sets out to hunt, and Adonis beaten by the huntress Venus who ought properly to have been the hunted. These correspondences reflect the personal sexual situation of Shakespeare himself (and of Stephen Dedalus?). Shakespeare, sexually wounded and killed by the huntress, Ann Hathaway, is the ghost of a sexually murdered man, not knowing (for he was 'poisoned' unawares, in his 'sleep') what it is that has destroyed him – except by a 162 divinely prophetic insight such as he reveals in the plays. Obsessed throughout his life as a poet, from the time of Tarquin's rape of Lucrece to the time of Iachimo's pretended, unachieved rape of Imogen, with a dream of masterful ravishing which he can never realize, he stalks through the world a ghost, a shadow, whose living self will be substantially made known only in his son. (The true Shakespeare made known only in his plays – of which he is the only begetter; the true Shakespeare to be made known only in the 'unliving' son Hamnet; the true Bloom to be made known only in the discovery of Stephen – and the re-emergence of unliving Rudy; the true Stephen to be made known only in the unwritten masterpiece; God made known only in His only begotten Son, consubstantial with Him: this is the mystery of paternity, reflected in artistic creation.)

253   An ironical 'Amen' from the doorway announces the arrival of Buck Mulligan, who punctures Stephen's pretentious theorizing (hence the 'enemy' of Stephen the intellectual poseur). Mulligan's cheerful mockery introduces an 'Entr'acte' between the two major acts of theorizing about Shakespeare. Stephen himself, mocking Mulligan's blasphemous mockery, mentally recites a burlesque creed. Here, as so often in Joyce, we must heed in advance Lyster's aphorism on the next page – 'The mocker is never taken seriously when he is most serious.' Stephen's burlesque creed speaks of a God who begets himself by means of the Holy Ghost and sends himself as a redeemer (Agenbuyer) between himself and others; one who is persecuted by those who should be his friends (but become 'fiends'), nailed up and 'starved on a crosstree'. This 'God' is recognizably the artist (Shakespeare or Joyce) who puts himself in his own work (Stephen and Bloom in *Ulysses* are Joyce's substantial self) and who is persecuted and starved for his pains. But fortunately he (Joyce) is now sitting on His own right hand (which held the pen that wrote *Ulysses*) and he will come (he is already here) to doom the quick and the dead, though of course, as Joyce foresaw, the quick are dead already (those who lived contemporaneously with him and starved him on the crosstree).

It should be noted that Stephen's superficially perverse insistence that Shakespeare is Hamlet senior *as well as* (not instead of) Hamlet junior is hint enough that Joyce has represented himself in both Bloom and Stephen. Indeed, the fullest emphasis (189) should be placed on the following correspondences: Joyce puts himself in *Ulysses* as both Father (Ghost–Father) and Son. Shakespeare puts himself in *Hamlet* as both Ghost–Father and Son. God enters His own world as Holy Ghost and as Son. As Son, God is crucified, then raised up by the Father: and this, too, is to be the pattern of Stephen's day. Joyce's created world, *Ulysses*, is like God's world – a world which one explores, seeking a pattern and a meaning, finding clues and threads which hint at an overall design and purpose, and ultimately realizing that it is a world into which its own creator has entered, in which he has suffered, and from which he has been raised up. But more of this later. (See especially p. 412/623.)

Lyster, Eglinton, and Best continue the polite airing of crit- 163 ical questions and conjectures about Shakespeare, which sound 254 tame after Stephen's performance. Wilde's wit is quoted and Stephen, while tempted to scorn the frail cleverness of the librar- 255 ians, reminds himself that he has not been very clever in getting rid of money this morning on a 'plump' of drinking pressmen, nor does his own cleverness compensate for the lack of youthful assurances and fulfilment which he recognizes in the face of Best ('lineaments of gratified desire'). There are many women in the world and the invitation is there for him to take one. But his image of Eve, the great mother, is a soiled one ('naked wheat-bellied sin') – as is Hamlet's image of Gertrude and of all women. She is coiled by the serpent. (Stephen's sense of the great mother as soiled is no doubt rooted in the prostitute's seduction of him in the *Portrait*. The archetypal meaning behind the Ghost–Father's announcement to Hamlet that he is born of guilty flesh is the revelation to man of original sin.)

164   Mulligan flourishes the telegram which Stephen sent him during the morning, quoting *Richard Feverel*. He then launches
256   into talk which fluently burlesques the dialogue of a Synge play, comically announcing, among other things, that Synge is looking for Stephen to 'murder' him. Stephen's thoughts reveal that he met Synge in Paris, and argued with him in a café. At this point an attendant comes in with a card to announce that a gentleman from the *Freeman* is here, wanting to look up the files of the
257   *Kilkenny People*. This, of course, is Bloom, in search of the adver-
165   tisement which contains the Key(e)s design. Lyster goes out and is heard politely shepherding Bloom to the files of 'all the leading provincial' papers. Mulligan recognizes Bloom as a Jew
(192)   and snatches up the card to discover his name. He is interested, as he has already seen Bloom in the museum, studying the buttocks of Aphrodite with his 'pale Galilean eyes'. ('Pale Galilean' is from Swinburne and strengthens the Jesus–Bloom correspondence.)
258   Eglinton, supported by Best, asks for more from Stephen on the subject of Shakespeare and Ann Hathaway – whom they had presumed to be a patient, chaste stay-at-home, another Penelope.

Stephen points out that Shakespeare lived richly in London for twenty years, taking his pleasures among court ladies, burgers' wives, and prostitutes (and the mention of Elizabethan
166   prostitutes, 'punks of the bankside', takes him back mentally to a conversation with a whore in his Paris days). What was Ann
259   Shakespeare, his 'poor Penelope', left at home in Stratford, doing meanwhile? Stephen's case is that Ann was unfaithful to Shakespeare, for his plays show him to have been obsessed with the theme of the wife's faithlessness, *Hamlet* most notably. The faithlessness of the 'court wanton' Shakespeare wooed in London cannot, Stephen argues, have been the cause of his obsession. To begin with, she spurned him for a lord who was himself loved by Shakespeare. (The sonnets establish that.) Moreover, she in her faithlessness 'did not break a bedvow'. Shakespeare's insistence, in *Hamlet* especially, on the broken vow, makes it clear that it was Ann who was faithless, and 'in
260   the fifth scene of *Hamlet* he has branded her with infamy'. The conclusive evidence of Ann's guilt is that for thirty-four years,

from the day of the marriage to the day of Shakespeare's death, there is no news of her except that she had to borrow forty shillings from her father's shepherd, and that Shakespeare, in his will, left her his second-best bed.

Eglinton repeats the stock critical reply to this case, which   167
would explain away the bequest of a second-best bed on subtle legal grounds: i.e. Shakespeare, well versed in the law, knew that the widow was legally entitled to her inheritance and that therefore there was no need to mention it specifically. To which the Satanic mocker, Stephen, now speaking in blank verse, replies ironically that Shakespeare omitted his wife's name altogether from the first draft of the will, while mentioning his other relations, and only when pressed to name her added the aston-   261
ishing bequest.

Eglinton and Best repeat the hackneyed excuses, that peasants had few possessions in those days, and that a bed might be a very fine and valuable one; but Stephen insists on Shakespeare's wealth and on the insult of the bequest,   (195)
comparing Shakespeare's will with Socrates's. Mulligan openly,   168
and Stephen mentally, mock the sentimental and squeamish   262
treatment of Shakespeare's character by Edward Dowden (author of *Shakespeare, his Mind and Art*), the Professor of English at Trinity College.

Stephen, warming to his theme, now proceeds by contrast to debunk Shakespeare as a man, to cite known incidents from his life which suggest meanness, cunning, and calculating selfishness; then, to cite instances from his plays which suggest that Shakespeare was always ready to climb on a band-wagon, to chime in with popular causes of the moment, however unprincipled. Thus he wrote a Jew-baiting play, *The Merchant of Venice*,   263
immediately after the execution of the Portuguese Jew Lopez who tried to assassinate Queen Elizabeth, jeered at the loss of the Armada in *Love's Labour's Lost*, and by implication at the recently imprisoned Jesuits in the porter scene of *Macbeth*. Moreover, he ignored artistic conscience and descended to the depths of writing a farce, *The Merry Wives of Windsor*, merely to satisfy the crude whim of Queen Elizabeth to see Falstaff in love.

That Stephen is not fully serious in pressing this case is plain from his unspoken self-congratulation, 'I think you're getting on very nicely. Just mix up a mixture of theologicophilolological.'

Eglinton, beginning to enjoy the fun, challenges Stephen to prove Shakespeare a Jew.

169   Taking up the challenge, Stephen cites St Thomas Aquinas and Mulligan collapses in mock horror, mouthed in the rhythmic
264   rhetoric of Synge. For Aquinas incest is an avarice of the emotions, Stephen says, by which love is withheld from hungry strangers and given to the near in blood, and the Jews, known as avaricious, are prone to intermarriage. Shakespeare, it is implied, is avaricious too – grasping over his rights as a property-owner and a creditor. Such a man is likely to be equally possessive over his rights as a husband. No 'Sir Smile, his neighbour' shall fish in his pond (*The Winter's Tale*, I, ii, 196). Ann
265   Shakespeare, Stephen adds, spends a forlorn old age and takes up with a puritanical gospeller.

Eglinton argues that Shakespeare is not the kind of 'family
170   poet' to whose work his own family life is relevant. Falstaff, the characteristic Shakespearean creation, is not a family man. Stephen sees this argument against the background of
(198)   Eglinton's own family situation. Eglinton is a shy man, anxious to forget his own family because his father is a rough country-man apt to turn up to visit his son on quarter-days, and shaming him with his crude rural appearance, 'a rugged rough rug-headed kern'. And what about your own father? Stephen asks himself. Eglinton can read your family situation too; for he knows old Simon, the widower. There sweeps back into Stephen's mind the memory of hurrying back to his mother's deathbed from Paris and being met on the quayside by his father. There is warmth and goodwill in old Simon's reception of his son; but Stephen is conscious of an unbridgeable chasm between them. His father's eyes 'wish me well. But do not know me'.

266   Stephen argues that (from the son's point of view) a father is a 'necessary evil'. Shakespeare wrote *Hamlet* immediately after his own father's death. It is absurd to identify Shakespeare, aged thirty-five, father of two marriageable daughters, wise and mature in experience, with the young undergraduate Hamlet, and Shakespeare's seventy-year-old mother with the lustful Queen Gertrude. Old John Shakespeare, the poet's father, is securely at rest, not an unquiet ghost. Stephen turns to formulate his doctrine of fatherhood. There is no such thing as an act of conscious begetting in which a man knows himself a father.

Rather fatherhood is a 'mystical estate' handed down from
begetter to begotten. This is the true mystery on which the
Christian Church is founded. Love of mother is grounded in an
evident physical relationship; but the mystery (in every sense)
of paternity grounds a son's allegiance on incertitude as the
world itself is founded upon the void.

Ignoring the voice within him which asks what this farrago
is all about, Stephen ploughs on. Father and son are sundered
by a steadfast bodily shame, the shame of knowing that what
links them physically is the single act of coition in which conception took place. There is no other connexion between them 'in
nature'. Therefore, though one hears of bestial and perverse
incestuous connexions between sons and mothers, fathers and
daughters, lesbian sisters, queens and animals, one does not
hear of such connexions between sons and fathers. The son is
the father's enemy, a rival to his masculinity, growing to   *267*
manhood with his father's decline.

The heretic Sabellius, Stephen continues, held that the Father   171
was Himself His own Son, a heresy refuted by Aquinas. (See
p. 17/25 for an earlier reference to Sabellius. This present cita-
tion of Sabellius indicates clearly that Stephen's study of *Hamlet*   (199)
is, among other things, an analogically theological one con-
cerning the operation of the three Persons of the Trinity. The
heresy of Sabellianism failed to do justice to the independent
existence of the Son, affirming that in the Godhead the only
differentiation was a mere succession of modes or operations.)
If a father who has no son (e.g. Shakespeare and Bloom after
the deaths of Hamnet and Rudy) is not a father, can a son who
hasn't a father (Shakespeare, Bloom, Hamlet, after the deaths
of John Shakespeare, old Rudolph, old Hamlet) be a son?
Shakespeare, no longer a son when he wrote *Hamlet*, was
consciously assuming the role of father in relation to all his
lineage, past and to come, grandfather and unborn grandson
alike. His message to the son is that he is dispossessed. (This
is also God's message to man – You are born of corrupted flesh.
The Devil has seduced your mother Eve. Thus the Holy Ghost,
the voice of the Father, makes plain to man that the ancestry
of his flesh is corrupted. Shakespeare, the father of all his
lineage, writing *Hamlet*, is God, the Father of all men, creating
his world. Into this world He enters as Ghost, announcing man's
original corruption; into this world He enters as Son to pay the

price of the corruption; ultimately to give his life in slaying the corrupter of the race.)

Mulligan mockingly proclaims himself (like son Shakespeare and son Hamlet) pregnant of a brain-child too – a play. He brings it forth later in the episode (p. 178/278).

Stephen continues. Shakespeare put his mother into *Coriolanus* as Volumnia; his son into *King John* as Arthur; his grand-

268   daughter into the last romances as Perdita, Miranda, and Marina; his wife into *Antony and Cleopatra, Troilus and Cressida*, and *Venus and Adonis* as the seductresses, Cleopatra, Cressida, and Venus. One other member of the family is also represented, for Shakespeare had three brothers. Gilbert Shakespeare was of little

172   account in the poet's story and is not represented in the plays. The names of the other two brothers, Richard and Edmund, however, both appear as the names of two of the three blackest villains in Shakespeare, Richard Crookback, and Edmund in *King Lear*. Moreover, *King Lear* was written while Edmund Shakespeare lay dying in Southwark.

269   As an Italian painter would set his own face in a dark corner of his canvas, so Shakespeare has hidden his own name away in such minor characters as the country fellow in *As You*

(201) *Like It*, though Shakespeare's application for a coat of arms proves that he set high value on his name. Our name is like the star under which we are born, the sign of our destiny. Shakespeare studied his (delta in Cassiopeia) as he walked by night from the arms of Ann Hathaway. Developing his theme,

173   Stephen mentally pursues a personal correspondence. Who will woo him as Ann Hathaway wooed Shakespeare? What is his own destiny? And there recurs to him the memory of that celebrated 'epiphany' in *Portrait of the Artist* when a visionary voice, calling, from 'beyond the world', was suddenly lost as the mocking shouts of his friends ('Bous Stephanoumenos') brought him back to the real world – the world of the kitchen at home, with its watery tea, fried bread, and nagging voices,

270   'Stephen, Stephen, cut the bread even.' Then, prompted by Eglinton, Stephen ponders the surname Dedalus, the name of the man who flew. He himself flew – by boat from Ireland to Paris, thence to be recalled. But it was the flight of an Icarus rather than of a Dedalus. He came back crying 'Father' (as Icarus did when his melted wings let him fall; as Christ did on the Cross).

Lyster presses Stephen to make clear which of Shakespeare's brothers his theory incriminates, but he is called away by an attendant to see Fr Dineen. Eglinton presses too. Stephen therefore returns to the brothers, nuncle Richard and nuncle Edmund, remarking that a brother is easily forgotten, recalling the role his own brother played, the role that Cranly, Mulligan, and now these librarians play – that of whetstone on which he sharpens his wit, Hamlet-like for ever talking, not acting.   *271*

Shakespare's Richard III, the only totally depraved and un-reverenced king in Shakespeare, 'makes love to a widowed Ann' in Act I, and the other four acts are but limply connected to it. Similarly the sub-plot of *King Lear*, dominated by the villainous Edmund, is artificially attached to the Celtic legend of Lear. These excrescences on the two plays are due to Shakespeare's obsession with the theme of the false, or usurping, or adulterous brother, and with the consequent theme of banishment from home. 'It was the original sin that darkened his understanding, weakened his will and left in him a strong inclination to evil.' (Joyce presses home again the double correspondence between the life of Shakespeare, the plays of Shakespeare, and the human situation in general, viewed theologically. Man is burdened by original sin 'committed by another in whose sin he too has sinned'.)   *174* *272*

Eglinton, trying to sum up the argument in a harmonious compromise, affirms that Shakespeare is both 'the ghost and the prince'. Stephen, meaning much more than Eglinton, agrees. Shakespeare is all in all: he is everyman. In love with an ideal, his intellect (Iago) tells him that the real woman (the Desdemona, the Imogen), is false and corrupted, and he destroys her. Thus man's brain, fretting Hamlet-like at the thought of discovered corruption, drives him to mutilate the part of himself which is simple, unsophisticated, trusting – 'the moor (Othello) in him'. (Note on 'hornmad Iago': Man is horn-mad, at least the intellectual part of man: i.e. he is cuckolded, for the flesh which the intellect is wedded to is corrupted: and he is wounded by the tusk of the pursuing boar, the sexuality which pulls Adonis to the earth and masters him.)   *(204)* *273*

Stephen sums up the story of Shakespeare's last days in such a way as to suggest the completion of his parable. Shakespeare returns home and dies. The epilogue ('if you like' it) is provided   *175* by *The Tempest*, the play in which the good man is rewarded and the bad man 'taken off to the place where the bad niggers go'. In other words, after death follows Heaven or Hell. 'Strong curtain.' The human pilgrimage is one in which men for ever meet themselves in others. The God who made this world 274 (as Shakespeare wrote his faulty folio), the crucified God ('hangman God', hanger and hanged), is no doubt in each one of us the summary of all things in this faulty world.

Buck Mulligan cries, 'Eureka!', having at last silently completed his travail and given birth to his play. He goes over to Eglinton's desk to get some paper and begins to write it down. Meantime Stephen reminds himself to take some library slips from the counter on the way out.

Asked by Eglinton whether he himself believes the theory about Shakespeare he has just propounded, Stephen says No. This is significant. It is not just that Stephen (and Joyce) are separating themselves from Stephen's cerebral display. 176 Rather we have an exploration here into the complexity of 275 faith. Stephen's thoughts reveal this. 'I believe, O Lord, help my unbelief.' Stephen's attitude to the dogma he has just recited, which by explained parable represents the Catholic view of man's situation and his destiny, is something which he (Stephen–Joyce) cannot believe: but then it is something which believers themselves believe only against the ever-present pressure of unbelief.

Eglinton remarks that, should Stephen write up his theory (205) for publication in *Dana*, he can scarcely expect payment if he doesn't believe what he is writing. The mention of payment and of Fred Ryan reminds Stephen that he owes Fred Ryan two shillings (a debt listed among his other debts on p. 25/37). Stephen offers Eglinton the right to publish the present 'interview' for a guinea, whereupon Mulligan begins to recite an imaginary journalist's write-up of an interview with 'the bard Kinch at his summer residence'. Then he urges Stephen to leave with him.

Eglinton and Mulligan talk of meeting again 'tonight' at George Moore's party from which Stephen is excluded. 276 Mulligan leads the way out. Stephen follows him out of the 177 librarian's office into the reading-room. They pass the librarian, quaker Lyster, engaged in 'book-talk' with the priest, Fr Dineen. Stephen follows an amused, pleased Mulligan. They go through the turnstile and Mulligan sings in Puckish mood. He also mocks the theatrical interests of the Eglinton group, who see themselves creating 'a new art for Europe' at the Abbey theatre. Stephen's mind returns to Shakespeare. He cannot believe that Shakespeare forgot Ann Hathaway – any more than he forgot Sir Thomas Lucy ('lousy Lucy') who punished him for poaching at Charlecote and whom he lampooned as Justice Shallow in *The Merry Wives*, punning on 'luce' and 'louse'. Shakespeare left Ann when she was thirty: there were no more children. 277

Mulligan continues his chatter about others he and Haines met on their visit to the Abbey theatre group's premises at the plumbers' hall. He scolds Stephen for getting across with the group by writing a hostile review of one of Lady Gregory's books. Why couldn't Stephen 'do the Yeats touch'? And he mocks the tactful flattery of a Yeats review. 'The most beautiful book that has come out of our country in my time.' 178 / 278

Now Mulligan reads the title-page and dramatis personae of his play, *Everyman His Own Wife*, a piece of obscenity whose theme is masturbation, and whose implications therefore identify Bloom as Everyman. (See *Nausicaa*.) Stephen, 'feeling one behind'* (it is Bloom, of course), stands aside. In his mind is the thought that the time has come to part with Mulligan. 'The moment is now.' There are seas between Mulligan's will and his. And through these seas, at this moment, sails Bloom, bowing, greeting. Meanwhile here, on the steps of the library, Stephen recalls how he stood watching the birds for augury as recorded in the *Portrait*. The mention of augury is noteworthy for the next thought is a recollection of last night's prophetic dream of the street of harlots, the man who offered him friendship, a melon, and a red carpet welcome (p. 39/58–9). And this recollection coincides with the passage of Bloom between himself and Mulligan – Bloom who tonight will bring him friendship and take him home, Bloom the melon-worshipper. (See pp. 49/72 and 604/867.) 279 / 179 / (209)

Mulligan calls Bloom the 'wandering Jew'. He is also the 'ancient mariner', another wanderer over the face of the earth, hungry for attention. Mulligan and Stephen follow the dark

* See p. 42/64, for a previous intuition of someone behind – three Crosses in the distance.

back of Bloom, with his 'step of a pard', out of the gateway.
280 The rising smoke from housetops brings back *Cymbeline* to
Stephen's mind, and the lines which express the resigned peace
of compromise, the note of ceasing to strive, on which
Shakespeare closes his work.

Chapter 10

The Wandering Rocks

This central episode of Joyce's book, built of nineteen short 180
sections, is both an entr'acte between the two halves and a
miniature of the whole. It is a small-scale labyrinth within which
most of the characters of *Ulysses* appear, moving about Dublin
between the hours of three and four. Their movements are set
against the background of two journeys by the representatives
of ecclesiastical and civil authority respectively – that of Fr
Conmee (section I) and that of the Earl of Dudley (section XIX).
Links and cross-references between the various sections abound.
Frank Budgen (*James Joyce and the Making of Ulysses*) tells us
that 'Joyce wrote the *Wandering Rocks* with a map of Dublin
before him on which were traced in red ink the paths of the
Earl of Dudley and Father Conmee. He calculated to a minute
the time necessary for his characters to cover a given distance
of the city.'

The Homeric basis for this elaborate experiment in virtuosity
is slight. In the *Odyssey* Circe warns Ulysses to avoid the
wandering rocks, which are a menace to navigation, and he
does so.

I

It is nearly three o'clock. John Conmee, once Jesuit rector of (210)
Clongowes Wood College, sets out from the presbytery in
Gardiner Street to walk to Artane. His mission is connected
with a letter from Martin Cunningham on behalf of young
Dignam, whose father was buried this morning.

A one-legged sailor comes by, singing and begging. Fr
Conmee, by the rules of his order, has no money except that

given him for his fare. He blesses the sailor and goes on his way, musing on the lot of soldiers and sailors wounded in action. He meets the wife of David Sheehy, MP, and greets her
281 politely. During their conversation she asks when Fr Bernard Vaughan will come to preach again. As Fr Conmee goes on his way, he recalls how Fr Vaughan exploits his droll eyes and cockney voice in the pulpit.

181 At the corner of Mountjoy Square he stops three little school-boys, Jack Sohan, Ger Gallaher, and Brunny Lynam. They are
282 Belvedere boys. He chaffs them and gives them a letter to post. It is to the father provincial.

(Mr Denis J. Maginni, professor of dancing, passes Lady Maxwell at the corner of Dignam's Court.)

Fr Conmee passes Mrs M'Guinness, who bows to him in gracious recognition. (She is the pawnbroker of p. 186/290.) Fr Conmee walks down Gt Charles Street and reads the notice on a shut-down free church, announcing the preacher. He turns
283 into the North Circular Road. He greets a band of schoolboys in the Christian Brothers' care. He passes St Joseph's Church, Portland Row, and the home for aged and virtuous females.
182 In the North Strand Road he passes Mr William Gallaher, the grocer, passes Grogan's, the tobacconist's, and reads a news-paper placard about a catastrophe in New York. He passes Daniel Bergin's public-house, H. J. O'Neill's funeral establish-
284 ment (where Corny Kelleher works at his books), a saluting constable, and Youkstetter's, the pork-butcher's. He sees a barge, tow-horse, and bargeman under the trees of Charleville Mall.
(213) On Newcomen Bridge he gets on to an outward-bound tram (unwilling to walk the dingy way past Mud Island) just as the Reverend Nicholas Dudley gets off an inward-bound tram.
285 Fr Conmee sees a couple on the tram, the husband an
183 awkward, nervous-looking man who reminds him of one of his communicants. At Annesley Bridge the tram stops and an old woman gets off. She almost misses her stop, and is recog-nized by Fr Conmee as one of those good but absent-minded souls who are never quite sure when their confession and absolution are over, and have to be told twice. A hoarding showing Mr Eugene Stratton, the Negro, turns Fr Conmee's thoughts to the problem of converting the coloured races
286 and, lightly, to the question whether their unconverted souls are wasted.

Fr Conmee gets off at the Howth Road stop and goes down Malahide Road. He muses on the history of the region, more especially the question whether the Countess of Belvedere had been unfaithful with her husband's brother (the *Hamlet* theme again). He pictures himself 'in times of yore' marrying the **184** nobility, then reading his office as he walked across the school **287** field at Clongowes where once he was rector. A young man **(215)** and a girl come through a gap in the hedge, the young man flushed, the girl bending to detach a clinging twig from her skirt. (They are to be identified on pp. 339–40/544–5.) Fr Conmee **288** blesses them as he reads his office.

II

Corny Kelleher (whom we and Fr Conmee have just seen at work in H. J. O'Neill's funeral establishment, p. 182/*284*) closes his day-book, examines a pine coffin lid, spinning it on its axle. Then he leans against the door-case and looks out. (Flashback **185** to Fr Conmee getting into the Dollymount tram on Newcomen Bridge, p. 182/*284*.) Constable 57c (presumably the constable of p. 182/*284* who saluted Fr Conmee) stops on his beat to pass the time of day. Corny Kelleher spits. (An arm emerges from a window in Eccles Street and flings a coin on the pavement for the begging sailor of p. 180/*280*. See also pp. 185/*288* and 192/*300*. The arm is Molly Bloom's.) Constable 57c tells Corny Kelleher he saw 'that particular party last evening'. (We remember that Bloom has his suspicions of Corny Kelleher as a possible informer, p. 134/*206–7*.)

III

The one-legged sailor jerks into Eccles Street, passes the Dedalus girls, Katey and Boody, growling, '*For England, home, and beauty*', **289** from the popular patriotic song, '*The Death of Nelson*'. (J. J. O'Molloy, seeking Ned Lambert, is told that he is in the warehouse with a visitor. This is a forecast of p. 189/*295* ff.) A stout lady gives the one-legged sailor a coin. Two barefooted urchins stand staring at him. His song stirs sympathy inside the house he is passing. A whistling within stops. The window blind is drawn aside, dislodging a card, '*Unfurnished Apartments*'. A woman's bare arm (Molly Bloom's, see p. 192/*300*) flings a coin

over the railings on to the path. One of the urchins picks it up
186　for the sailor.

IV

Katey and Boody Dedalus arrive home. Maggy is boiling clothes
at the range. Boody asks whether Maggy has managed to get
290　anything for the books (Stephen's, of course). Maggy says they
wouldn't take them. (Flashback to Fr Conmee walking through
the grass, p. 184/*287*.) She tried M'Guinness's in vain. Boody
(217)　and Katey hungrily inspect the pans on the hob. One contains
shirts, the other pea soup; the latter begged from Sister Mary
Patrick. (The lacquey – by the door of Dillon's auction rooms
– rings his bell. This is a forecast of p. 195/*304*.) The girls eat
and talk. Maggy says that Dilly has gone to meet father. 'Our
291　father,' Boody comments bitterly, 'who art not in heaven.'
　　(The crumpled throwaway, with its slogan 'Elijah is coming',
which Bloom dropped into the Liffey, p. 125/*192*, rides under
Loopline Bridge and sails eastwards.)

V

187　In Thornton's shop the blonde assistant makes up a basket of
fruit for Blazes Boylan, who gives her a bottle (port – see
p. 615/*884*) and a jar (perfume?) to put under the fruit. Boylan
is sending a present in advance to Molly Bloom, to prepare
the way for his four o'clock visit. (The sandwich-board-men
advertising HELY'S – see p. 127/*194* – file past Tangier Lane.)
Blazes Boylan asks the girl to send the fruit by tram immediately.
(Bloom – a dark figure in the background – studies books on a
hawker's car under Merchant's Arch. This is a forecast of p. 193/
302. While Boylan moves towards active adultery with Molly,
Bloom is seeking erotic literature to satisfy her at the 'ideal' level.)
292　Boylan gives the girl the address. As she bends to reckon up the
bill, he studies the contents of her blouse, flirtatiously takes a red
carnation for himself, then asks to use the phone.

VI

188　Stephen is in conversation in the street with Almidano Artifoni,
the music teacher. Two carfuls of tourists pass, gazing at Trinity

College and the Bank of Ireland. Artifoni wants Stephen to pursue his musical career in Dublin. An Inchicore tram stops 293 and unloads 'straggling Highland soldiers of a band'. Stephen is touched by Artifoni's warmth as he takes his leave and trots after the Dalkey tram, holding up a baton of rolled music. But Artifoni's gesticulations are not noticed: he is lost among the bare-kneed Highland instrumentalists and misses the tram.

VII

Miss Dunne, Blazes Boylan's secretary, hides a library copy of (220) Wilkie Collins's *The Woman in White* in her drawer and takes up her typing. She thinks there is 'too much mystery' in the 294 book. (Forecast of Tom Rochford's machine, p. 191/297.) Miss Dunne types the date. (Flashback to Hely's sandwichboard-men again, pp. 127/194 and 187/291.) She stares at the poster of 189 Marie Kendall, soubrette; doodles, and day-dreams about her coming night out. The phone rings. It is Boylan (ringing from the fruit shop, p. 187/292). Having taken a message, she tells him that Lenehan has called, and will be in the Ormond at four. (Where Boylan meets him, p. 217/340.)

VIII

Ned Lambert is showing a visitor the ancient council chamber of 295 St Mary's Abbey by the light of a match. Someone approaches in the darkness. It is Jack O'Molloy. He joins Ned and his visitor, a clergyman. Ned explains that this is 'the most historic spot in all Dublin'. It was once the site of the Jewish synagogue. It was the place where silken Thomas proclaimed himself a rebel in 1534.

The clergyman, who is writing a book on the Fitzgeralds, asks permission to bring his camera and take photographs. It is 190 granted. (Forecast of John Howard Parnell at the chessboard, 296 p. 204/319.) He takes his leave. Ned Lambert and J. J. O'Molloy follow him out into the daylight. Ned reads the visitor's card – 'The Rev. Hugh C. Love, Rathcoffey'. (Flashback to the young woman detaching the twig from her skirt, p. 184/287.) Ned and J. J. O'Molloy walk away. They pass the horses, which start nervously. Lambert slaps and quietens one. Then he sneezes 297 violently, and blames a cold caught the night before last and worsened by attending Dignam's funeral this morning.

IX

191   Tom Rochford shows Nosey Flynn, Lenehan, and M'Coy how his machine works which indicates what turn is in progress at the music hall.

(Richie Goulding, carrying the firm's cost-bag, passes from the consolidated taxing office to Nisi Prius court. An elderly lady in a black silk skirt rustles from the admiralty division of king's bench to the court of appeal.)

298   M'Coy leaves, and Lenehan, too, goes off to meet Boylan in the Ormond. As they go down Sycamore Street together, Lenehan shows M'Coy the manhole for the sewer from which Tom Rochford rescued a man half-choked with sewer gas. Rochford went down, roped, and roped the other man to

299   himself. Lenehan slips into Lynam's to check *Sceptre*'s starting-
192   price. M'Coy, waiting for him, kicks a banana peel into the
(224)   gutter. (The gates of the viceregal lodge open to make way for the viceroy's cavalcade. This is a forecast of the procession detailed in section XIX, p. 207/324.)

Lenehan returns to announce that Bantam Lyons is in there backing a horse that 'hasn't an earthly'. At this moment they pass the dark back of Bloom, scanning books on the hawker's cart under Merchant's Arch. He, of course, is the 'someone' who unwittingly put Bantam Lyons on to *Throwaway*, the horse that hasn't a chance. (See p. 70/106.) Lenehan and M'Coy see Bloom. M'Coy says Bloom is mad on sales, and tells how he paid two

300   bob for a book on astronomy. They cross the bridge and go along Wellington Quay. (Young Master Dignam comes out of Mangan's carrying a pound and a half of pork-steaks. Forecast of p. 206/323.)

Lenehan tells M'Coy his story of the Glencree Dinner, ten years back when Val Dillon was lord mayor. We have already learned about this from Bloom's own musings (p. 127/196). (Flashback to 7 Eccles Street, Bloom's house. The card *'Unfurnished Apartments'* is replaced on the window-sash. See

301   p. 185/289.) Lenehan describes the drive back from the party
193   on a gorgeous winter night, Bloom and Chris Callinan sitting on one side of the car, Molly Bloom and himself on the other, Molly well primed with port. As the car jolted, Molly was thrust against him and he made the most of it, exploring her bosom under cover of keeping the rug well tucked round her.

Meanwhile Bloom was pointing out the stars and the comets to Chris Callinan. Lenehan collapses with laughter over this story. M'Coy is not so amused. He grows grave. Lenehan senses his mistake and changes his tune, praising Bloom as 'a cultured allroundman'. 'There's a touch of the artist about old Bloom.'   *302*

X

Mr Bloom is looking in a bookshop for something for Molly to read. (She asked him to get another book this morning, p. 53/*78*.) He picks up *The Awful Disclosures of Maria Monk*, Aristotle's *Masterpiece*, Masoch's *Tales of the Ghetto*, then, at the shopman's suggestion, *Fair Tyrants* by James Lovebirch (but he has already   *194* had it), and *Sweets of Sin*. (Flashback to Professor Maginni, now walking on over O'Connell Bridge, p. 181/*282*.) He samples *Sweets of Sin*, a luridly written sex novel based on the triangle – husband, wife, and lover (Raoul). Its crude phrases recur to   *303* Bloom's mind frequently later in the day, and the three excerpts   (*226*) given here should be noted. They evoke in Bloom a mood of mental surrender to gushingly sensuous images of feminine curves, nudity, and sweat. (The elderly lady leaves the courts, having listened to cases in the lord chancellor's court, in the admiralty division, and in the court of appeal. On p. 191/*223* we caught sight of her moving from the second to the third of these.) Bloom decides to take *Sweets of Sin*.   *304*

XI

The lacquey outside Dillon's auction rooms rings a handbell,   *195* which we have already heard (p. 186/*290*).

(Another bell marks the start of the last lap of the Trinity College bicycle race: four cyclists – Jackson, Wylie, Munro, and Gahan – negotiate the curve by the college library. W. E. Wylie, the second-named here, is the brother of Reggy Wylie who occupies a place in Gerry Macdowell's thoughts in episode 13. See p. 287/*454*.)

Dilly Dedalus meets her father, Simon Dedalus, whom she has come to call home. He mocks her stance, urging her to stand erect. (Mr Kernan walks along James's Street. Forecast of   *305* p. 197/*308*.) Dilly manages to get a shilling out of him, though he curses his children drunkenly in handing it over. The

196   lacquey's bell interrupts their talk. Dilly presses for more money.
306   Mr Dedalus claims that he got two shillings only from Jack Power and spent twopence of it on a shave 'for the funeral'. When Dilly suggests that he might try to get more, he mocks her, then parts with another twopence. (The viceregal cavalcade passes out of Parkgate. See pp. 192/*299* and 207/*324*.)

XII

307   Tom Kernan, commercial traveller (we met him at Dignam's funeral, pp. 86–7/*132–3*), is walking towards James's Gate, looking back with pleasure on the deal he has just done with the firm of Pulbrook Robertson through a Mr Crimmins. His chat with Mr Crimmins turned on the General Slocum explo-
197   sion , the loss of life, the failure of the lifeboats and the fire-hoses, and Mr Crimmins's suspicion that only bribery could account for the fact that inspectors ever allowed the boat to go to sea. Kernan took up Mr Crimmins's hint and blamed the rottenness of the Americans.

308   Moving on, aware of Mr Crimmins's admiration of his frock-
(230)   coat, Kernan attributes his commercial success today to his smart suit as well as to his conversation. (Forecast of Simon Dedalus meeting Fr Cowley, p. 200/*313*.) He dwells in self-admiration on his appearance and his achievement. (Flashback to Bloom's throwaway, 'Elijah is coming', pp. 125/*192* and 186/*291*, now floating westward in Sir John Rogerson's Quay.) Kernan dwells on his own image in a hairdresser's window, on a figure across the road who looks like Sam Lambert (Ned's brother), on the good gin Mr Crimmins gave him, and on the site of Emmet's
309   execution. (Robert Emmet, martyred Irish revolutionary, 1778–1803. See p. 238/*375*.)
198   Kernan turns into Watling Street. (Denis Breen, weary of waiting for an interview in John Henry Menton's office, is now going with his wife over O'Connell Bridge, carrying his law-books, and making for Messrs Collis and Ward. See pp. 129/*198* and 131/*201*.) Kernan is musing on the stirring days gone by, and more particularly on Lord Edward Fitzgerald who was arrested just round the corner at 152, Thomas Street. (Lord Edward Fitzgerald, 1763–98, soldier, rebel, patriot, joined the United Irishmen, was captured and died in Newgate of wounds inflicted when he was arrested.) He recalls, too, John Kells

Ingram's* ballad on the Battle of New Ross during the 1798
Rising, in which Lord Edward took part, and Ben Dollard's
touching way of singing 'The Croppy Boy' ('At the siege of Ross   310
did my father fall'). We are to hear him singing this ballad in
the next episode (pp. 232 ff./365 ff.)

The viceregal cavalcade passes along Pembroke Quay (see pp.
192/299; 196/306; and 207/324). Mr Kernan hurries forward,
but is too late to catch a glimpse of 'His Excellency'.

XIII

Stephen Dedalus stares at the stones and jewels in a lapidary's
window. They are stars from the brows of fallen archangels, flung
into the dirt, thence to be uprooted and upwrested by the muddy
snouts of swine or by groping hands. He recalls seeing a naked   (232)
girl dancing in a dim room before a drunken sailor, a huge ruby
flapping on her belly. As the lapidary, Old Russell, polishes a gem,
Stephen sees his own poetic work as wresting buried images from   199
the earth. (Flashback to the two old women of the *Proteus* episode,
Florence MacCabe and her companion – p. 31/46. Now they   311
trudge through Irishtown after their walk on the seashore. Mrs
MacCabe has eleven cockles in her mid-wife's bag.)

The noise of the machines in the power-house near by impels
Stephen to move on. He sees himself caught between 'two roar-
ing worlds' of inner and outer compulsion. He is tempted to
strike out at them both, at the God within and the God without,
the God whom he called 'Bawd and butcher' in his *Hamlet* dis-
course (p. 175/274). But the time is not yet. He is frightened.
He withdraws from his own blasphemy, asking God for a little
more time, meanwhile praising God's clockwork creation, 'keeps
famous time' and quoting Hamlet, 'You say right, sir . . .' Thus
Stephen detaches himself from his own violent utterances, as
Hamlet does on the approach of Polonius, pretending that his
mind is occupied with conventional trivialities.

He goes down Bedford Row, notes a faded print of heavy-
weight boxers in Clohissey's window, then stops to examine the
books on a book-cart at the roadside. He wonders whether he

---

* John Kells Ingram, 1823–1907, Regius Professor of Greek, Trinity College,
Dublin, as an undergraduate wrote a poem, 'The Memory of the Dead' or 'Who
fears to speak of Ninety-Eight?'.

may find one of his pawned school prizes here. (Flashback to
Fr Conmee walking through Donnycarney, reading Vespers,
312   p. 184/*287*.) He picks up a book by Peter Salanka, full of charms
and invocations. The thumbed pages, much consulted by the
book's former owner, deal with the questions, 'How to soften
chapped hands', and, more interestingly to Stephen, 'How to
win a woman's love'. He is reminded again of Abbas Joachim's
comminations and gives us, in 'Down, baldy-noodle, or we'll
wool your wool', a new translation of 'Descende, calve . . .'
(p. 33/*49*). Suddenly his sister Dilly appears. Her long face and
200   lank locks remind him of Charles Stuart. He remembers how
she crouched before the fire, trying to get heat by burning old
boots, while he told her of Paris.

Dilly has bought a book for a penny. Stephen looks at it. It
is a French primer. In the midst of all the meanness and squalor
and misery of the girls' life with their father, Dilly is hoping to
(233)   learn French. It is a touching moment, one of the most compassionate in the book. Stephen senses acutely but silently the irony
of the girl's suffering and poverty, and her trusting reliance
313   upon his own judgement and influence. 'She is drowning.' His
conscience calls him to come to her aid, but he feels that everything is against them. If he were to return home he would be
dragged down to drown with her. The torment of remorse for
his failure to do anything for the family in their suffering
conflicts with his determination not to be destroyed himself,
and the tension remains unresolved.

XIV

Simon Dedalus meets Fr Cowley outside Reddy and Daughter's.
Fr Cowley is in difficulties. Reuben J. Dodd, the money-lender
(see p. 78/*118*), to whom he owes money, has sent two bailiffs to
his house, and Fr Cowley has barricaded the place against them.
Fr Cowley is waiting for Ben Dollard, who has gone to see the
sub-sheriff, Long John Fanning (see p. 203/*317*), on his behalf, in
the hope that Dodd can be induced to take his men away. Ben
201   Dollard comes along now. He and Simon greet each other chaf-
314   fingly ('Hold that fellow with the bad trousers. . . . Hold him now
. . .') in phrases which are to recur later.

(Flashbacks to Cashel Boyle O'Connor Fitzmaurice Tisdall
Farrell, p. 131/*201*, now striding past the Kildare Street club;

and to the Reverend Hugh C. Love, p. 190/*296*, now walking   *315*
away from the old Chapterhouse of St Mary's Abbey, in imagination in the company of the Geraldines.)

Ben Dollard has met John Henry Menton and cleared up
Fr Cowley's legal position satisfactorily. Fr Cowley's landlord
has already distrained for unpaid rent. (The landlord is none   *202*
other than the Reverend Hugh C. Love.) He has the prior claim
upon Fr Cowley's property. This means that Dodd the money-
lender's writ for possession of it is not worth the paper it is
written on.

XV

Martin Cunningham and Mr Power are passing through the   *316*
Castleyard Gate. Cunningham signs to the waiting cab to move
on while they walk. (Forecast of Misses Douce and Kennedy
looking out through the window of the Ormond Hotel, p. 211/
331.) He tells Power that he had laid the case of the orphaned
Dignam boy before Fr Conmee (hence Fr Conmee's preoccupation on p. 180/*280*). Power suggests touching Boyd for   (236)
help. Cunningham thinks it useless. John Wyse Nolan catches
them up. (Councillor Nannetti meets Alderman Cowley and
Councillor Lyon on the steps of the City Hall.) Nolan knows
that Bloom has put his name down for five shillings on the
subscription list for the Dignam orphans. Cunningham remarks   *317*
that he has paid it too. Nolan agrees that 'there is much kindness in the jew'. They turn down Parliament Street. Power sees
Jimmy Henry heading for Kavanagh's. (Boylan meets 'Jack
Mooney's brother-in-law'* outside La Maison Claire.) Nolan falls
back with Power, while Cunningham takes the arm of Jimmy
Henry, the assistant town clerk, who is walking uncertainly (his   *203*
corns are troubling him, Nolan says), but he cannot interest
Henry in the subscription list.

In the doorway of Kavanagh's wine rooms they meet Lord
John Fanning, the sub-sheriff, who talks of the council meeting.
Cunningham tries to interest Fanning and Jimmy Henry in the   *318*
Dignam Fund. Jimmy Henry gets out of it by pretending that
his corns are troubling him. Fanning claims not to have known
Dignam. Power and Cunningham describe him.   *319*

* i.e. Bob Doran. (See 'The Boarding House', *Dubliners*.)

204   There is a clatter of horse-hooves. They turn to see the Lord Lieutenant-General's procession passing Parliament Street.

XVI

Buck Mulligan and Haines are in a Dublin Bakery Company's restaurant. Mulligan points out John Howard Parnell, brother of the great man and city marshal, who is in a corner playing chess (picture anticipated on p. 190/296). Mulligan and Haines

320   discuss Stephen. Haines implies that Stephen's mind is unbalanced. (Flashback to the one-legged sailor of pp. 180/280 and 185/288, now begging outside 14 Nelson Street.) He wonders what is the particular obsession that has unbalanced him. Mulligan gravely tells Haines that the Jesuits put the fear of Hell into him and 'drove his wits astray' (like Hamlet's). As a result he cannot experience the joy of creativity.

205   Haines swallows this readily. He realized from this morning's conversation about belief (p. 16/23) that there was something on Stephen's mind. It is odd that eternal punishment should be Stephen's obsession, since the idea of Hell is not present in Irish myth. He asks whether Stephen is writing anything for the Irish

321   movement. Mulligan reports, laughingly, that he is going to write something in ten years' time. Haines, prophetically, says he shouldn't wonder if he did after all.

(Flashback to Bloom's 'Elijah' throwaway of pp. 125/192; 186/291; and 197/308 – now sailing eastward in the docks past

(240)   the three-masted schooner, *Rosevean*, which Stephen saw from the beach this morning in the *Proteus* episode, p. 42/64.)

XVII

Almidano Artifoni, who talked with Stephen and missed his tram in section VI (p. 188/293), is now walking past Holles Street. Farrell, of pp. 131/201 and 201/314, is behind him.

322   Farther behind is the blind stripling whom Bloom guided across the street in *The Lestrygonians* episode (p. 148/231). Farrell turns at Werner's window and walks back. As he passes the blind

206   stripling, his coat knocks the boy's cane against his body. The boy curses him.

XVIII

Master Dignam dawdles along Wicklow Street with the sausages, reluctant to go back home where the adults sit behind drawn blinds, talking and sighing and sipping sherry. He looks in the window of Madam Doyle, milliner, and sees himself, in mourning, duplicated in the side mirrors. He reads the advertisement for a boxing match, only to realize regretfully that the bout has already taken place. (We get a journalist's write-up of   323 the engagement in *The Cyclops* episode, pp. 261–2/412–4.) He muses on Bob Fitzsimons's world title victory over Jem Corbett in 1897. In Grafton Street he sees a toff with a red flower in his mouth, listening to a drunk. This is clearly Blazes Boylan and 'Jack Mooney's brother-in-law' (p. 202/317), Bob Doran.

Young Dignam, meeting schoolboys with satchels, indulges reflections on his temporary superiority to the common herd. Do they notice he's in mourning? Will his name be printed in tonight's paper with news of the funeral? Other images of the bereavement succeed: his dead father's face in the coffin, the   207 laborious business of getting the big coffin downstairs, the last   324 memories of his father, standing on the landing and bawling for his boots so that he could go out and get himself drunker, then muttering a final message on his deathbed.

XIX

The Lord Lieutenant and his lady, William Humble, Earl of Dudley and Lady Dudley, are driven with their cavalcade through the streets of Dublin. They are going from the viceregal lodge to inaugurate the Mirus Bazaar in aid of funds for Mercer's Hospital. In the course of their ride they pass, and are   (242) variously seen by, stared at by, saluted by, ignored by, or missed by, the following: Mr Thomas Kernan, Mr Dudley White, Richie   325 Goulding, Miss Kennedy and Miss Douce, Simon Dedalus, Rev. Hugh C. Love, Lenehan and M'Coy, Gerty MacDowell, John   208 Wyse Nolan, Tom Rochford and Nosey Flynn, Buck Mulligan   326 and Haines, Dilly Dedalus, John Henry Menton, Mr and Mrs Breen, HELY'S sandwich-board-men, Professor Maginni, Blazes   327 Boylan, Cashel Farrell, Hornblower, Master Dignam, the blind   209 stripling, the man in the brown mackintosh, the two midwives,   328 Almidano Artifoni, and various other persons unnamed.

Chapter 11

The Sirens

210 In the *Odyssey* Ulysses and his men manage to sail past the sirens, with their irresistibly luring songs, because they have defended themselves in advance. Ulysses has had himself tied to the mast, and his followers' ears are stuffed with wax. There would appear to be no point-for-point correspondence here, but the episode contains two charming siren barmaids as well as much song, and the style represents an elaborate attempt to imitate musical form in words. The musical devices parodied include: structural development of small figures and phrases; a continuous symphonic manipulation of sharply identifiable themes; the use of emphatic rhythmic figures and patterns; varied tonal contrasts; rich onomatopoeic orchestration which mimics the interplay of strings, brass and woodwind; repetition and partial repetition; echo and semi-echo; contrapuntal play of phrase against phrase; percussive explosions; recapitulations in different 'keys'; and so on. This technical experimentation apart, Joyce peppers the episode with lines and phrases taken from opera and operetta popular at the time, from Victorian and Edwardian drawing-room ballads, from music-hall favourites and from traditional songs.

329 The introductory flourish has been said to represent the tuning
(245) up of an orchestra. It seems more sensible to regard it as an
330 overture, for it lays before us, in concise form, many of the
211 themes (fifty-seven, to be exact) to be fully and richly explored in the body of the episode.

331 It is close on four o'clock in the bar of the Ormond Hotel. Two barmaids, bronze-haired Miss Douce and gold-haired Miss Kennedy, stare through the window at the viceregal cavalcade ringing by in the street outside. Miss Kennedy admires Lady

Dudley, sitting at the side of his ex(cellency) in pearl grey and *eau de Nil*. Miss Douce's eyes are on one of the accompanying gentlemen in the second carriage, who wears a tall silk hat (the Hon. Gerald Ward, ADC, p. 207/324). He sees her – or she thinks he sees her – 'killed' by her glance. She laughs delightedly, while Miss Kennedy comes sadly away from the window. Bloom goes by on Wellington Quay with *Sweets of Sin* under his arm.

212
(247)

The boots brings in the girls' tea, banging the tray down on the counter. He wants to know who Miss Douce is looking at through the window. She rebuffs his 'impertinent insolence' and he mocks her big words ('Imperthnthn thnthnthn') as he goes.

332

Miss Kennedy pours out the tea. The girls settle down on stools behind the counter. Chatting about sunburn, Miss Douce tells how she asked the old fogey in Boyd's for something for her skin, and he said, 'For your what?' She mimics his snuffling grunt and the two girls are son rocking with laughter, recalling an encounter with the old fogey one night in the Antient Concert Rooms.

333
213

Bloom, passing the 'blessed virgins' in the window of Bassi's statuary shop, broods mistakenly on Roman Catholic dogma ('God they believe she is: or goddess'), on the goddesses he has recently inspected in the museum, and on the fellow who interrupted his inspection and whom he saw later with Stephen Dedalus. Rightly he conjectures that this was Mulligan.

334

Miss Douce and Miss Kennedy are still overcome with the giggles. Hysterical laugher reaches its climax as Miss Douce pictures the horror of being married to the greasy-eyed fogey in Boyd's.

214
335

Bloom now sees pictures of the Virgin in the window of Ceppi's, the frame-maker's shop; he recalls how Nannetti's father hawked religious pictures, remembers he must see Nannetti again about the Keyes advertisement, but feels the need for food first. Molly's appointment with Boylan at four still haunts him. Related images collide: the wish to make five guineas to buy new underwear for Molly with it, and the triangle in *Sweets of Sin* where the woman decks herself at her husband's expense, all for the pleasure of her lover, Raoul (see p. 194/302–3).

Simon Dedalus comes into the bar, picking chips off his thumbnails. He flirts lightly with Miss Douce and orders a whisky.

336

Lenehan comes in to keep his appointment with Boylan (see p. 189/294).

215

Bloom crosses Essex Bridge, remembering that he must reply to Martha. He will buy some notepaper at Daly's, on Ormond Quay, where the girl is civil.

337   Lenehan asks whether Boylan has been in. He hasn't. Lenehan tries flirtatiously to get Miss Kennedy's attention, but she goes on reading, though he teases her, mockingly, as a teacher

(251)   teaching a child to read. ('Ah fox met ah stork . . .') His efforts are fruitless: he is ignored. So he turns his forced jocularity on Simon Dedalus. 'Greetings from the famous son of a famous

216   father.' Simon inquires dryly after Stephen. Lenehan reports the

338   gathering for drinks in Mooney's this morning when Professor MacHugh, Myles Crawford, and O'Madden Burke hung upon Stephen's lips, as he puts it.

Simon, unresponsive to Lenehan, remarks that the piano has been moved. Miss Douce praises the playing of the tuner who has been in today. He is clearly the blind stripling Bloom helped across the road (p. 148/*231*). Miss Douce speaks sadly of his misfortune, whereupon there is inserted an echo of the blind man's curse upon Farrell for bumping him as he passed. ('God's curse on bitch's bastard.' See p. 206/*322*.)

339   We hear a diner tinkling a bell for service in the dining-room next door. Pat, the waiter, comes in for a lager. Simon examines the newly tuned piano.

Meantime Bloom buys notepaper and envelopes in Daly's, recalling how he once worked for Wisdom Hely's in stationery. Phrases from Martha's past letters recur to him. He sees a poster with a swaying mermaid, advertising cigarettes, and the sensu-

217   ousness of it takes him back to *Sweets of Sin* again. In the distance, on Essex Bridge, he catches a glimpse of Boylan's car. The jaunty, jingling adulterer intrudes on the mind once more. Bloom feels the urge to rush from the shop and follow, and almost forgets to pay for his purchase. The winsome friendli-ness of the shop assistant is received with a hint of suspicion against the background of his wife's four o'clock infidelity. Women smile at you as though you're the only pebble on the beach; but they do the same to all.

340   In the saloon Miss Kennedy still reads. Someone strikes the tuning-fork accidentally left behind by the blind tuner. Simon plays on the piano the song, '*Goodbye, sweetheart, goodbye*', which begins '*The bright stars fade, the morn is breaking,/The dewdrops pearl each bud and leaf*'. Lines from it – '*I could not leave*

thee, though I said/Goodbye, sweetheart, goodbye' – thread themselves appropriately through the movements of the drama here.
Meanwhile Miss Kennedy finishes her book and Lenehan gets
a reply out of her at last, but it is a snub. 'Ask no questions
and you'll hear no lies.' Blazes Boylan (the conquering hero)
comes in and Lenehan greets him.

Bloom (the unconquered hero) comes along, sees Boylan's car
outside the Ormond, and Richie Goulding, raising his bag in   *341*
recognition. Bloom is surprised that Boylan has 'not yet' gone   218
for his appointment, and wonders what he is doing in the   (254)
Ormond. The meeting with Goulding gives him a chance to
watch Boylan in the Ormond without being seen, and he tacks
himself on to Goulding.

Inside Miss Kennedy smiles at Boylan, but Miss Douce out-
smiles her, winning his eye with her richer hair, her bosom, and
the rose. (Note that the wire bringing the result of the Ascot
race is expected at four; significant hour.) She reaches up for a
flagon, and Boylan makes the most of the satin stretched tightly
over her bust. Lenehan and Boylan drink to each other. Lenehan
says he has backed *Sceptre* to win the Gold Cup. As Boylan
pays for the drinks, the clock strikes four. ('Clock clacked.'   *342*
Cocklike it heralds a betrayal – and a false sunrise. 'Look to
the west.') Bloom, following Goulding to a table near the door,   219
wonders whether Boylan has forgotten his date or whether his
delay is a device to whet the appetite – a trick of which Bloom
thinks pathetically, 'I couldn't do.'

'Let's hear the time.' Lenehan has been pressing Miss Douce
to perform her party trick. Humming, she eyes Blazes Boylan.
'Please, please' Lenehan pleads; Miss Douce hesitates coyly,   *343*
then, while Miss Kennedy is out of earshot, coquettishly obliges,
catapulting her elastic garter against her thigh with a warm
smack. 'Sonnez la cloche!' Lenehan cries, delighted, but Miss
Douce's eyes are on Boylan, not on him. Boylan has his drink,
his eyes following Miss Douce's movements; then he leaves (and
for Bloom it is *'Sweetheart, goodbye!'*). Lenehan follows him, at   *344*
the doorway meeting Ben Dollard and Fr Cowley coming in –   220
and still discussing Fr Cowley's financial difficulty. Simon
Dedalus comes through the saloon and Ben asks him to sing.
Pat, the waiter, takes orders for drinks from Goulding and
Bloom.

Ben Dollard sits on the piano stool and thumps a few chords.

345   Blazes Boylan's jaunting car is heard jingling off outside, and Bloom sighs. Miss Douce watches Boylan's departure from the window, pensive, disappointed, wondering whether he is smitten with her. Ben Dollard, Simon Dedalus, and Fr Cowley together recall a memorable concert at which Professor Goodwin, worse for drink, thrashed the piano. Ben Dollard was due to sing on this occasion, but had no evening suit.

221   Bob Cowley saved the situation, remembering that the Blooms
346   carried on a little business in secondhand clothes on the side – a business represented by the significantly ambiguous advertise-
(258) ment, 'Mrs Marion Bloom has left off clothes of all descriptions.' They searched out Bloom's house to equip Ben Dollard. As they reminisce about buxom Marion Tweedy, 'Daughter of the regiment', Boylan's car jingles down the quays, while Bloom orders liver and bacon, his mind on Molly and this morning's conversation with her in the bedroom about metempsychosis, the burning kidneys, and the novelist Paul de Kock.

347   Misses Douce and Kennedy pine pensively at the bar. Pat serves Bloom his liver and bacon, Richie his steak and kidney,
222   and they eat in silence. Boylan jingles by Bachelor's Walk.

Ben Dollard thumps some chords and booms out a few words
348   of a song in his deep bass voice. Miss Kennedy serves two gentlemen, who ask polite questions about the purpose of the lord lieutenant's journey across the city. Bloom, hearing Ben Dollard's voice, himself recalls the night when he and Molly lent him the suit, with the trousers so tight that 'all his belong-ings' were on show, and Molly couldn't contain her laughter when he'd gone. (Molly herself recalls this occasion in her solil-oquy, p. 636/920.)

349   The solicitor George Lidwell comes in, and greets Miss Douce suavely, who tells him that his friends are inside. Bloom's
223   thoughts roam widely – from Ben at the piano to string players in the orchestra, Molly's snore, the brass, the night at the theatre in a box (recalled again on p. 233/367, and by Molly in her monologue on p. 632/914), the jigging of the conductor's legs and the jingling of the harpstrings (coinciding here with the jigging and jingling of Boylan's jaunting car towards its goal), cool hands of the harpist, the afternoon in the sunshine on Ben Howth when he was young (a much remembered day, the day of Molly's first and final Yes, p. 644/933), his own age now, and Boylan's youth.

Ben Dollard and Fr Cowley press Simon Dedalus to sing
'M'appari' from Flotow's *Martha*. Simon sits at the piano and   350
begins, but Fr Cowley comes forward to accompany him.

Boylan jingles through the streets of Dublin towards Molly,
while Bloom eats. Richie Goulding reminisces about Joe Maas   (261)
singing '*All is lost now*' from Bellini's *La Sonnambula*. Bloom
studies him, a near physical wreck with no appetite, indisci-   224
plined, rambling, inventing his own reminiscences and believing   351
them. Richie whistles the tune and Bloom recalls the situation
in the opera when the innocent Amina, walking in her sleep,
goes at night to Rodolfo's room. The image of the woman
walking blindly into danger, unable to be halted, converges with
the jingling of jaunty Boylan towards his goal. Indeed, all is
lost now.

Bloom catches sight of his own dejected face in the wall   352
mirror. Richie's stale jokes and broken personality complement
the vision. Meantime Simon is at last prevailed upon to
sing the aria from *Martha* (significant name for Bloom). Bloom   225
signs to Pat the waiter to set the door of the bar open so that
all in the dining-room can hear. The song touches Bloom with   353
a soft nostalgia and, while his fingers wind and unwind an
elastic band in his pocket, his thoughts wander from the sexual
appeal of tenors to the crude music-hall songs of Boylan who
'can't sing for tall hats', from Martha's letter to the imagined
moment of Boylan's arrival at his home – the jingling of his
car, the knock on the door, Molly's last look in the mirror – and
so to the crisis moment in *Sweets of Sin* where 'hands felt for
the opulent curves'.

Bloom admires Simon's glorious tone with its soft Cork
flavour; thinks of Simon's silliness in failing to make a career,
wearing out his wife. Then rational reflection is submerged   354
under an emotional surrender to the gushing flow of the sentimental tune.

Bloom realizes the coincidences that this is Lionel's song to   226
his lost Martha and he himself was just about to write to his
own Martha. The repetition of the first words and theme of the
aria, '*When first I saw that form endearing*', takes Bloom back to   355
his first meeting with Molly in Terenure, when they came
together in a game of musical chairs; then of how she sang
'*Waiting*' while he turned the pages for her, luxuriating in her
full voice, her full bosom.

The song moves out of strict repetition towards the climax –
the repeated, agonizing, lonely cry, '*Martha, Martha*', reflecting
Leopold's lost, lonely dream-correspondence. The rush of
emotion produced by the prolonged dominant seventh of the
perfect cadence is represented in a riotous, mounting rhetoric
227   appropriately emotive and meaningless. As the dominant is
resolved in the tonic, the tension of expectation is released
356   in fulfilment. '*Come to me.*' The momentary total involvement
of Bloom's being in Simon's (and, in the opera, Lionel's)
emotional assertion is represented in the sudden fusion of the
three names. Simon, Lionel, and Leopold, as 'Siopold'. All clap.
(265)   The '*Come*' answers all Bloom's needs – 'She ought to' – but
the joy of the shared fulfilment is not exclusive, rather
communal, 'To me, to him, to her, you too, me, us.' (See p.
411/622–3 for further light on the resolution of dominant into
tonic in the perfect cadence.) All applaud, while the reader
catches up on the progress of Blazes Boylan, quickly recapitu-
lated. He has passed the Nelson monument and is now all
impatience as his mare climbs more slowly up the hill by the
Rotunda, Rutland Square.

Fr Cowley continues to play the piano. Tom Kernan comes
357   in. Richie Goulding drivels on, ramblingly, repeating himself in
reminiscence of a memorable night when Simon sang '*'Twas
rank and fame*' at Ned Lambert's. Bloom knows of the family
rift between Simon and Richie, who admires Simon's voice none
228   the less. Bloom dwells on the theme of the song – the cruelty
of parting, the suddenness of death, Dignam's funeral, the rat
in the graveyard (p. 94/*145*), his contribution to the fund for
the Dignam orphans, the funeral liturgy, Fr Coffey's belly (p.
85/*130*) . . . Yet too much happiness would be boring.
358   Boylan jingles into Dorset Street.

Miss Douce coquettishly rebuffs George Lidwell's approaches.
(We hear increasingly Miss Douce's Christian name, Lydia, and
Miss Kennedy's Christian name, Mina.) Bloom decides to write
his letter to Martha here and now, asks Pat the waiter for pen,
ink, and blotting-pad. He maintains his conversation with
Richie while planning his reply to Martha and extracting the
359   notepaper from his pocket. He dwells mentally on the mys-
229   terious nature of music, rooted as it is in mathematics. Fr Cowley
continues to improvise, and Bloom's mind moves quickly over
the pleasures of listening to music, learners' scales excepted,

more particular memories, and the fact that daughter Milly, unlike her parents, has no musical taste.

Pat brings pen, ink, and blotting-pad.

Simon Dedalus recalls his boyhood in Cork and the singing of the Italian sailors who used to call there.

Bloom opens his newspaper in order to conceal what he writes   *360* from Richie Goulding and starts his letter to Martha. Half bored with it though he is, he thanks her, then, calculating the day's expenditure so far and what he can afford to give, mentions his enclosed present of a half-crown postal order, keeps the 'baby talk' going, adds a plea that she 'must believe' him, then stops to ask himself whether the whole thing is not foolish. Why does he do it? Is it because he is kept away from his wife   (268) physically? The thought of Molly induces the determination that she must not find out.

Boylan has now parked his own car and is being carried in   *361* a hackney cab past Dlugacz's pork-shop which Bloom called at   230 for his breakfast kidney this morning.

Richie's curiosity is aroused; he asks Bloom if he is answering an ad. Bloom says he is, meantime signing himself off and taking care to disguise his handwriting with Greek ees. The continuing music inspires him to add a sentimental PS, 'How will you punish me? Tell me. I want to know.' and a PPS, 'I feel so sad today, so lonely.' He addresses the envelope, then blots the blotting-pad so that Richie cannot read the address after he has gone. Might he not win a prize from *Titbits* for a story in which a detective solves a mystery by deciphering the words imprinted on a blotting-pad?

Second thoughts suggest that the PS was too poetical – a product of the music. 'Music hath charms.' Shakespeare, he reflects, has a quotation for every purpose, every occasion. (There is a flashback to Stephen's mental picture of 'greyedauburn'   *362* Shakespeare in London, p. 166/259. This apparently telepathic parallelism foreshadows the latter meeting of minds and hints at consubstantiality between father and son. NB 'One life is all. One body.')

Bloom's meal is over. He intends to get a postal order and stamp for his letter to Martha on the way to Barney Kiernan's, where he is to meet Martin Cunningham about the Dignam fund. He wants his bill and calls Pat the waiter, but Pat doesn't hear. There is too much talk. Bloom, in his present mood, would prefer music to talk: it keeps his mind off the Molly–Boylan meeting.

Lydia Douce is telling George Lidwell of her gorgeous holiday, showing him the shell she has brought back. Tom Kernan is

231 claiming that Walter Bapty lost his voice when his mistress's husband took his revenge. Lydia demonstrates the virtues of

363 the shell in George Lidwell's ear. The sight of the shell brings back seaside memories to Bloom and Boylan's song of the seaside girls; then the thought of sunburn, cold cream, and the skin lotion he has forgotten to buy.

The recurring 'tap' signals the gradual approach of the blind stripling who is coming back to recover his forgotten tuning-

(270) fork. Boylan sways in the cab, turning the corner by Larry O'Rourke's. Lydia Douce continues her flirtatious by-play with the shell and George Lidwell.

Fr Cowley plays a tinkling, tripping tune: Bloom recog-

364 nizes the Minuet from *Don Giovanni* (opera of seduction), and pictures court dancing in a castle while the starving faces of peasants stare in from outside. (An apt imaginative rein-forcement, this, of Bloom's own position, starved of Molly, miserably locked out from her fun with Boylan.) He broods on

232 the relationship between music and joy; on the contrast between Molly's voice and Mrs M'Coy's; then on the sexual quality of a woman's voice, which seems to open a vacancy yearning to be filled.

Boylan's cab comes to a stop and he steps out.

Bloom puns mentally on chamber music, thus bringing together the music imagery and that of flowing water in a way which anticipates the later picture of Molly enthroned on her chamber pot (p. 633/914–5).

Boylan knocks on Molly's door and the cockcrow theme

365 recurs. The blind stripling taps on the pavement.

Fr Cowley suggests that Ben sing '*Qui sdegno*' (from *The Magic Flute*). Tom Kernan asks for '*The Croppy Boy*': Simon supports him. Bloom is still trying to catch Pat's attention so that he can pay his bill and go. Bob Cowley starts the piano introduction to '*The Croppy Boy*' in the key of F sharp major. The ballad tells a story of betrayal. The croppy boy has lost his father at the Siege of Ross and his brothers at Gorey. The 'last of his name

366 and race', he seeks a priest in order to make a final confession before himself going to join the rebels at Wexford. He is tricked

into confessing to a redcoat in priestly disguise, and executed on the strength of his own statements.

Bloom tells Richie he must go. He pays his bill and tips Pat. The rich chords introducing 'The Croppy Boy' cause him to linger. As the story of the ballad unfolds, Bloom thinks of Ben Dollard's ruined carer: Dollard's ships' chandler's business failed to the tune of £10,000. Now he inhabits a cubicle in the Iveagh home – first wrecked by drink, then cared for by the brewer. His brain is a bit addled now and he nourishes hopes of a win in one of *Answers'* competitions; but he still has a good voice. 'No eunuch yet . . .' 233

All listen, touched by the pathos of the ballad – Miss Kennedy and the customer with the tankard, Lidwell and Miss Douce, Tom Kernan, Simon Dedalus. The boy's confession is recounted. One item in it, a miniature betrayal – the boy's failure on one occasion to pray for his mother's departed soul – reflects Stephen's archetypal act of disobedience at his mother's deathbed. The correspondence is to be pressed home later (pp. 484–5/ 691–2). Bloom watches Lydia Douce and knows that, though looking away, she is conscious of his gaze. He catches sight of her in the mirror too; then remembers that last moment of titivation in the mirror before Molly opens the door to a visitor. It is an apt recollection. At that moment the cockcrow announces Boylan's phallic, strutting approach to Molly. It announces too the betrayal of Bloom and the betrayal of the croppy boy – as the cockcrow announced St Peter's betrayal of Christ. 367 (272)

Bloom, wondering how women respond to music, remembers a night in the box at the opera when Molly wore a low-cut dress that attracted the men's opera glasses, and he held her 'hypnotized, listening' by his talk of Spinoza. (The comic irony of this emerges in Molly's monologue, pp. 632–3/914, where she remembers the same evening. She was not hypnotized by Leopold's talk. Sitting in a swamp, she was intent on the fact that her menstrual period had just started. Bloom has already dwelt on this evening before, p. 223/349.) 234

The ballad moves to its close, reminding Bloom that he, too, is 'the last of his name and race', sonless. About to go, he looks again at Lydia, reflecting on the dangers of falling for sirens such as her, who might land a man in court with a breach of promise action, having his love letters read out in evidence. Bloom's capacity to detach himself from his own 368 sentimentality in the relationship with Martha emerges here. It keeps his feet on the ground. His pseudonym, Henry, is a protection.

Still the tapping of the blind stripling's stick approaches.

Lydia poses as enraptured by the music. Bloom appreciates her apparent freshness and virginity. The body of a woman becomes for him a three-holed woodwind instrument, and she is only too ready to be played. There lies the secret of the success 369　of an assured philanderer like Boylan. Bloom dwells on the tacit understanding so quickly and naturally reached between the philanderer and the flirt. 'Will? You? I. Want. You. To.'

The climax of the ballad approaches. The yeoman captain throws off his priest's disguise, vents his fury on the boy, and dooms him. Images of tears, dying, suffering, Mrs Purefoy, converge with the present reality of Lydia's eyes, bosom, rose, 235　and hair. Lydia's gaze melts into a smile of tenderness; yet it (274)　is given, not to Bloom but to Lidwell. Her fingers move to and fro, in sexual gentleness, over the beerpull.

The cock of betrayal crows again as the innocent, fatherless 370　son of the song is condemned and the usurper takes over Bloom's house.

The tapping of the blind stripling recurs.

The pathetic climax of the ballad is reached. The boy is executed at Geneva Barracks and buried at Passage. The last verse urges the hearers to breathe a prayer, drop a tear, for the croppy boy.

Bloom gets up; remembers the soap, the forgotten lotion, the card inside his hat; purposely leaves his *Freeman*. He passes out of the dining-room doorway, through the bar, past the barmaids. Then he moves into the Ormond hallway where, behind him, he hears the shouts of applause greeting the end of the song. He is not sorry to have missed it.

371　Tom Kernan, Fr Cowley, Lidwell, Simon Dedalus, all gather 236　round Ben Dollard in praise of his performance. Richie Goulding meanwhile sits in neglected solitude. Mina Kennedy and the man with the tankard murmur together intimately.

372　Outside Bloom feels the gassy effect of the cider. Our Leopold, Henrietta's Lionel (of Flotow's *Martha*), Martha's Henry, Molly's Poldy, walks up the quay, thinking how Fr Cowley inebriates himself with music in the intensity of his piano-playing. Playing 237　music is a mode of self-expression. Bloom recalls Old Glynn

on his organ in his cock-loft with the most violent contrasts of
sound at his disposal.

Back in the Ormond Simon Dedalus and Lidwell are
discussing the departed Bloom and his wife, while Lydia talks   *373*
of the piano-tuner, and his tapping stick draws nearer. Simon
Dedalus stares at a last sardine on bread under the sandwich-
bell. It symbolizes the loneliness of Bloom. The tapping recurs.

Bloom, longing to rid himself of accumulating gas, ponders
the vocation and lot of the tympani player, and poms on the
drum begin to punctuate his thoughts, which run on instru-
ments, Molly in shift, hunter with horn, barmaid with chiming   *374*
garter, shepherd with pipe, policeman with whistle; then on the
nightwatchman's cry 'Four o'clock's all's well', which leads to   238
'All is lost now', a phrase marking Boylan's encounter with
Molly (and see p. 224/*351*).

So, brooding and breaking wind, he meets the whore of the
lane, the last and least tempting siren in the episode, with whom   *(278)*
he has previously had an encounter, the less satisfying in that
she revealed a dangerous knowledge of Molly at a crucial
moment. To avoid meeting her face to face, Bloom stares in   *375*
Lionel Marks's antique shop window.

The friends at the bar, Lidwell, Simon, Cowley, Kernan, and
Dollard, the perfect fifth, drink to one another. The blind
stripling arrives at last. Meanwhile Bloom stares in the antique
shop window at a picture of Robert Emmet, the martyred patriot
(see p. 197/*308–9*). When the whore has gone by and there is
a passing tramcar to drown the noise, he breaks wind climac-
tically – and simultaneously reads from the portrait Emmet's
heroic last words. '*When my country takes her place among the
nations of the earth, then and not till then let my epitaph be written.*   239
I have done.' Rhetoric and 'gas' are blended once more (cf. p.   *376*
104/*160*).

Chapter 12

The Cyclops

The Homeric parallel is Ulysses's encounter with the gigantic one-eyed Cyclops, Polyphemus. Ulysses escapes from Polyphemus's cave by blinding him. The Cyclops hurls a rock at him as he sails away, but misses him. The citizen in this episode has Polyphemus's one-eyed crudity. He can see no point of view other than his own. He is arrogant, cruel, and stupid. Polyphemus's gigantic stature is reflected in the citizen's grossly inflated ego and his equally exaggerated claims. The episode is soaked in another form of gigantism too. For though the events are recounted by a nameless narrator, the narration is punctuated by a series of commentaries in vastly different styles – but each style an inflated caricature of the legal, the epic, the scientific, the journalistic, and so on. The total effect is to set the gentle, pacific, charitable Bloom in lonely opposition to a barbaric, bigoted, and aggressive nationalist – and likewise to place Bloom's mildness and commonsense in lonely isolation within a world given over to vast excesses. The intemperate inflations represent many aspects of culture, many movements in our civilization, that are irrational, violent, or pretentious. The fact that the reader, as well as Ulysses–Bloom, feels swamped under it all is appropriate and of course intentional.

We must remember throughout that the Cyclops is a one-eyed creature. The citizen, who approximates to Polyphemus, has a one-eyed view, a fanatical, unreasoning nationalistic passion that makes him incapable of seeing any other side to a question. Bloom is always able to see two sides to a question. He is two-eyed throughout. We have reason to believe that the one-eyed–two-eyed dichotomy was very important to Joyce. Each of the interpolations in this episode has a one-eyed quality:

it represents a single style, a single fashion of utterance pushed to its extremist limits: each is a gigantic inflation of a one-eyed approach. Joyce's peculiar quality as an artist is that he rejected all one-eyed outlooks. In *Portrait of the Artist* he refuses to take (280) his hero at his own valuation. While one eye sees with Stephen in deep sympathy, the other eye judges Stephen's egoism and vanity. This two-eyed view is persistent in Joyce. He will never totally surrender himself or his reader to a single mood or style: the tragic and the comic moods exist side by side; poetic and 'vulgar' styles are intertwined. The one-eyed–two-eyed dichotomy may yet have a good deal to tell us about *Ulysses*. One notes that it is one-eyed Nelson who presides over Dublin as the symbol of the British imperium.

The narrator is talking with Troy of the Dublin Metropolitan Police at the corner of Arbour Hill, when a passing chimney-sweep almost catches him in the eye with his gear. This little miniature of the blinding of Polyphemus by the stake which Ulysses drives into his eye is the first in a series of light-hearted correspondences that echo the more serious Homeric parallelism. Turning to curse the sweep, the narrator sees Joe Hynes and explains that he is now working as a collector of bad and doubtful debts. He has just tried to get a payment from a plumber, Gerachty. Gerachty stole tea and sugar from Herzog's, 377 was charged and ordered to pay three shillings a week. Now Gerachty has rebuffed the narrator, saying that if Herzog pursues him for the money he will summon Herzog for trading without a licence. This story is presented to us partly in the lively dialogue of the narrator, partly through an interpolation 241 in exaggerated legalese. Gerachty, caught by Herzog and the law, yet about to wriggle out by cunning, is of course in the situation of Ulysses in Polyphemus's cave. 378

The narrator and Joe Hynes decide to go to Barney Kiernan's for a drink. Joe Hynes has been at a meeting of cattle traders about the foot-and-mouth disease, held at the City Arms, and he wants to report to the nameless citizen about it.

In another interpolation, whose style parodies Celtic saga, 379 Dublin's market is pictured in immense hyperbole, drawing 242 produce from the whole country.

The narrator and Joe Hynes turn into Barney Kiernan's and 380 find the citizen there, sitting thoughtfully in a corner, with 243 his terrifying dog, Garryowen. Drinks are ordered. Then an 381

382   interpolation in mock-epic style of farcical extravagance builds
383   up a picture of the citizen, gigantic in stature. His nationalistic
       fanaticism is laughed at in a riotous list of 'Irish' heroes and
244   heroines that eventually incorporates Charlemagne, Napoleon,
       and William Tell along with Buddha, Lady Godiva, and Dick
(285) Turpin. The one-eyed fanatic knows no restraint in the claims
       he makes for his cause.
384   Terry the barman brings the drinks. Joe Hynes pays, tendering
       a sovereign. The narrator is astonished, but Hynes explains that
       he is in the money because of a hint given him by 'the prudent
245   member'. A brief interpolation in mock-epic style identifies this
       member as Bloom, whom Hynes met this morning in the
       Freeman office and who reminded him that the cashier was avail-
       able if he wished to draw from him (p. 99/*151*). The narrator
       has already himself seen Bloom by Pill Lane, staring at the fish
       'with his cod's eye'. (Bloom's cod's eye is God's eye. He has
       the charitable two-eyed view. He seems to have 'greasy' (gracey)
       eyes too, p. 214/*334*.) In the eyes of the citizen Hynes works
       for 'the old woman of Prince's street' (*Freeman's Journal*). He is
       angered too by today's *The Irish Independent*, a paper founded
       by Parnell, because its list of births, marriages, and deaths
385   contains so many English names and addresses, which he reads
       out contemptuously. Joe, in a more relaxed mood, hands round
       the drinks and they partake.
          First in mock-epic, then in homely Dublin idiom, we have
       the entry of Alf Bergan. He sneaks in, laughing, to point out
       the tragi-comic couple passing by outside – Denis Breen,
       carrying his law-books with his wife at his heels, still insanely
386   intent on bringing a libel action against the person who sent
       him the anonymous postcard with its cryptic message, 'U.p.'
246   Alf Bergan tells how Breen is being pushed around from one
       office to another in pursuit of legal vengeance. (Like the obscen-
       ities at the expense of English people named in today's *The Irish
       Independent*, the mockery of unbalanced, innocent Breen is both
       narrow-minded and uncharitable, in key with all that fair-
       minded Bloom is up against in this episode.)
          Bob Doran, who has been sitting up in a corner drunk, puts
       in a few words for the first time. He is incapable of intelligent
       conversation. (We have already heard that he is on his annual
       drinking spree, p. 137/*212*.) Terry hands Alf a drink – ale brewed
       by Guinness brothers, here mock-epically transformed into

Bungiveagh and Bungardilaun (Lords Iveagh and Ardilaun).
Alf, in his own mock-epic transfiguration, meets hospitality with   387
hospitality, presenting to Terry a romantically transfigured
Queen Victoria jubilee mug.

Joe Hynes's question about the coming hanging of a prisoner
in Mountjoy jail causes Alf to produce a bundle of hangman's   (288)
letters from his pocket. Joe takes them up. Meantime Bob   247
Doran's repeated drunken question, 'Who are you laughing
at?' with its surly air of spoiling for a fight, is one of the
little touches that add to the intermittent sense of impending
violence characteristic of this episode. As Joe looks at the letters,   388
the narrator talks to Alf. Alf's astonishing remarks, that he has
just seen Willy Murray in Capel Street with Paddy Dignam,
causes consternation. Joe assures Alf that Dignam is dead.
Question and counter-question, confusion and astonishment, all
punctuated by Doran's dim, drunken interjections, establish
the unsettling flavour of the den into which Bloom is shortly
to enter. The place begins to assume a slightly sinister air.

The interpolation which follows, in the burlesqued idiom of   389
pseudo-scientific spiritualist literature, is hilarious rather than
sinister: it hinges on Alf's mistaken idea that he has just seen
the deceased Dignam, and expands the notion of contact with
the dead. After this 'spiritualist voice' has spoken of a message   248
from the deceased, a 'business voice' records that the matter   390
will be 'attended to', and then the 'epic voice' is heard again,
lamenting the lost O'Dignam, 'Patrick of the beamy brow'. Thus
in three distinct idioms three of Joyce's one-eyed Cyclopean
personae make themselves felt.

As the citizen remarks on the fact that Bloom is passing to
and fro before the bar outside, Alf tries to get over the shock
of hearing of Dignam's death so soon after 'seeing' him, and
Bob Doran blasphemes from his corner against Christ for taking   391
away 'poor little Willy Dignam'. Terry warns him against such
talk and he begins to blubber sentimentally about the deceased.
The narrator can't take it seriously. He thinks Bob Doran should   249
go home to his wife, and recalls the story of their marriage, a
story fully recounted in *Dubliners*: 'The Boarding House'.

Bloom comes in and asks Terry if Martin Cunningham is here.
Joe Hynes reads aloud one of the hangman's letters, an appli-   392
cation for employment from H. Rumbold, a Liverpool barber.
Rumbold, whose application is addressed to the Dublin High

Sheriff, cites his previous experience as hangman. Joe then greets
250 Bloom and, under pressure, Bloom accepts a cigar from him.
393 Alf gives details of how hangings are carried out and Bloom
launches into what the narrator scornfully calls his 'codology'
in criticism of capital punishment. Alf tries to keep the talk on
a lower level, saying how the penis of a hanged man becomes
(292) erect at death. Bloom, with his scientific interests, is prepared
to explain this phenomenon technically in spite of the crude
394 and mentally alien company around him. An interpolation
transfigures Bloom into a German professor explaining the
phenomenon with a mouthful of medical technicalities.

The citizen and Joe Hynes launch into excited nationalistic
chatter about the revolutionaries and their martyrs. The dog
251 wanders over to Bob Doran, who tries to get his paw, drivels
395 about treating dogs kindly, and is only prevented from falling
on top of the brute by Alf. Then Bob Doran asks Terry to bring
him a Jacob's biscuit tin, and he scrapes a few bits of old biscuit
out of it for the dog. (That the biscuit tin is *Jacob's* emphasizes
its part in the gathering symbolism of this episode, later to
become more explicit.)

Meantime Bloom and the citizen argue the politics of Irish
revolution. The narrator is scornful of Bloom's superiority of
speech and understanding. He recalls how Bloom tried to ingratiate himself with an old woman (Mrs Riordan, Dante of the
Portrait, see pp. 143/221–2 and 258/408) who had some money
to leave, and how he tried to put her young nephew off drink
by taking him on a round of pubs calculated to make him so
drunk as to be sickened off for life. The old woman, and Molly,
and Mrs O'Dowd (keeper of the City Arms where the Blooms
were staying at the time) were all angry about this. And small
396 wonder, for the plot failed of its object. The young man was
soon being carried home drunk five times a week.

The citizen drinks to the memory of the martyred revolutionaries with a note of hostility in his voice which seems to
bode no good to Bloom.

252 At this point Joyce interposes an account of a revolutionary's
execution in a style which is richly packed with the clichés of
contemporary journalism and cheap literature. It is one of the
397 funniest pieces of sustained writing in *Ulysses*. Like the other
burlesque interpolations, it gathers absurdity as it proceeds. It
cuts deeply into contemporary pretentiousness and hypocrisy,

especially at the official and ceremonial level; also into the false sentimentality and sensationalism of current journalism. Its linguistic effect is surely to render unusable dozens of hackneyed phrases and worn artifices. *398* *253*

Rumbold, the illiterate barber–hangman from Liverpool (p. 249/392), is metamorphosed into a 'world renowned headsman' and public idol who steps on to the scaffold in 'faultless morning dress' to the acclamation of the spectators. Fantastic inflations of this kind swamp the tense seriousness of revolutionary passion and of the official 'establishment' which suppresses it, under a flood of humour which is neither cynical nor destructive but kind, even indulgent. The social effect of such passages, if heeded, ought surely to be to render untenable many one-eyed political postures which tear society with fruitless dissensions. Joyce makes much of the protest literature of our age look shallow and redundant, the output of one-eyed writers no more humane than the paraphernalia of the one-eyed governments they assail. Rebel and conservative alike are here cut down to size. The machinery of state officialdom and the effervescence of mass-taste which together express the futility of our century are here held before a mature and humane comic gaze. *399* *(295)* *400* *254* *401* *255*

The citizen, Bloom, and Joe continue talking politics. Bloom speaks approvingly of the anti-treating league as a means of tackling the drink problem. The narrator scoffs at this, both because he thinks Bloom is only too ready to avoid buying drinks for others and because he once attended a musical evening given by the anti-treating league where the temperance speeches and the lemonade put him off. *402*

The old dog has now finished with the biscuit tin, and begins to mouse around threateningly. The citizen calls him and talks to him while he growls ominously. The narrators thinks he ought to be compulsorily muzzled. *403* *256*

There follows another interpolation, journalistic (magazinish) in tone. 'Years of training by kindness' have metamorphosed the brute Garryowen into an almost human exhibition dog (Owen Garry now) who performs in public – reciting verse of his own composition which bears 'a *striking* resemblance to the ranns of ancient Celtic bards'. A specimen of his lyrical utterance is sub-joined, rendered into English. (NB Cynanthropy – 'a species of madness in which a man imagines himself to be a dog'.) *404*

405
257   Terry brings more water for the dog. Joe orders more drinks all round. The narrator thinks the citizen does well for himself in free drinks by means of the moral blackmail of his nationalistic zeal and his frightening dog. Bloom alone refuses a drink, explaining that he is here only to meet Martin Cunningham over insurance difficulty in connexion with the Dignam estate. A Freudian trap-door opens when Bloom speaks of 'the wife's admirers' in mistake for 'the wife's advisers'. At this moment, when Bloom is in such unsympathetic company, the slip of the
(300)   tongue pathetically underlines his loneliness.

The narrator, who hates Bloom's superior intelligence and vocabulary, scoffs at his technical explanation of the insur-
406   ance position, recalling an occasion when Bloom himself nearly got into legal difficulties through selling tickets for a Hungarian lottery. Bob Doran lurches over to Bloom, offering maudlin drunken condolences to be conveyed to Mrs Dignam and shaking his head emotionally. An interpolation metamorphoses this incident into an inflated exchange of formal courtesies in an elaborately artificial diction which pushes the
258   proprieties of Victorian dignity and politeness to a high point of absurdity.

Bob Doran staggers out. The citizen recalls an incident when
407   Doran, blind drunk, had his pockets picked by two prostitutes, contrasts Doran's anti-Catholic outbursts when he is drunk with his former youthful piety and his present attendance at church on Sundays. (For more of Mrs Mooney and Jacky Mooney, see 'The Boarding House': *Dubliners*.)

Terry brings the drinks. There is talk of Nannetti (Nannan) who is running for the mayoralty and whom Bloom met this morning in the *Freeman* offices (p. 99/192). Joe Hynes has
408   just seen Nannetti with William Field, MP, at the meeting of the cattle traders, and the talk turns to the foot-and-mouth disease question again. Once more Bloom can speak knowledgeably because he worked for a time as an overseer in a knacker's yard. (In 1893–4 Bloom, then resident at the City Arms Hotel, was for a time a clerk in the Cattle Market, employed by Joseph Cuffe. See pp. 326/521–2; 334/535; and 556/795.) He lost the job, the narrator claims, for being a 'Mister Knowall' and 'giving lip to a grazier'. (Cf. Molly Bloom's account of the affair in her monologue, p. 619/891.)
259   Other recollections of the Bloom family life in the City Arms

days* help to build up the narrator's scornful picture of Bloom as an interfering busybody wanting to give the doubtful benefit of his help or his wisdom to everyone. 'Old cod's eye' (God's eye) hints at a divine parallel. Bloom's gentleness comes under the narrator's judgement. 'Gob, he'd have a soft hand under a hen.' Immediately an interpolation presses home the point, concretizing the image in an infants' reading-book account of Uncle Leo taking a fresh egg from Black Liz, our hen.   (302)

Joe Hynes announces that Field and Nannetti are going over tonight to London to raise the treatment of cattle issue in the House of Commons. Bloom, who has yet to finish his business with Keyes and Nannetti over the advertisement, is unwilling to believe that Nannetti is going on this errand, but Joe Hynes   *409* insists that Nannetti is indeed going too – with a commission from the Gaelic league to ask a question about a recent ban on Irish games in Phoenix Park.

An interpolation, mock-Hansard in style, records a burlesque exchange in the House of Commons at question time.

Joe Hynes praises the citizen as the man who 'made the   *410* Gaelic sports revival', and this identifies him as Michael   260 Cusack, founder of the Gaelic Athletic Association, who sometimes called himself 'Citizen Cusack'. There is talk of various athletic activities and Bloom's contribution, much to the narrator's annoyance, deals with the damage that over-strenuous exercise may do to health. Thus Bloom again inserts a voice of temperance and gentleness into a colloquy concerned with force and violence. An interpolation expands this exchange to the dimensions of a public meeting, at which Mr Joseph M'Carthy Hynes pleads eloquently for 'resuscitation of the   *411* ancient Gaelic sports' and is opposed by L. Bloom. Bloom's case has a 'mixed reception' and the chairman concludes proceedings by singing '*A nation once again*' by Thomas Osborne Davis.

The subject of violence is pursued farther. The Keogh–Bennett   261 fight is talked of, and the story that Blazes Boylan, its promoter   *412* and the 'traitor's son' (cf. p. 262/*414*), made £100 out of it. He is said to have swayed the betting by spreading a rumour that Myler Keogh was drinking beer, when in fact he was in strict

---

* The doings of the Blooms when resident at the City Arms are referred to obliquely many times. Something like a complete picture can be built up by reference to pp. 81/*122*; 143/*221–2*; 251/*395*; 277/*439*; 326/*521–2*; and 556/*795–6*.

training. Here Bloom's quiet, rational attempt to press the claims of the gentle game of lawn tennis as fully valid for training the eye and the body is submerged under the crude chatter of the others. In a few brutal phrases Alf Bergan tells how Myler Keogh
(305) knocked out Percy Bennett.

413   A journalistic interpolation, parodying the style of the sports columnist, expands this account in vivid detail. Myler Keogh, the Irishman, 'Dublin's pet lamb', whose blood is 'lively claret', lacks the weight and power of Percy Bennett, the English artilleryman, but he beats him by sheer agility and skill. It is notable that the English soldier fights with his right eye nearly
262 closed. Two eyes can run rings round one eye any day, even though the one-eyed have the superior violence and thrust, and anyway Ireland's representative is a 'lamb' whose blood is wine. (We have heard of the fight from Nosey Flynn, p. 142/220, and young Dignam, p. 206/322–3.)

414   Alf mentions Boylan's coming concert tour. Bloom agrees that his wife is to sing on it and is at pains to speak naturally of it, praising Boylan's ability to organize. The narrator sees through the cover-up to Boylan's design. (We learn that Boylan's father, Dan Boylan, sold horses to the British during the Boer War. For Molly on this, see p. 617/886.)

       An interpolation in the poetic idiom of a prose saga praises the beauty and purity of Molly Bloom, 'pride of Calpe's (Gibraltar's) rocky mount'. The entry of J. J. O'Molloy and Ned
415 Lambert is announced in the same style. More drinks.

263   The narrator speaks with his customary scorn of J. J. O'Molloy and Ned Lambert, ridiculing J. J.'s attempts to conceal his failure and poverty. (For O'Molloy's story, see p. 103/159.) He hobnobs with the toffs, then pawns his watch under a false name, 'Dunne'.

       The talk turns to Breen. Everyone laughs at the poor man's
416 insane obsession and the effect of the unknown joker's post-card – everyone, that is, except gentle Bloom, who sees the suffering of Mrs Breen. In the eyes of the others she deserves all she gets for having married a 'half and half', a 'pishogue'. The narrator recalls how proud Mrs Breen was to have married
264 a man whose father's cousin was 'pew opener to the pope'
417 (Signor Brini). As the drinkers have their fun, the poor lunatic Breen passes the door again outside, his wife at his side, and Corny Kelleher with them, playing up to Breen's lunacy.

Talk turns to the Canada case (in which a swindler collected payments through a press advertisement for imaginary passages to Canada) and to the Recorder who tried it and whose reputation is for generous and compassionate judgements. ('You can cod him up to the two eyes' – *sic* – and he has a 'heart as big as a lion' – as another *Leo* indeed.) All except Bloom scoff at the recorder's human sympathy, Alf and Ned mockingly reproducing a court dialogue between Sir Frederick Falkiner and 'poor little Gumley' who is 'minding stones for the corporation, there near Butt Bridge'. Reuben J. Dodd has sued Gumley, but the recorder dismisses the case when he hears Gumley's tale of woe. It is the moneylender who gets the rough side of the recorder's tongue. (We heard of Gumley in connexion with the 'Invincibles' on p. 112/172. We hear more of him on pp. 503/708; 505/712; and 522/739) An interpolation in archaic epic diction presents a heroic picture of the recorder, now metamorphosed into Sir Frederick the Falconer, coming to administer justice amid the princes of the 'twelve tribes of Iar'.

The citizen tries to provoke Bloom by insulting him, but Bloom ignores him. Quietly he comes to an understanding with Joe Hynes: he will forget the three shillings Hynes owes him (see p. 99/152) 'till the first' of the month: in return Hynes will fix up the renewal of the Keyes advertisement with Myles Crawford. Meanwhile the citizen persists in his rude attack on the strangers admitted to Ireland. Like Mr Deasy (p. 29/43) he blames the adulterous Devorgilla and her paramour for bringing 'the Saxon robbers' here. (The 'dishonoured wife' is the 'cause of all our misfortunes' – Parnell's, Ireland's, Bloom's.) Bloom is silent. Alf brings the adulterous to light, displaying a 'smutty yankee picture' relating to a Chicago misconduct case reported in the *Police Gazette*.

At this point John Wyse Nolan and Lenehan come in. Nolan brings news of the City Council Meeting about the Irish language. The citizen's fury against England and the English mounts. J. J. O'Molloy and Bloom try to mollify him, speaking coolly and rationally of English civilization. The citizen resorts to venomous curses on the English as a nation with 'no music and no art and no literature', with no part in European culture. Lenehan, backing him up, drinks against 'Perfide Albion' and a mock epic interpolation puts this act into its proper barbaric setting.

418

(309)

265

419

266

420

421

267

422

Lenehan brings news that *Throwaway* has won the Ascot
Gold Cup. Those, like himself, Boylan, and his 'lady friend'
(Molly) who backed *Sceptre* are 'all in a cart'. As for *Throwaway's*
victory, it 'takes the biscuit'. All this contributes to a significant cluster of symbolic overtones. The Gold Cup itself is
the vessel of refreshment, the woman, the womb, the chalice.
Bloom's associations with *Throwaway* are manifold. He threw
away thoughtlessly both the 'Elijah is coming' throwaway
and the racing tip. Both have gone sailing down the river of
Dublin's life today; prophecies to be fulfilled. And Bloom
himself, a 'rank outsider' rebuffed by the Dubliners, is a
throwaway from Dublin society. Moreover, sexually discarded
by his wife, he is a domestic throwaway. The Dubliners do not
appreciate the prophetic voice, the Jesus and Elijah present
in Bloom's tolerance and charity. But he wins in the end – with
(312)   Molly even – while Boylan, flourishing his Sceptre (plainly
a phallic symbol here: Molly Bloom's monologue later leaves
us in no doubt of that), is left in the cart. 'Frailty, thy name
is *Sceptre*', Lenehan says and we know how true that is.
Throwaway Bloom 'takes the biscuit'. Bloom has the *Jacob's*
tin thrown at him later in this episode. Lenehan here finds
the tin empty.

Meanwhile J. J. O'Molloy and the citizen argue, Bloom occa-
sionally inserting a word or two on a tolerant, liberal note.
'Some people can see the mote in others' eyes, but they can't
see the beam in their own.' This is not only Jesus–Bloom
423   speaking; it is also Ulysses–Bloom who sticks the stake in the
Cyclops's eye. From the beginning of the episode, when the
sweep nearly stuck his gear in the narrator's eye (p. 240/376),
the pages have contained numerous echoes of this act, many
of them phallic, and several of those carrying overtones of
gigantism. (See references to the Jew's penis sharpened by circumcision, p. 240/377; to the erection that occurs at execution,
p. 250/393; to the enlarged penis in the American magazine,
p. 266/420; to 'syphilization', p. 266/421; to the telescope in
Nelson's blind eye, p. 266/421; and to Mr Verschoyle's ear-
trumpet and Mrs Verschoyle's 'turnedin eye', p. 273/433.) The
268   citizen launches into a diatribe against England for depopu-
lating Ireland, destroying her ancient arts and industries, and
reducing her land to a treeless swamp. John Wyse Nolan and
424   he agree on the need for reforestation.

An interpolation in the style of a gossip article in a smart journal transfigures Nolan into the 'chevalier Jean Wyse de Neaulan, grand high chief ranger of the Irish National Foresters' who has just married 'Miss Fir Conifer of Pine Valley'. The parody of a fashionable wedding write-up, in which the forest theme repeats itself in the names of the guests and the descriptions of the dresses, finally establishes the bride and bridegroom *269* on a quiet honeymoon where they can settle down to the task *425* of reforesting their country. The marital picture of a land covered with upstanding tree trunks, flourishing and fruitful, carries an implicit contrast to the theme of dead wooden stakes sharpened destructively and of male organs erect in death, enlarged by disease, or mutilated by circumcision.

The citizen speaks rhetorically of the day when an independent Ireland will again meet on equal terms with European powers, her harbours thick with 'masts'. The cynical, scoffing *(314)* narrator notes that the citizen's high-flown rhetoric is 'all wind and piss'. He grabbed the holding of an evicted tenant in *426* Shanagolden and the peasants hate him for it.

There are more drinks. And there is more violence in the air as Alf Bergan looks at a picture in the paper of a butting match and another of a Negro lynching. The headline *'Black Beast Burned in Omaha, Ga.'* reminds us that Bloom is a 'dark horse'; he is in mourning; he is the 'black panther' of Haines's nightmare (p. 4/3) and of Stephen's delirium (p. 496/701). Remember, too, Stephen's theory that Shakespeare's 'unremitting intellect is the hornmad Iago ceaselessly willing that the moor in him shall suffer' (p. 174/273) which establishes the symbolism of the Negro as simple, unsophisticated, trusting humanity exploited and destroyed by the white man's intellectualism. Bloom is Sambo–Othello. And the narrator here thinks they ought to have crucified the Negro too, as the citizen later would like to crucify Bloom. Thus the Crucifixion theme, recurring throughout this episode, plainly draws all who suffer persecution into the common relationship with Christ. And note that the 'crucifixion' – coming so soon after the picture of a living wood – is the work of 'Deadwood Dicks'. The image of wood merges with the phallic theme in this act of brutality. Then the talk turns to English brutality in a vivid, scathing description *270* of naval flogging. Pretentious English claims to freedom and *427* liberalism are mocked as hypocrisies covering brutalities in an

empire 'on which the sun (Son?) never rises'. The citizen's astonishment that the English actually *believe* their own hypocritical
claims is taken up in a venomous interpolation which parodies
the Apostles' Creed as translated in the English Book of
Common Prayer, turning it into an act of faith in brutality,
assumed to be more in keeping with the English character than
the real creed.

428
271
The citizen continues his tirade against the English, recalling
the poverty, starvation, and depopulation that followed the
potato famine of 1846. John Wyse Nolan tells how the Irish have
spilt blood for other nations, England, France, Spain, only to be
betrayed. The citizen scoffs at the French, Joe Hynes at the
429
Germans, and especially the German–English monarchs. Queen
Victoria is represented as an old drunkard, Edward VII as a
diseased lecher.

430
(317)
272
431
More drinks: and amid the mounting intemperance of liquid
intake and verbal output Bloom puts in his quiet protest against
the futility of persecution and national hatred. The others niggle
Bloom the Jew, asking him what a nation is, then laughing at
his definition – 'the same people living in the same place'. When
Bloom claims Irish nationality, the citizen spits; then dries
himself with his handkerchief. An interpolation humorously
transforms the citizen's handkerchief into an 'intricately embroi-
dered Irish face-cloth', a treasured relic on whose corner-pieces
are symbols of the four evangelists, and on whose 'emunctory
field' are famous Irish buildings and beauty spots – everything
from the lakes of Killarney to the Guinness's brewery.

273
432
Bloom, almost burning his fingers with the butt of his cigar
(like Ulysses with his sharpened, red-hot stake), refers to his
own hated and persecuted race. John Wyse says the Jews
should resist force with force, and the narrator mocks Bloom
as a 'lardy-face' incapable of standing up to a gun. Bloom
himself points the futility of 'force, hatred, history, all that'.
He preaches love, 'the opposite of hatred'. Then off he goes to
look for Cunningham, leaving behind the mockery of himself
as 'a new apostle to the gentiles'. Bloom, linked thus ironically
with St Paul, has a second name, 'Paula' (p. 594/852; and see
commentary on p. 497/702).

433
An interpolation, in the idiom of comic scribbles on a wall,
lists a series of love relationships which sum up current usages
of the verb *love* on the sexual and sentimental levels. 'Gerty

MacDowell' takes us forward to the next episode: 'Mrs Norman W. Tupper' takes us back to the pages of the *Police Gazette* (p. 266/420).

The citizen inveighs against England's use of sanctimony as a cover-up for self-enrichment. Cromwell's Irish campaign is cited; then a skit in today's *United Irishman* on the supposed   274
visit of a Zulu chief to Manchester. The convenient British proce-   434
dure of spreading the word of God and British trade at the same time is the target. The image of the exploited Negro is further strengthened.

J. J. pushes the theme farther, mentioning the Casement report   435
on Belgian atrocities in the Congo rubber-fields. Into this talk of raping and flogging Lenehan inserts the crucial information which finally turns the fury of the drunk and violent Cyclops against Bloom – and this information is, of course, false. Lenehan imagines that Bloom must now have gone off to collect his winnings on the Gold Cup. Bantam Lyons's mistake, that Bloom gave him *Throwaway* as a tip (p. 70/106), has travelled a long way. Bloom is now a 'white-eyed kaffir', 'a bloody dark horse'.   (321)
It is imagined (and *believed*: the unfortunate yahoos believe it!) that Bloom must have won £5 on *Throwaway*. The narrator retires   275
to the lavatory where, relieving himself, he dwells on Bloom's imaginary winnings, recollects Pisser Burke's stories of Molly Bloom at the City Arms (see p. 258/408, etc.), and mentally ridicules Bloom's claim to Irish nationality. The urinal is indeed   436
the right place for these musings. The combination of heavy micturition, falsification, scorn, and ridicule reflects the coming together of physical bestiality and violence and unreason in the Cyclopean threat to Bloom.

Back in the bar John Wyse is arguing that Bloom gave the idea to Griffith* for certain attacks in the *Freeman* on British corruption. The narrator hates to think of 'old sloppy eyes' (two of them) thus 'mucking up the show'. He claims that Bloom's father swamped the country with baubles and penny diamonds before poisoning himself with prussic acid. (Leopold himself hawked the trinkets from door to door. See pp. 337/540 and 545/778.)

---

* For study of the difficulties and apparent inconsistencies in the connexion between Bloom and Griffith, see Robert M. Adams: *Surface and Symbol*, pp. 100–4.

Three more men arrive, Martin Cunningham, Jack Power, and
an Orangeman, whose name the narrator forgets (he is Crofton
437   of 'Ivy Day', *Dubliners*). An interpolation presents this arrival,
276   suitably enlivened, in the pseudo-archaic lingo and trappings
of comic-strip medievalism. Questioned, Martin Cunningham
438   confirms that Bloom has tried to help Sinn Fein. 'It was he
drew up all the plans according to the Hungarian system.'
Cunningham also explains how Bloom's father changed his
name from 'Virag' by deed poll.

277   The citizen says, 'That's the new Messiah for Ireland!' and
once more his irony misfires, but the Bloom–Messiah correspondence sticks. 'They're still waiting for their redeemer,' says
439   Martin. The light-hearted talk of Jewish fathers-to-be hoping for
a messiah–son reminds us that Leopold himself is in search of
a son, and Ned Lambert's comic account of how nervously and
fussily Bloom waited for the arrival of little Rudy, eleven years
ago, reinforces the image of the searching, unquiet father. The
narrator scorns Bloom as 'one of those mixed middlings' (half
man, half woman, that is) 'lying up in the hotel ... once a
(323)   month with a headache like a totty with her courses'. The feminine streak in Bloom is to be richly exploited later in the *Circe*
episode.

The citizen continues to abuse the absent Bloom. Martin
Cunningham appeals for charity. Drinks are called for again.
440   Martin raps for his glass, 'God bless all here is my prayer', and
the drinkers say Amen.

This moment of religiosity is expanded, in an interpolation,
278   into a massive religious ceremony. A vast procession of reli-
441   gious and saints with all the paraphernalia of Catholic ritual
(and a good deal besides) converges on Barney Kiernan's where
442   the Reverend Fr O'Flynn (Malachi and Patrick attending him)
pronounces a formal liturgical blessing upon all. Among the
saints in this remarkable gathering one should note St Martin
of Todi (Martin Cunningham), St Alfred (Bergan), St Joseph
(Hynes), St Denis (Breen), St Cornelius (Kelleher), St Leopold
(Bloom), St Terence (Terry), St Edward (Ned Lambert), St Owen
Caniculus (Garryowen), St Anonymous (the narrator), and of
279   course St Marion Calpensis (Marion of Gibraltar – Molly).
443   At this point Bloom comes in again, hurriedly and apologet-
ically, saying he has just been round to the court-house. The
narrator assumes this to be a lie; is sure Bloom has been to

collect his winnings and is too mean to stand drinks. The citizen thinks the same and gibes at Bloom accordingly. 'Don't tell anyone.' Martin Cunningham and Jack Power, sensing the sharp hostility, hurry out with Bloom and Crofton, and jump on to Martin's jaunting car. Martin orders the jarvey to be off. An interpolation, with the flavour of Greek poetry translated, transforms the jaunting car into a Homeric vessel, with golden   444
poop and bellying sails, standing off amid sporting nymphs. The citizen gets up and waddles cursing to the door. Joe Hynes   280
and Alf try to stop him, but he shouts out, 'Three cheers for Israel!'

The narrator, sour about everything else, is sour about this exhibition too. People gather round the door. Martin orders the jarvey to drive off. The citizen bawls out and loafers join in. Bloom makes his brave and fully reasonable reply, 'Mendelssohn   was a jew and Karl Marx and Mercadente and Spinoza. And   445
the Saviour was a jew. . . . Your God was a jew. Christ was a jew like me.' For this the citizen determines to 'crucify him' and goes for the biscuit box.

An interpolation builds up this fracas in a farcical journalistic account of Dublin's farewell to Nagyaságos uram Lipóti Virag (Bloom). The ironical juxtaposition of the superficial 'manners'   281
of our civilization and the reality they cover is powerful and   (328)
searching.

The citizen gets the tin. Little Alf hangs on to him. The   446
narrator is determined to 'be in for the last gospel'. But the jarvey has got the nag's head round and the car moves off. The citizen flings the tin, but the sun is in his eyes and he misses.

An interpolation, in mixed styles, inflates the event as a   447
seismic disturbance with atmospheric repercussions that seem   282
to be, prophetically, in the megaton range.

The citizen sends his dog in pursuit of the escaping car, while   448
oaths reinforce the Jesus–Bloom and Moses–Bloom parallels.

A last interpolation, in the style of the English Bible, trans-figures Bloom, and jaunting car too, into Elijah and his chariot,   449
which ascend to heaven amid clouds of angels at the call of the   283
divine voice.

Chapter 13

Nausicaa

284   In the *Odyssey* Nausicaa, daughter of Alcinous, king of Phaeacia, comes to the beach, accompanied by her maids, to wash her linen. The girls play ball, laughing and shrieking, and wake up Ulysses who is lying there, worn-out, storm-tossed, naked, cast up by the waves. The girls are frightened and embarrassed, but Nausicaa takes charge, cleans Ulysses and clothes him, then leads him home.

This episode offers respite to the 'storm-tossed heart of man'; respite to Bloom after his violent departure from Barney Kiernan's; respite to the reader from the inflated and disorderly stylistic excesses of that interlude. Here Joyce adopts a sentimental, woman's magazinish style which, viewed as literary burlesque, is devastating. Yet the farcical, satirical strain does not wholly determine the temper of the passage; for the vulgar idiom of the novelette, when exploited to articulate a young, uneducated girl's thoughts and dreams, becomes peculiarly touching by virtue of its sheer aptness to her adolescent self-dramatization. Joyce's linguistic virtuosity and psychological sensitivity together present the two-eyed reader with a feast of blended satire and pathos.

(331)   Gerty MacDowell (Nausicaa), Cissy Caffrey, and Edy Boardman are sitting on the rocks on Sandymount shore, where Stephen Dedalus walked and mused this morning. They are looking after Cissy's two brothers, Tommy and Jacky,

450   twins of four years old, and little Baby Boardman. In the background is Howth Hill (for Leopold and Molly Bloom the place of youthful love realized) and, near by, the parish church dedicated to Our Lady as Star of the Sea. Gradually, in this episode, an important parallel is unmistakably established between Gerty

MacDowell and the Virgin Mary. Each of them is 'in her pure
radiance a beacon ever to the storm-tossed heart of man'.

Tommy and Jacky dabble in the sand: Cissy plays with baby,
eleven months old, trying to get him to talk. Tommy and Jacky   (332)
begin to quarrel over their sand-castle: Cissy has to reprove   285
Jacky and to comfort Tommy.   451

Gerty MacDowell, meanwhile, sits lost in thought. She is   452
beautiful, slight in build, graceful, pale in complexion. The   286
description of her, voiced in the sentimental idiom of her own
thinking and dreaming, is as much a piece of self-revelation
as of objective picturing. (The use of words and phrases
like 'graceful', 'almost spiritual in its ivory-like purity', 'veined
alabaster', 'queenly', and 'glory' reinforces the implicit correspondence with the Virgin Mary.) The reader moves in Gerty's
mind, richly aware of its absurdities, its naïvetés, and its
pathos, piquantly stirred simultaneously to laughter at her and
sympathy for her. Her eyes, beautiful and yearning, have a   453
seductive power that owes something to the advice on make-
up given in the Woman Beautiful page of the Princess novelette.
Her dark-brown hair waves naturally. Her ready blush adds
to her loveliness. It is due to Edy Boardman's playful remark
to little Tommy. 'I know who is Tommy's sweetheart, Gerty is
Tommy's sweetheart.'

Or *is* it wholly playful? Gerty sees more to it. We hear of   454
Reggy Wylie, whose father is now keeping him in of the   287
evenings to study. (We heard of his brother in the bicycle race
on p. 195/*304*.) Reggy, it seems, has ridden his bicycle much
past Gerty's window, but now has ceased. To Edy this marks
the end of Gerty's romance. To Gerty it is a mere phase, a
'lovers' quarrel'. Tenuous as the foundations seem, the relationship with Reg has been built up in Gerty's mind to the
stature of a romantic attachment.

Gerty's dress is described as seen by Gerty herself, in all its   455
neatness, grace, and good taste, with some emphasis on the
points where she has the edge on Edy Boardman. Her greatest
pride is her 'four dinky sets' of undies; and today she is wear-   288
ing the blue set 'for luck'. Blue, 'her own colour', is of course   456
the Virgin Mary's colour. There are many, many 'blues' in this
episode.

A romantically dramatized vein of doubting sorrow runs
through Gerty's rich dreams of a fashionable marriage to Mr

457   Reggy Wylie. Doubt and dream alike take their origin from a hurried peck on the end of her nose which Reggy (still at the short-trousered stage) snatched at a party long ago. A new dream of an older, more commanding suitor, more worthy of

289   her girlish self-giving, supersedes.

(337)   Then Gerty pictures herself as wife, drenching her husband's
458   days in the hominess of good cooking, warm fire, well-furnished drawing-room, and (less obviously attractive to the reader) 'photograph of grandpapa Giltrap's lovely dog Garryowen' on the wall. Against this background moves the tall, broad-shouldered, home-loving husband, complete with sweeping moustache and glistening teeth.

Edy completes the supervision of Tommy's evacuation. Cissy
459   retrieves the boys' ball from baby, whom she jigs and cuddles, laughing and chattering; for Cissy is the gay extrovert, frank
290   and unselfconscious, who shames Gerty's sensitivities by speaking of baby's 'beetoteetom' loudly enough for 'the gentleman opposite' to hear. This is only the second mention of Bloom, the Ulysses cast up on the shore.

460   In the background we hear the singing and the organ from the church, where Reverend John Hughes, SJ, is conducting a men's temperance retreat. (The symbolical significance of this will emerge later.) The sounds touch Gerty sadly, for her father's addiction to the bottle has cast a shadow over her home. As the retreatants have a sentimentalized simplicity of heart and equality before Our Lady; so the MacDowell home sounds for a moment like the stock drunkard's household of the Victorian temperance novel. It has seen violence and a man's hand lifted
461   shamefully against a woman.
291   But that is not all. The paragraph which begins with a liturgical echo about the 'Virgin most merciful' tells us that, in spite of his faults, Gerty loves her father still – for his songs (NB 'Tell me, *Mary*, how to woo thee') and for the happy family parties together.) Thus the correspondence between Gerty and Our Lady is gradually pressed home.) And Mrs MacDowell has lately been able to impress on Father the dangers of drink by reference to the sudden demise of Mr Dignam.

Gerty is the home's 'ministering angel', looking tenderly
462   after her mother when ill, turning the gas off at the main every night, tacking up a sentimental picture in the lavatory, 'Halcyon Days'.

The two boys still play with the ball. Jacky kicks it hard   292
towards the rocks. Bloom intercepts it, then throws it back to
them, and it comes to rest at Gerty's feet. She kicks it, misses,   *463*
blushes, then catches sight of Bloom's face, 'the saddest she had
ever seen'.

The sugary, mellifluous prose flows on; and it catches the
verbal echoes of Benediction ('spiritual vessel . . . honourable
vessel . . . vessel of singular devotion') through the open window   (341)
of the church. The twins play merrily. Cissy has lots of laughs   464
and hugs and baby-talk for Baby, and capably attends to his
needs at both ends.   293

Gerty, tired of the squalling baby, indulges an emotional   465
surrender to the influence of sea and sunset, distant music and
the perfume of incense, and above all to the searching eyes of
Bloom fixed upon her. The dark eyes, the pale intellectual
face, the hint of foreign-ness, and the mourning clothes, convey
the appeal of mystery and sorrow. She is aware of her own
transparent stockings and kicking legs. He becomes the focus
of pent-up longings and unrealized girlhood dreams; the suffering dream-husband in need of a woman's comfort; the power-   *466*
ful male seeking a womanly woman to crush to himself in his   294
arms.

The phrases of Benediction flow on, pressing the correspondence between Gerty and the Virgin Mary, for Gerty
has just now, in her own words, imaged herself as a 'refuge
of sinners' and 'comfortress of the afflicted'. Gerty's mood of
emotional self-indulgence carries her mind smoothly from the
dark-eyed dream-husband to the saintly figure of Fr Conroy at
the altar, to his white hands in the confessional, and his
kind, quiet words after hearing her over-scrupulous confession.
(Fr Conroy's comforting words explicitly draw a parallel be-   467
tween Gerty and Our Lady.) Here, as throughout, Gerty holds
off at a distance references to her own sexuality, self-consciously
taking refuge in euphemism and evasion. All this indicates her
alert sexual sensitivity.

The twins quarrel again and go rushing down to the sea.
Cissy pursues them; and it is through Gerty's mind that we see
Cissy's tomboyish, headlong chase that rashly risks so much in   295
the way of exposure before Bloom. Catching the twins, Cissy   *468*
is ladylike enough not to clip them with Bloom watching.
But Gerty well knows that Bloom is *not* watching Cissy; he is

watching her own shapely legs. (At this point the meaning of the correspondence between Gerty and Our Lady becomes clearer. The priests in the church are 'looking up at the Blessed Sacrament'. Bloom on the shore is looking up at Gerty's legs. We are involved in a double act of adoration.) Cissy, unkempt,

469   drags the children back. Gerty takes off her hat and settles her nut-brown hair, rejoicingly conscious of Bloom's admiration. She puts her hat back so that she can watch him from under the brim, then swings her legs enticingly, blushingly aware of the appetite she has roused.

296   Edy becomes aware of the silent duologue between Bloom
470   and Gerty. Cissy goes over to ask him the time and Bloom's
(345) look of longing is transformed into one of grave self-control. But his watch has stopped, significantly at the hour of Boylan's encounter with Molly (see p. 303/482).

The *Tantum ergo* and the censing of the Blessed Sacrament proceed in the church behind them, and one of the candles threatens to set fire to the flowers. Gerty swings her leg more, as the censer swings in the church. Bloom's hands go back into his pockets, and the flow of instinctive understanding between the two of them rises farther. Gerty is conscious of an

471   approaching period and of dark eyes fixed in her worship. It would seem plain that just as the temperance men in the church are given up to adoration of Our Lady and the Blessed Sacrament, so Bloom (an abstainer from actual marital coition as the temperance retreatants are abstainers from actual wine) is given up to adoration of a virgin's womb, a 'vessel' now holding the blood soon to be spilt. Benediction is a service which stops short of real 'communion'. The Virgin is hymned; the sacrament is exposed; but no one partakes. Even so adoring Bloom's only fulfilment is to be a fruitless emission, and Gerty's mounting excitement and increasing exposure are to culminate in the frustration of menstruation.

297   Edy and Cissy prepare to go. Edy teases Gerty about her lost sweetheart, and the mood of tormented abandonment returns,
472   bringing the sting of tears to her eyes. But she covers her pain in banter and straightway a new mood is upon her, that of the proud, injured woman shrivelling a male trifler with her scorn. Drama upon drama. Gerty reads defeat and rage and jealousy of superiority in the fallen face of Edy. Cissy and Edy, busy
473   with the youngsters, complete the preparations to go.

Hackneyed images of gathering twilight, evening bells, ivied   298
belfry, and the like introduce another surge of emotionalism in
Gerty. Her mood is stimulated by all that is most cheaply
sentimental in memories of books, souvenirs, personal treasures,
journalistic poetry, and the like. (Note the 'child of Mary badge'.)
The passion rises, touched pathetically by a veiled first refer-   474
ence to her one shortcoming – the lameness due to an accident
on Dalkey Hill; it rises in a cliché-drenched rapture of girlish
devotion that idealizes Bloom into the tragic male in need of
woman's aid, and herself into the pure woman who gives all   299
but that which honour forbids her to give.   475

In the church the Blessed Sacrament is restored to the taber-
nacle. Over the trees beside the church coloured fireworks from   (348)
the Mirus bazaar shoot into the sky. Cissy and Edy and their
charges run off to watch them. Gerty stays, held by a sense of
Bloom's stirred passion, glad to be left alone to answer it. And   476
answer it she does, leaning so far backward, in order to watch   300
the fireworks, that her legs and thighs and knickers are on
display. In a few moments of imaginary consummation she is   477
glad and fulfilled in giving herself visually, feeling no shame;
for she draws a clear line between the pure fervour of this heartfelt encounter and the exhibitionism of the stage. At the crisis
she yearns to have a 'little strangled cry' wrung from her in
his arms, and a Roman candle (like the candle on the altar
in the church) bursts in gushes of green and gold.

She bends forward quickly, a mood of pathetic shy reproach   478
seizing her in her post-crisis moments. From reproach the mood
changes to forgiveness, and then to the knowledge of a secret
shared between herself and a stranger. Cissy calls her. Gerty   301
takes the perfume-soaked wadding from her handbag and
waves in reply, thus sending an olfactory greeting on the wind
to Bloom (as the smell of incense was wafted from the altar to
the worshippers). She sends a half smile too; then stands and
moves away, walking slowly, for the first time revealing her   479
lameness. (The exact nature of the lameness is not explained.
Must we assume that Gerty's heel was bruised that day on
Dalkey Hill? p. 298/474.)

The lameness shocks Bloom: he is glad Gerty didn't spoil his
experience of her by revealing it earlier. He rightly guesses
that pale Gerty is 'near her monthlies' and muses on women's
oddities and moodinesses at such times. We gather that Bloom's

self-indulgence as a voyeur has given him a crisis and an emission which compensates for what he missed when the tram
blocked his view of the lady mounting her cab this morning
(p. 61/90), a frustration already recalled once (p. 132/203), and
480   to be magnified later in the *Circe* episode (p. 355/567). He muses
302   on the readiness of women to give these pleasures so freely, on
their excitement in dressing themselves up for the purpose of
being undressed, on the charm of changing fashions, then on
the changeless dress of the east – Mary and Martha (Marion
and Martha?), unchanged and unchangeable.

Bloom has summed up the relationship between Gerty and her
companions, and dwells upon women's superficial friendliness
481   with one another that covers bitter envies and jealousies.
(352)   His mind runs over aspects of the encounter, touching on
the oddities of women when approaching their monthlies,
wondering what Gerty thought of him, appreciating how she
took off her hat to show him her hair, them remembering how
he once sold some of Molly's combings for ten shillings when
303   they were 'on the rocks in Holles Street'. Which leads to the
veiled question – does Boylan pay Molly? 'Why not? . . . She's
worth ten, fifteen, more, a pound,' says Bloom the businessman.
Mentally he sees Boylan's letter to 'Mrs Marion' again and then
is soon diverted to the question whether he correctly addressed
482   his own love-letter to Martha. He thinks it 'funny' that his watch
stopped at half past four and feels that it must have been the
very moment when Boylan and Molly committed adultery.
'O he did. Into her. She did. Done.'

He adjusts his shirt, wet from his emission. He thinks how,
after this singular achievement, Gerty goes home to the evening
activities of innocent girlhood; dwells on men's need of women
idealized by dress, lights, music, and assumed purity; wonders
whether he might have started a conversation when Cissy came
to ask the time; then recalls an occasion when he nearly put
his foot in it by mistaking Mrs Clinch at night for a prostitute.
So to memories of the girl he took in Meath Street, making her
483   say dirty words; and to how a single girl will pretend to be
shocked when taken by a married man, though 'that's what
they enjoy. Taking a man from another woman.' As for Leopold,
he is 'glad to get away from other chap's wife'. Nevertheless,
he pictures himself embarking on an affair and surveys the
304   seductive techniques of women and of men.

Meanwhile he sees Gerty in the distance with the others, watching the fireworks; dwells on Cissy's whistle, her mouth, *484* her over-affectionate attention to the little boy. Gerty didn't look back at him when she was going; but Bloom knows that she knows what has happened. Women have a sharp instinctive awareness and self-awareness. Unlike men, you 'never see them sit on a bench marked *Wet Paint'*. They notice people; they know when they are themselves noticed. So to further reflections on the minor instinctive seductive devices of the female. At the end of it Gerty, with her shapely limbs, comes out of it better *485* than the frump with the rumpled stockings he saw earlier with *305* A. E. (p. 136/*210*).

A rocket bursts. The children and the girls reappear in the distance and there is a moment of telepathic acknowledgement between Gerty and Bloom. Bloom is grateful for what she has *(355)* given him. Boylan's song about the seaside girls is indeed right; they make your head 'swirl'. There has been an unspoken dialogue between them, and at least he has heard her name, 'Gerty'.

Now he muses on the brevity of a young girl's flowering and *486* on how quickly women must settle down to the female role of washing children, potting babies, laying out corpses, giving birth. He remembers that he must call at the hospital and inquire after Mrs Purefoy (link with the next episode); wonders if Nurse Callan is still there, recalls that the marriageable girls like her turn into the Mrs Breens and the Mrs Dignams, coping with drunkenness and the like. Perhaps the women are in part to blame. But not Molly. Bloom compares her Moorish beauty and her 'opulent curves' with the fading wives of other Dubliners. *306* So to the incongruities that the destiny of marriage produces. *487*

Bloom's thoughts return to his stopped watch. He wonders whether some kind of magnetism caused it to stop at the moment of Molly's encounter with Boylan. So to the magnetism 'back of everything' and especially that which draws the sexes together, as he and Gerty were drawn, as Molly and Boylan have been drawn.

He smells the perfume wafted his way from Gerty's cotton- *488* wool. Thoughts move to Molly's scent, to the night she first danced with Boylan, her black dance dress, the mysterious nature of her perfume, especially the odour given off by women *307* and clinging to their clothes. From the sniffs with which dogs *489*

recognize each other thought moves back again to the ubiqui-
tous subject (in this episode) of women's menstruation; then to
the question whether men themselves give off comparably
meaningful odours for women. He experiments, inserting his
nose into his own waistcoat, and is rewarded by the scent of
the soap in his pocket. And so back to the forgotten lotion,
Hynes's unpaid three-shillings debt, and the fate of debtors.

490   A 'nobleman' passes by for a second time. Bloom thinks he
is enjoying an after-dinner constitutional. (By the way, we learn
now that Bloom was aware this morning how the newsboys
mockingly aped his walk behind him, p. 107/*164–5*.) The man
is a 'mystery man', like 'that fellow today at the graveside in
308   the brown macintosh' (p. 90/*138*).

Bloom counts the flashes from Bailey's light-house on Howth
promontory. So to thoughts of wreckers, to fear of the dark,
491   night travel, stars, clouds, and Ireland, the land of the setting
(359)   sun. The dew is falling. Bloom remembers the unwisdom of
sitting on damp stone; then begins to envy the rock Gerty sat
on; notes his growing fondness for young girls; how they open
like flowers in romantic situations; and so back again to Molly
– in Matt Dillon's garden, where he kissed her shoulder (on a
yet much-to-be-recalled occasion). That was June too. And now
the month had come round again and he has adored another,
the lame Gerty.

He sees the quiet Howth Hill. 'Where we' – thus briefly he
recalls the day of romantic union with Molly there (already
recalled on p. 144/*224*). Feels 'a fool perhaps' in that now Boylan
enjoys what it is his right to enjoy. 'He gets the plums and I
the plum-stones.' (Once more Bloom's thoughts touch Stephen's.
See Stephen's 'Parable of the Plums', pp. 119–22/*183–5* and also
561/*802*.) Gerty has left him feeling tired, drained of manhood.
The mind switches back to Molly, who kissed him on Howth
Hill when he still had youth, and Molly had too. He might
revisit Howth Hill – but no; returning doesn't work. He needs
492   the new. So to Martha and the clandestine correspondence
carried on c/o PO, Dolphin's Barn, and then immediately
309   back to Molly and the party at Dolphin's Barn in 1887 when
they played charades, acting the words 'Rip van Winkle' in
three episodes – tear in overcoat for 'rip', breadvan for 'van',
and periwinkles for 'winkle'. 'Then I did Rip van Winkle coming back.' He will do so again, for this charade marked the

memorable party with prophecy. The tear in the overcoat forecast the tear in Stephen's coat after the climax in night-town
(p. 553/791). As for breadvan, the connexion between Bloom,
Jesus, and the Bread of Life is strengthened here. (See p. 125/192,
and commentary on p. 561/802.) Bloom's performance as Rip
van Winkle forecast the theme of the wanderer's return which
occurs repeatedly in episode 16.

A bat flies around. Bloom ponders where he lives. Thus
thought moves to the church belfry, to the bell, to what he calls
the 'mass' (it was Benediction, of course), the liturgy, the priest
at his evening meal, till the bat catches his eye again and he
studies its appearance, then dwells on the way colours depend   493
on the light: so to the light-house on Howth. The mind moves
quickly: from bats to insects, to birds, to the way they follow
ships, to the dismal lot of sailors, 'storm-tossed' and separated   310
from their wives, to the protective tokens they carry, to death   494
by drowning, to the moonlit calm which ironically follows
storm.

A last stray Roman candle shoots up from the bazaar. It is   (361)
the hour of tryst, of the evening postal delivery, of lamp-lighting,
of the late *Evening Telegraph* with its racing news of the Gold
Cup. Howth Hill settles for slumber. On Kish bank the light-
ship twinkles.   495

Bloom muses ever more drowsily – on life at sea, on a pleasure
cruise in the *Erin's King*, an occasion of much seasickness and
of fear in the eyes of the women. But Milly enjoyed it, too
young to fear death – at the age rather of fearing to be lost.
He recalls how once they frightened her by hiding from her –
and so wonders about the relationship between child's play
and seriousness, between mock battle and real war. (The ideal–
real dichotomy is again a theme implicit throughout this
episode, for Bloom's purely visual relationship with Gerty
parallels his purely verbal relationship with Martha. The disintegration represented in Bloom's partial relationships with
Molly, Martha, and Gerty seems to reflect a Joycean judgement
on modern life.) Memories of Milly's childhood predominate   311
here – her hand in his, her hand at his waistcoat buttons, her
little paps, her puberty and the effect of it on her mother,
bringing back her own girlhood. So we return mentally with
Bloom again to Molly and what she has told him of her Gibraltar
days.   496

Thoughts become sketchier as sleepiness grows. Looking back on his day's activities so far, Bloom sees the row at Barney Kiernan's in a detached, balanced light. The beer-swillers 'ought to go home and laugh at themselves'. Thus Bloom recommends the two-eyed self-critical attitude which Cyclopean mentalities can never achieve. He even manages to consider the argument from their angle. 'Not so bad then. Perhaps not to hurt he meant.' The citizen's cry, 'Three cheers for Israel' (p. 280/444), becomes in Bloom's mind three cheers for the citizen's extremely ugly sister-in-law, and we are back with the theme of the unattractive wife that keeps recurring in this episode. Thought moves, via Dignam, to widowhood, widow-
497   erhood, plain women, Denis Breen and his U.p. postcard, the quirks of Fate by which 'he' (Breen), not Bloom, is the husband of Mrs Breen, and, as ever, thought returns then to Molly – to
312   last night's dream of her in Turkish trousers (which has a connexion with Stephen's dream, p. 39/58–9), and to the intention to get the Keyes ad fixed up and to buy Molly petticoats with the proceeds.

Idly he turns over a piece of paper on the strand. Then he
(364)   picks up a bit of stick, thinks of writing a message in the sand
498   for Gerty, and gets as far as 'I. AM. A.' leaving the reader's curiosity aroused. He effaces the letters with his foot and flings the stick away, reflecting on the transience of all things, but grateful for Gerty. By an odd coincidence the stick falls into silted sand and sticks upright. There seems to be one more hint of the Cross in this symbol. Correspondingly there appears to be an anticipatory joke, 'I AM A ... stick in the mud.' (See p. 359/571, 'Poldy, you are a poor old stick in the mud', and p. 513/724.) Subsequent half-formed thoughts ('And she can do the other. Did too. And Belfast. I won't go. Race there, race back to Ennis') reveal the old preoccupation with Molly's coming tour and the opportunities for adultery with Boylan which it will provide. Bloom's apprehension gives place to acceptance, even forgiveness ('Let him' ...'No harm in him'), which reinforces the view that Bloom's writing in the sand carries overtones of Christ's act when He was asked to condemn the woman taken in adultery. ('I. AM. A.' suggests the divine 'I AM' and 'I am Alpha'.)

Meantime the desire to snooze has become conscious, amid thoughts and half thoughts of Molly, Gerty, Martha, undies, and the lines from *Sweets of Sin* about Raoul, the frillies, and the 'heaving embonpoint', and so on.

The cuckoo clock coos the hour in the priest's house near by. 313 Gerty MacDowell is near enough to hear it. Bloom is now asleep: *499* but the bird, giving its threefold message thrice, presses home the fact that Bloom has been cuckolded once more. Like the ninefold chime of the Angelus, it marks an annunciation. Like the cockcrow in *The Sirens* episode (p. 233/367), like the cock-crow in the gospels, it announces a betrayal.   (365)

Chapter 14

Oxen of the Sun

314   The Homeric parallel to this episode is the visit of Ulysses and his followers to the Isle of the Sun. Ulysses warns his men against killing the sacred oxen of the Sun for food, but they disobey him when he is asleep. Retribution for this impious sacrilege follows. Ulysses's ship is struck by a thunderbolt and all lives are lost but Ulysses's own.

The general drift of the correspondence here is that the ribald and riotous students in the Maternity Hospital commit a kind of sacrilege against the hospital's patients who, like the Oxen of the Sun, are symbols of fertility. Bloom alone dissents from the inappropriate behaviour of the young men; and Bloom alone remains sober.

More detailed correspondences between the subject of fertility outraged and the matter and form of this episode will emerge. They are numerous, complex, and perhaps too elaborately contrived. For instance, the theme of embryonic growth is reflected in a series of often brilliant parodies (or pastiches) of English prose style from Anglo-Saxon days to the twentieth century. Formally there is a division into nine parts (like the nine months of gestation), and these parts have a special reference to earlier episodes in the book. Moreover, there is a highly technical connexion between the detailed development of the foetus and allusions in the respective sections of this episode which only those who have considerable medical knowledge will appreciate.

One must add to these formal correspondences more material ones. The theme of contraception, as a crime against fertility, recurs frequently. And Joyce himself refers in his letters to an allegory in which 'Bloom is the spermatozoon, the hospital the womb, the nurse the ovum, Stephen the embryo' (Letters, 138–9).

We are in the Maternity Hospital in Holles Street. The location is given us in a threefold introductory incantation of which Stuart Gilbert (*James Joyce's Ulysses*) writes, 'The first (366) of these formulas means simply "Let us go south to Holles Street." The second is an invocation to the Sun, Helios, personified by Sir Andrew Horne, the head of the Lying-in Hospital, the "House of Horne". The third is the triumphant 500 cry of the midwife as, elevating the new-born, she acclaims its sex' (p. 291). By its ninefold pattern, this opening constitutes one more Angelus-like annunciation. Hornblower gave us the first (p. 70/107) and 'horn' is now a heavily laden word.

The style of the following three paragraphs is pre-English. ①️ Latinical in syntax and vocabulary, it is purposely indisciplined, turbid, and confused. It represents the chaos which precedes creation (in evolutionary terms) and perhaps the restlessness which precedes coition (in sexual terms). Paraphrased, the paragraphs say – 'Every decent and intelligent person knows that it is our duty to increase and multiply. For this reason the Celts 501 have always respected and cultivated the study of medicine and 315 have established maternity hospitals so that women, whatever their financial means, should be properly attended in childbirth. It is a praiseworthy thing in a people thus to honour procreation and to cherish the mother in the mother-to-be.'

'Before born babe bliss had.' An alliterative Anglo-Saxon 502 flavour is added to the prose as we see the midwives and their apparatus, the guardians of the fertile women. The ponderous ②️ Anglo-Saxon idiom becomes predominant as Bloom is introduced, the wandering Jew, brought by sheer compassion ('stark ruth') to visit the hospital where Mrs Purefoy lies in labour. Sir Andrew Horne is in charge of the hospital of seventy beds. Two sisters govern the wards day and night.

The sister on duty admits Bloom. She is Nurse Callan, an old 316 acquaintance (see p. 305/486). Bloom apologizes for once having 503 failed to respond to her greeting when they met at the docks, and she blushes. She is concerned about what his mourning suit signifies, until he reassures her. Bloom inquires about Dr O'Hare and is told that he died three years ago of a stomach complaint ('bellycrab'). The Anglo-Saxon flavour gives place to

(3)
504 a Middle English one as the moral of Dr O'Hare's early death is pressed home: we must look to our last end at all times.

Bloom asks after Mrs Purefoy, who is still in labour after three full days. Bloom is touched by the suffering of women in child-birth; likewise by the pathos of the nurse's childlessness. The *317* student doctor, Dixon, comes in. He it was who treated Bloom's *(369)* bee sting at the Eccles Street Hospital (p. 133/*206*). He wants Bloom to join himself and others at a party within. Bloom hesi-*505* tantly agrees.

In a style which smacks of the fourteenth century, and of Mandeville in particular, the dining-table is described, and espe-cially a tin of sardines (in 'oily water' in a 'vat of silver') and the ale. The students pour out beer for Bloom, who does not *506* want any, but accepts some in order to be friendly and then gets rid of most of it in his neighbour's glass.

The sister, at the door, begs them to restrain their roistering *318* for Mrs Purefoy's sake, and Bloom hears a cry from the labour ward. He remarks to Lenehan that perhaps Mrs Purefoy's trial will be over soon, and they toast each other. The style of this paragraph is unmistakably Sir Thomas Malory's.

507 The convivial company consists of Dixon, Lynch, and Madden, who are medical students, Lenehan, Crotthers, Punch Costello, and Stephen. Mulligan (Malachi) is expected, but has not yet arrived. Leopold Bloom joins them out of friendship for Stephen and his father.

The young men are discussing what should be done when choice has to be made in childbirth between the life of the *508* mother and the life of her baby. All agree that the mother should *319* be saved and deplore the official view to the contrary. Madden cites an actual case in which the mother's life was sacrificed – in accordance with the religious scruples of her husband. Stephen comments ironically that now 'both babe and parent glorify their Maker', the one in limbo and the other in purga-tory. Pursuing the ironic vein, he states the Catholic view against *509* contraception as a sinful abuse of our true nature. Bawdy talk and laughter follow, though Bloom is too concerned for the suffering of Mrs Purefoy above to be able to share in it. Stephen expands the Church's condemnation of abortion, noting that the foetus is endowed with a soul by the end of the second month. When Bloom is appealed to for an opinion, he takes refuge in a joke, that Holy Church is well advised to get the financial advantages of both a birth and a death from the dilemma of a dangerous labour.

Nevertheless, Bloom is inwardly worried by the thought of Mrs Purefoy's suffering, by the memory of Rudy's birth and death eleven days afterwards, and of how Molly knitted a lamb's-wool vest for him to be buried in. The various references to this vest carry overtones establishing Rudy as the sacrificial lamb (see p. 497/703). Bloom's lack of a son gives him a touching fatherly affection for Stephen, and he is sorry to see him living in wasteful debauchery.

Stephen calls for a toast to the pope in this wine which embodies his (Stephen's) soul, leaving the bread, the more physical element, to 'them that live by bread alone'. Then he preaches a brief sermon. The word is made flesh in a woman's womb: but our flesh, through the power of the Holy Spirit, becomes the undying word. The first Eve, to whom we are linked by the chain of navel-cords (cf. p. 32/46), sold us for an apple. Our Lady, the second Eve, gave us the Redeemer. Either Our Lady knew Jesus as God, in which case she was daughter of her own son. Or she did not know him and thus shared in St Peter's denial of Him; for our Lord had a parallel or a joint substantiality with his Father; He did not have an inferior substantiality.

Punch Costello strikes up a bawdy song, but Nurse Quigley comes to the door and asks for restraint. She is anxious that if Sir Andrew Horne should come, he shall not find a riot in progress during her period of duty. The others drunkenly rebuke Costello.

Dixon and Lenehan tease Stephen about his unfulfilled early religious vocation and his rumoured sexual adventures. They describe a Madagascar rite for deflowering a wife to song and ritual, and Stephen responds with the hymeneal lyric, 'To bed, to bed', from *The Maid's Tragedy* by Beaumont and Fletcher. ('Beau Mount' and 'Lecher' Dixon prefers to call them.) Stephen says the two of them shared one mistress and then achieves a high point of drunken blasphemy in misquoting, 'Greater love than this no man hath that a man lay down his wife for his friend' as the teaching of one Zarathustra, professor of French Letters. He expands the theme of the usurping adulterer who betrays and despoils, in the style of the Authorized Version of the Old Testament, echoing *Lamentations*

320
510

(373)

511

321

512

513
322

514

and the *Reproaches* from the Good Friday liturgy. Overtones associate Molly Bloom with Ireland in adulterous betrayal. The 'kiss of ashes' takes us back to the recurrence of Stephen's mother to him in a dream, 'her breath bent over him . . . a faint odour of wetted ashes' (p. 9/10). Finally, changing his idiom to
515
323
a burlesque of Sir Thomas Browne, Stephen rounds off his homily with reflections on the circular rhythm of life from cradle to grave.

Costello starts to sing again, but a thunderclap interrupts him. Lynch bids Stephen take note that his blasphemies have been
(376)
516
heard. Stephen is genuinely frightened (we are told that Joyce was terrified of thunderstorms), but tries to cover up his fear in further arrogant blasphemies to the effect that old Nobodaddy (God), too, is drunk. Bloom senses Stephen's genuine fear and tries to calm him with the scientific explanation of the phenomenon of thunder.

'But was young Boasthard's (Stephen's) fear vanquished by Calmer's (Bloom's) words? No,' for Stephen has in his bosom a 'spike named Bitterness'. Bunyan is the object of parody now, as Stephen's moral and spiritual condition is analysed. He has lost the bottle Holiness and lacks the Grace to find it again. The thunder reminds him that he is within the natural order and
324
517
must one day die. But he knows nothing of Heaven (the land called Believe-on-Me) for though Pious told him of it and Chastity showed him the way to it, he has been beguiled by the flatteries of Bird-in-the-Hand and led astray into her grot – 'Two-in-the-Bush' or 'Carnal Concupiscence'.

The whole company disbelieves in Believe-on-Me and lusts after Bird-in-the-Hand, who entices them to her grot with its four pillows labelled Pickaback, Topsy Turvy, Shameface, and Cheek-by-Jowl. They use contraceptives ('a stout shield of oxengut' named Killchild) to preserve themselves from Allpox.
518
325
519
In a style strongly reminiscent of Pepys the thunderstorm and the cloudburst are described. Outside Justice Fitzgibbon's door Buck Mulligan, bound for the Maternity Home, meets Alec Bannon, fresh from Mullingar and full of talk about a 'skittish heifer, big of her age and beef to the heel'. This is plainly Milly Bloom, for Bannon is the student she refers to in her letter to her father received this morning (p. 54/80). Mulligan and Bannon make for the Maternity Hospital together, and we are given a fresh, seventeenth-century picture of the convivial

company there and of Mrs Purefoy, still labouring of the 'ninth chick to live', not to mention the three who died and whose names are written out 'in a fair hand in the king's bible'.

Lenehan, described in a sharp, earthy seventeenth-century prose as 'merryandrew or honest pickle', speaks of Mr Deasy's letter on the treatment of foot-and-mouth disease which has appeared in the evening paper (thanks to Stephen). Frank Costello joins in and his career is summed up. He has made many false starts in life, but always returns penniless to his father. Bloom (once employed in the Cattle Market – see p. 258/*408*) can scarcely believe that all the cattle he has seen today heading for the docks and Liverpool must be slaughtered, and Stephen reassures him, speaking of the Russian expert Rinderpest who is to come and give the cattle anti-foot-and-mouth treatment.

520
326

521

(381)
327
522

Lynch suggests that Rinderpest would be rash to meddle 'with a bull that's Irish', whereupon ensues a complex parable of bulls in a conversation between Lynch (Vincent) and Dixon. The first bull 'sent to our island by farmer Nicholas' is presumably the papal bull of Hadrian IV (Nicholas Brakespear) which gave the country into Henry II's hands. 'So be off now, says he, and do all my cousin german the Lord Harry tells you.' The bull becomes a symbol of the Irish Church and the parable unfolds how he is spoilt, petted, enriched, overnourished, and indulged in every whim. The course of history runs on. The Lord Harry quarrels with farmer Nicholas, and it is plain that Henry VIII is now intended and 'Nicholas' stands for the papacy in general. Thus Henry discovers in himself 'a wonderful likeness to a bull', pronounces himself Bos Bovum, boss of the show, boss of the bull, John Bull lord of the Irish and papal bulls. The end of it all is that the wearied Irishmen load themselves 'on shipboard', set sail, and make for America.

523

328
524

The style assumes an eighteenth-century flavour strongly reminiscent of Addison and Steele. Mulligan and Bannon appear. Mulligan displays a printed card advertising himself as '*Fertilizer and Incubator, Lambay Island*' and holds forth on his project to counter the ill-effects of nuptial sterility by setting up on Lambay Island a national fertilizing farm named Omphalos, where he will personally act as fertilizer to all female comers. He embellishes his statement with a 'classical quotation', mock-Ciceronian in style – 'Such and so great is the depravity of this

525

329
526

527

age that our women greatly prefer the lascivious titillations of
330   any kind of half-man to the weighty testicles and lofty erec-
tions of the Roman centurions.'

Mulligan attends to his clothes which have suffered from the
storm. Bannon, 'overjoyed as he was at a passage that had
befallen him' (his encounter with Milly Bloom), talks about it
to his neighbour. Mulligan asks who the 'loaves and fishes' are
for and whether Bloom ('the stranger') is in need of professional
assistance (obstetrical). Bloom speaks seriously of Mrs Purefoy's
528   condition, and Dixon throws Mulligan's mockery back at him,
asking him to account for his swollen belly. Mulligan obliges
with characteristic ribaldry.

Crotthers ('the Scotch student') who has been listening to
(385)   Bannon's confidences, congratulates him and offers him a drink.
Bannon responds ('*et mille compliments*') in words which hint
529   again that Milly Bloom is the person concerned in his adven-
331   tures. Then he produces a photograph of Milly and sings her
praises in a more mannered eighteenth-century style clearly
influenced by Sterne. He speaks of buying a cloak to protect
530   his lady 'from wetting'. Mulligan (called here 'Le Fécondateur')
gives George Moore as his authority that they have a rain in
Cape Horn which will wet through 'even the stoutest cloak'.
Lynch prefers umbrellas. It is plain that we are in the midst of
a web of double-entendres (reminiscent of *Tristram Shandy*) in
which raincoats and umbrellas stand for contraceptives. The
fertility theme thus recurs. Nakedness is advertised as the proper
human condition for two activities of which bathing is one.

332   Nurse Callan comes in and whispers to Dr Dixon. Her appear-
531   ance puts a brief temporary brake on the ribaldry, but as soon
as she has gone out Costello declares her a 'monstrous fine bit
of cowflesh'. Lynch joins him in mockingly indecent chatter of
the ways of doctors with nurses till Dixon ('the young surgeon')
rises and rebukes them in the more dignified, sober prose of a
Goldsmith or a Cumberland for these insults to the 'ennobling
532   profession' of medicine. Then he goes out, leaving behind 'a
murmur of approval'. It should be clear, at this point, that Joyce
adopts not only the styles of various periods but also something of the modes of behaviour appropriate to them.

333   Bloom's tolerance of the young men's high-spirited obsceni-
533   ties comes near to being overstrained only by Costello, whose
ugliness repels him. For Bloom has learned to control his temper,

much as he dislikes the cruder wit and ribaldry at the expense
of a poor woman in labour. He is very relieved to learn that
Mrs Purefoy's ordeal is over, since she has been in such pain   *534*
'through no fault of hers'. The others mockingly explore the
question whose fault it is, some doubting whether 'old Glory   334
Allelujurum', her husband, 'an elderly man with dundrearies'
could be capable of the achievement and preferring the claims
of some priest, 'linkboy', or 'itinerant vendor of articles'. Bloom
is astonished to reflect that frivolous medical students like these
can so quickly be transformed into respectable practitioners.

A passage follows in the style of late eighteenth-century polit-   *535*
ical oratory in which Bloom's right to criticize Irish medical
students, even silently, is questioned. A dignified barrage
of rhetoric is brought to bear upon Bloom. He is an alien,
graciously admitted to civil rights. He is open to criticism him-   (389)
self on several grounds. He has ceased to fulfil his marital
obligations to his wife. He tried to seduce a servant-girl (for a
fuller account of this incident, see pp. 375 ff./*586* ff; and for
Molly's view of it, p. 609/*873*). The charge that he has 'nearer   *536*
home a seedfield that lies fallow for want of a ploughshare'
recalls how Mr Deasy's letter attacked 'the doctrine of *laissez
faire*' and 'the pluterperfect imperturbability of the department
of agriculture' (p. 27/*40*). Moreover, Bloom discredited himself
when working at Cuffe's, and he is a masturbator. In short, his
attempt to pose as a moralist is hypocritical. The implicit satire   335
here of high-flown politico-moral polemic is searching.

The announcement of the Purefoy birth is repeated in the
grave idiom of a Gibbon. The occasion has now acquired the
trappings of a royal nativity and the students have become
waiting delegates. Hearing the news, vainly discouraged by
Bloom, they burst into a 'strife of tongues',* discussing a long
series of obstetrical problems and natal abnormalities, and for   *537*
good measure touching on such related questions as artificial
insemination, menopausal involution of the womb, and impreg-
nation by rape. Eventually they move on to monstrous freaks   *538*
and the theory of copulation between women and animals, with   336
special reference to the Minotaur. (NB Dedalus was the artificer
of the Cretan labyrinth. He also manufactured a metal shell in

---

* The theological overtones suggested by these pentecostal hints are dealt with
in the commentary on p. 345/*554*.

the shape of a cow into which Pasiphae could enter in order to indulge her lust for the bull.)

539   A sudden switch to the style of the Gothic novel, comically burlesqued, gives us Mulligan's tale which freezes them with horror. It conjures up the apparition of Haines. Haines, a ghastly figure, again blames history for his cool reception (see p. 17/24). He confesses himself the murderer of Samuel Childs, haunted by remorse, doomed to dope and destruction. 'This is the *337*   appearance is on me.'* He sees a vision of the black panther and vanishes; then briefly reappears – 'Meet me at Westland Row station at ten past eleven,' and is gone.

540   Meanwhile Bloom, in a dreamy mood (and in a style reminiscent of Charles Lamb), sees himself in memory first as a schoolboy, then as a young traveller in trinkets for his father *541*   (see pp. 275/*436* and 545/*778*), then in his first full sexual encounter – with a shilling whore, Bridie Kelly. It was a fruit-*338*   less encounter. Then and now Bloom remains sonless.

Bloom's reverie assumes the fantastic flavour and high *542*   colouring of an opium-eater's vision from De Quincey's pen. *(394)*   His soul is wafted away among stars and phantoms, and some of today's recurring images and memories are strangely metamorphosed. Agendath (p. 49/*72*) becomes a waste land. Netaim, 'the golden, is no more', and the cattle herding to the docks (p. 80/*122*) are magnified into a vast threatening zodiacal host tramping to the dead sea. Then appears the everlasting virgin bride, radiant and resplendent, who is both Martha, 'thou lost one' of '*M'appari*' (the ideal and unattainable) and Milly his daughter, the symbol of youth, whose jewelled veil is trans-*543*   formed into a ruby triangle (see p. 340/*545*: he is looking at the label on a bottle of Bass) on the forehead of Taurus. (Bloom's thoughts touch Stephen's again. See Stephen's memory of a dancing girl with a ruby on her belly, p. 198/*310*. The red triangle is, of course, another pentecostal image – tongue of flame. See p. 345/*554*.)

Costello (Francis) reminds Stephen of their schooldays *339*   together under Fr Conmee. Stephen boasts himself a poet able to bring back the lost past and its inhabitants. Lynch (Vincent) suggests that the pose is premature from the author of a mere

---

* The theological overtones suggested by these pentecostal hints are dealt with in the commentary on p. 345/*554*.

'capful of light odes' and hopes that his great work will indeed
be written (thus the creation of *Ulysses* is forecast once more).
This, and Lenehan's mention of Stephen's mother, puts Stephen
into a sombre mood. Meanwhile the others speak of the Gold
Cup race on which both Lenehan and Madden have lost money.
Lenehan tells how *Sceptre* was overtaken by the dark horse
Throwaway in the straight (as Bloom beats Boylan in the end).
Lynch speaks of a romp in the fields today with his girl friend   *544*
and tells how, coming away through the hedge, they met Fr
Conmee, and to cover her confusion the girl concentrated on   *340*
removing a slip of underwood clinging to her skirt. (The couple
noted by Fr Conmee on his walk are now identified. See pp.
184/*287* and 190/*296*.)

Lenehan is going to take up a bottle of Bass when Mulligan   *545*
restrains him, pointing out that Bloom is lost in reverie with
his eyes fixed on its scarlet label. But Bloom is by no means
mesmerized. His boyhood reminiscences have in fact given
way to more mundane thoughts on 'two or three private trans-
actions'. Now, seeing Lenehan's eyes on himself and the bottle,   *546*
he helps him to a drink.

Stylistically we are now firmly established in the nineteenth-
century, and Stuart Gilbert cites Landor, Macaulay, Dickens,   *341*
Newman, Pater, and Ruskin as among the models here
imitated. But Joyce's experiment is not a simple, chronological   *(397)*
series of pastiches. There are sentences which recall Meredith
and Carlyle, and sentences which carry the flavour of quite
other ages.

There is one more description of the assembled drinkers. Since
Dixon has gone out ('The chair of the resident indeed stood
vacant') there are nine of them. The debate, both in subject   *547*
and style, seems to reflect an increasing disorder. It is as though
Joyce wished to represent clearly the collapse of the old patterns
of culture and the decay of literature begun in the nineteenth-
century and accelerated in the twentieth. Thus the pseudo-
scientific attack on Stephen's 'transcendentalism' founders in
a bog of bogus physiology. The discussion of infant mortality   *548*
runs riot in a series of arguments chaotically freed from the   *342*
disciplines of scholarship, logic, or even common sense.
The juxtaposition of the pseudo-medical with the sociological,
the comic, and the irrationally sentimental ('Nature, we may   *549*
rest assured, has her own good and cogent reasons for whatever

she does') produces an effect of intellectual chaos whose nadir
is reached in Stephen's image of God as an 'omnivorous being'
who devours human creatures at their death and needs to vary
550   his indigestible diet of 'cancrenous females emaciated by partu-
rition, corpulent professional gentlemen', and the like, with the
343   gastrically more acceptable babies ('staggering bob').

Meanwhile Dr Dixon has supervised the accouchement and
551   a burlesque of Dickensian sentiment pictures the mother and
her ninth baby, lacking only Theodore ('Doady') Purefoy to
344   complete the idyllic scene. Theodore is congratulated. He has
552   'fought the good fight'.

As Bloom hears Stephen's bitter words, the memory arises
in his mind of a May evening at Roundtown on the bowling
green (the evening which John Henry Menton recalled on pp.
87–8/134, and which Bloom himself recalled on pp. 94–5/146),
when Menton took offence because Bloom's ball sailed inside
his. Molly and Floey Dillon were there 'linked under the lilac
553   tree'. Molly, wearing ear-rings ('Our Lady of the Cherries'),
Floey, Atty, and Tiny were gathered round a little boy of four
or five, standing on the urn. The child kept looking at his mother
with a look of remoteness and reproach. This was Stephen,
whose present facial expression of 'false calm' reminds Bloom
of the childish parallel of 'seventeen golden years ago'. (See also
pp. 556/795 and 637/922.) It is noteworthy that in this episode,
(401)   so much concerned with growth and development, both Bloom
(p. 337/540) and Stephen are glimpsed in their early childhood.
It is significant too that here, after the long philological preparation, culminating in the mounting linguistic turbulence of
pp. 341–3/547–50, we have reached for a brief spell a comparative verbal calm. The child has been born. The word is made
flesh. The image of the infant Stephen (dressed in 'linsey-
woolsey' so as to establish a correspondence with the dead little
Rudy and the sacrificial lamb; cf. pp. 320/510 and 497/703) and
his mother as 'Our Lady of the Cherries' constitutes an archetypal 'Nativity' scene.

There is a sudden calm among the drinkers in the 'ante-
345   chamber of birth' like the calm of shepherds and angels about
the crib in Bethlehem. But it is shattered as by the flash and
peal of a thunderstorm when at last the Word is uttered. Stephen
554   utters it, and it is the name of a pub, 'Burke's!'

The scriptural correspondences hinted at in this episode are neither precise nor predominant, but they should not be over-looked. The revellers are not in an upper room, but there is a point when Stephen's words and actions seem to parallel those of Christ at the Last Supper (p. 320/*510–11*). Later more defi-nite pentecostal correspondences emerge. The apparition of Haines (p. 336/*539*) suggests the appearance of the risen Christ in the Upper room. The scarlet triangle on the Bass's beer bottle (p. 340/*545–6*) which both mesmerizes and releases a vast ima-ginative fertility, recalls the tongues of flame on each apostle's head. None of these parallels, taken singly, would constitute an evident and intentional symbolism. But the incarnation of the word in the new birth calls out an evident correspondence with Christ's nativity, and Stephen's utterance of the Word produces an unmistakable pentecostal phenomenon as the young men dash out, drunkenly, to proclaim Alexander J. Dowie and to 'shout salvation in King Jesus' (p. 349/*561*). Moreover, from this point forward they have plainly received the gift of tongues.

Stephen leads them capering out through the hall into the street. Dixon follows them. Bloom lingers only to send a kind word to Mrs Purefoy through Nurse Callan, and gently to cheer the tired nurse with a well-meant if characteristically clumsy joke ('Madam, when comes the storkbird for thee?').

Like the Word, the fresh air is intoxicating. The prose achieves now, not only a pentecostal vitality but also a pentecostal unin-telligibility. We are in the twentieth century at last. Prose style disintegrates into a violent, explosive chattering in which slang, dialect, and the utterance of illiteracy go side by side with the sensational vulgarity of press and hoarding. (402)

Theodore Purefoy is eulogized for his prolific achievement over twenty years; for giving his wife 'beef-steaks, red, raw, bleeding'; and is urged to drink Mina's flowing mother-milk by the udderful. The verbal riot is at first a rich celebration of fertility. 555 346

In the street the comments of passers-by, some of them angry ('Righto, Isaacs, shove em out of the bleeding limelight') mingle with the delirious shouts of the revellers and what sounds like Stephen's mockery of an artistically produced Yeats volume ('calf covers of pissedon green') from the Druiddrum Press. 556

Arrived at Burke's, they order their drinks – two whiskies ('mead of our fathers'), five number one Basses, ginger cordial, two Guinnesses ('ardilauns'), and amid the ceaseless chatter 557

347   Dixon seems to be talking of Molly Bloom ('none of your lean
      kine'), Bloom seems to be winding up his 'ticker', and Mulligan
      is mockingly telling how his aunt is still concerned lest 'Baddy-
      bad' Stephen should lead him astray.
          Much of what is said in this farrago of tangled and abbrevi-
      ated utterance touches again on familiar themes – Bannon and
558   Milly at Mullingar, Lynch and Sara on the road to Malahide,
      the Rose of Castille, the Gold Cup race, but there is much, too,
      which would tax ingenuity to interpret and attribute to its
348   speaker. Amid the welter it seems clear, however, that they all
559   drink absinthe at Stephen's expense, with the exception of Bloom
      who has a glass of wine ('Rome boose for the Bloom toff'), and
      that Bannon identifies Bloom as Milly's father ('Photo's papli,
      by all that's gorgeous').
560   The landlord calls Time. The mysterious man in the macin-
      tosh appears again. Whether seriously or not, he is accused of
      drinking Bovril, and someone says, 'Bartle the Bread we calls
      him,' which scarcely advances his identification much.
          It is interesting that as they are turned out of Burke's at
349   closing time, 'there's eleven of them', the true apostolic num-
      ber. Is this because Bantam Lyons has joined them? ('Look at
      Bantam's flowers', p. 347/558.) There were only ten at the
      hospital (Stephen, Crotthers, Lynch, Costello, Madden, Bannon,
      Mulligan, Lenehan, Dixon, and Bloom). Someone is noisily
561   sick. Stephen and Lynch go for the train to take them to night-
      town and the brothels. They see the advertisement for the
(406) hot-gospeller on the Merrion Hall, and mockingly proclaim
      themselves 'washed in the Blood of the Lamb'. On this note
      the episode ends. The idiom is that of an American hot-gospeller
      advertising salvation and kingdom-come in the vulgarest
      button-holing commercialese.

Chapter 15

Circe

Homer's enchantress, Circe, entertains the followers of Ulysses
in her palace, drugs them at a feast, then with her wand transforms them into swine, to join previous victims of her witch-
craft. Ulysses, who sets out to rescue his men, is aided by
Hermes. Hermes gives him a magic drug which immunizes
him against Circe's enchantments, so that when she tries to
bewitch him he is able to draw his sword and master her.
The men are restored and feast at Circe's table, while Ulysses
is taken to Circe's bed.

The withdrawal of the rational element, represented in Homer
by the bestializing of Circe's victims, has its contemporary
counterpart in both the content and the form of this episode.
Its nightmare quality is appropriate to the hour and to the condition of Stephen, who is drunk after his potent mixture of drinks,
culminating in absinthe. Joyce's technique is striking. What
passes in the mind is expressed in dramatic form exactly as
what happens externally is expressed. This technique makes
difficulties for the reader, but it would be a mistake to overes-
timate the novelty of Joyce's experiment in this respect. It is
doubtful whether much is done in this episode, in the way of
materializing imagery and concretizing mental sequences, which
is not anticipated in, for instance, Shakespeare's *Macbeth*. The
weird sisters themselves exemplify the process of personifying
the spiritual and mental forces at work in man's inner life.
The brew they concoct from tiny fragments of newts, toads,
frogs, Jews, birth-strangled babes, and the like, illustrates how
imagery expressive of disorder and disintegration in the system
of Nature may be concretized and bodied in dramatic form.
We hear, too, of horses that eat each other. Macbeth's dagger,

if it does not assume a voice, like Bella Cohen's Fan or the Bracelets, exercises a personal influence even more extravagant. And the apparitions in the Witches' Cavern are surely no less outrageous than the apparitions here of Edward VII and Alfred Lord Tennyson.

It is significant that Shakespeare, in what is considered to be his profoundest study of evil and his most sensitive poetic investigation of the human status, should have had recourse to just such devices as Joyce uses here. If further evidence is needed that Joyce's work is neither freakish nor inordinately experimental, one should consider the literary devices utilized in Spenser's *Faerie Queene*, in Milton's *Paradise Lost*, and in *Comus*. That one should naturally justify Joyce's *Circe* by reference to major works of Shakespeare, Milton, and Spenser itself establishes the true category of *Ulysses*.

(408) We are at the Mabbot Street entrance to night-town, Dublin's
562 brothel area, already known to Stephen and to Joyce's readers from *A Portrait of the Artist*. Stunted men and women gather ghoulishly round an ice-cream cart. Under the gaslight their ice-cream sandwiches look like 'lumps of coral and copper snow' wedged between wafers. It is murky. Calls and whistles from unseen mouths establish the atmosphere of mysterious, furtive, illicit encounters in the dark background. A deaf-mute idiot who has St Vitus's Dance is teased by a gang of children. Other pictures image slum squalor and misery – a figure sprawled
351 against a dustbin, grinding teeth and snoring; a stunted fellow ('gnome') searching for rags and bones in a rubbish-tip; an old hag with a smoky oil lamp helping him, and a bandy child to complete the family. In the background are the sounds of crude, sordid slum-life – crashing plate, screaming woman and child,
563 cursing man, and the voice of Cissy Caffrey, the harlot, singing an indecent ditty.

Two British soldiers, Private Carr and Private Compton, march drunkenly in and mouth a fart. Stephen and Lynch come
352 through the crowd and the soldiers mock Stephen as 'the parson'. This is not surprising, for Stephen and Lynch process together in a pantomime of the opening of the Mass, Stephen
564 chanting the introit. A bawd in a doorway tries to interest them in a maidenhead she has for sale, is ignored, and spits after them angrily. They are Trinity medical students, she assumes, 'all prick and no pence'. Meanwhile, crouched in a doorway

with Bertha Supple, Edy Boardman is gossiping about a recent verbal victory over one of her rivals.

Stephen is drunkenly proclaiming gesture as a possible 353 universal language, a new 'gift of tongues' by which the structural rhythm at the heart of things might be given utterance. He seems to imply, in what Lynch calls his 'pornosophicial (411) philotheology', that verbal language gives us nothing more 565 essential than the fruits of sexual repression in women-dominated men like Shakespeare and Socrates. He hands Lynch his stick so that he can illustrate in a single gesture the bread and wine which Omar needs so many words to proclaim. (The notion of surrendering language is, of course, in tune with the movement back from rationality to animality in the Homeric basis.) We gather, by the way, that Stephen is making for the arms of Georgina Johnson (the whore on whom he spent the pound borrowed from A. E., p. 155/242). Lynch, returning 354 the ashplant to Stephen, tells him to take his crutch and walk. The drunken navvy near by, lurching against a lamp, immediately takes it up on his shoulder and miraculously walks away with it. In Stephen's mind, he and Lynch are St Peter and St John who, soon after receiving the gift of tongues at Pentecost, healed the lame man.

Through the fog and fumes Bloom appears, 'cramming bread and chocolate into a sidepocket'. He is panting and has a stitch in his side through struggling to keep up with Stephen. He goes 566 into Olhausen's, the pork butcher's, and buys a pig's crubeen and a sheep's trotter. He wonders at a glow in the sky, then realizes that it is a fire. He can take this cheerfully because it 355 is on the 'south side anyhow' and his own house is in Eccles Street, on the north side of the Liffey. He even indulges a momentary hope that it 'might be his house' (presumably Boylan's). As the navvy lurches his way, Bloom darts across the road and there is a brief moment of crisis as urchins shout and cyclists flash past, missing him narrowly. The next moment he 567 is almost run down by a sand-strewer on the tram-track – a 'dragon' with red headlight and hissing trolley. The motorman curses him as he blunders off the track. Plainly this monster dragon sand-strewer is a metamorphosis of the tram which this morning cost him his view of the girl mounting the cab (p. 61/90), a frustrating incident which he has already recalled in annoyance ('Think that pugnosed driver did it out of spite',

p. 132/203). Thus Bloom is a stumbling, harried, frustrated
356 figure among the monsters of the night. He jumps to safety on
the pavement. The close shave has miraculously cured his stitch.
Prudent as ever, he notes the need to take up his physical exercises again, likewise to insure himself against street accidents;
then recalls earlier close shaves, such as the day the wheel of
(415) the Black Maria peeled off his shoe. He wonders. Was the tram-
driver the same one who came between his vision and the
horsey woman this morning? The lameness theme recurs in the
memory of a cramp and a joke about the 'stiff walk'.

Surrendering wearily to 'brainfogfag', Bloom has a brief
568 exchange in Spanish and Gaelic with an imaginary sinister figure
identified by him as a Gaelic league spy 'sent by the fire-eater',
the citizen who reviled him at Barney Kiernan's. It is not
surprising that the memory of this violent encounter should
recur thus transmuted. Further frustrations, after the pattern of
Bloom's experiences today, follow, as a ragman bars his path
357 and has to be evaded, and as the chasing Caffrey children collide
with him. (Did not their presence on the shore impede his
yearning for Gerty MacDowell?) In Bloom's mind suspicion
matches frustration. The ragman is probably a fence, he thinks;
the Caffrey children are pickpockets playing the collision gambit.
His hand goes to his watch and his pockets, checking on purse,
book (*Sweets of Sin*), potato, and soap.

569 To frustration and suspicion guilt is added. The voice of
conscience takes the form of Rudolph Bloom, Senior, in his habit
as he lived, scolding Leopold for wasting half a crown on drinks
for companions. Old Rudolph has to feel his son's face to assure
himself of his identity – in a re-enactment of the recognition
scene between Isaac and Jacob ('the scene he was always talking
about where the old blind Abraham recognizes the voice and
358 puts his fingers on his face', p. 62/93). A past paternal scolding
is then reproduced. The occasion was when Leopold went on
the spree with the harriers, and Bloom is mentally reclothed for
the sprint as the scolding is re-enacted. Bloom's mother returns
570 to re-enact the shock of seeing her son come home muddied
and damaged.

359 Now that judgement of guilty Bloom has asserted itself as
the dominant mental theme, it is natural that Molly should add
herself to those who arraign him. She appears costumed as she
was in last night's dream (pp. 311–12/497), oriental, remotely

yashmaked, superior, and condescending. As Bloom stands in panting agitation, full of apology and desire, he sees the gleam of a coin on her forehead (he wondered whether Boylan paid her, p. 303/*481*) and a camel patiently waiting her will. At a word and a slap it plucks a mango fruit from a tree and offers it to her. Bloom quibbles in nervous ambiguity, 'as your business menagerer ... Mrs Marion' and the key words 'manager' (Boylan), 'ménage', and 'menagerie' coalesce. Marion becomes indulgent, maternal, to her 'poor little stick in the mud' (see p. 312/*498*), while Leopold apologizes for forgetting to buy the lotion. He will go for it 'first thing in the morning'. This promised visit to the chemist's materializes immediately. Tomorrow's sun rises in the form of a cake of soap in which the face of Sweny, the chemist, emerges: the purchase of the forgotten lotion is prophetically accomplished. (Note that the Sunrise theme, an archetype of fulfilment, is here securely, if indirectly, tied to the Sonrise theme, by the face in the sun.) Molly softens for a moment in response; but Bloom, still humble and deferential, addresses her as 'ma'am', and she leaves him, humming her part from *Don Giovanni* disdainfully.

571

(418)
360

We return to reality. The bawd is still hawking a ten-shilling maidenhead. A burly tough chases Bridie Kelly into the gloom. She is a mental recall of Bloom's past, the girl with whom he had his first sexual encounter (see p. 338/*541*). The chasing tough, like so many of the 'halt and the lame' in this episode, stumbles on the steps. The bawd presses her wares. Her mention of the virgin next brings into Bloom's mind a leering, limping Gerty MacDowell, whose earlier romantic appeal ('With all my worldly goods I thee and thou') is now blended with the slobbering sordidness of a cheap whore. Sentimentality is transformed into squalor.

572
361

Another of today's encounters recurs in Bloom's mind as Mrs Breen appears, wearing a man's overcoat and a roguish smile. Bloom first addresses her in a parody of the remote polite language which nowadays cloaks their memories of earlier intimacy; but Mrs Breen, another recall of Bloom's guilt, comes to scold him for his presence in night-town. Vainly Bloom tries to restrain her, to shift the too frank conversation back on to the level of frigid politeness about the weather, to pretend that his interest in night-town is philanthropic. Mrs Breen is not suppressed: she threatens to tell Molly. Fearful, Bloom claims

362
573

that Molly, too, has an interest in slumming, in the 'exotic', even in Negroes. And immediately the Negroes materialize, two coons with banjoes who dance and sing.

574   Bloom's approaches to Mrs Breen at this point give us a fascinating linguistic representation of his complex attitude to her.
363   His unsureness, his awareness of the cold demands of propriety,
(422)   and the lingering warmth of their old intimacy jostle one another in a verbal ensemble subtle in its blending of the inner and outer personae. It is the warmth of shared reminiscence which eventually predominates. Mrs Breen becomes 'Josie Powell that was, prettiest deb in Dublin': they recall a party at Georgina Simpson's, and Bloom becomes again 'the lion of the night', giving a champagne toast in dinner jacket. Wallowing deeper in sentimentality about the 'dear dead days', they lapse into the
575   childishness of the 'teapot' game they used to play (in which
364   the word 'teapot' is substituted for words which must be guessed at). Fully back now in mind, they fondle each other as they did, Bloom in a purple fancy hat, Mrs Bloom in a moonlight blue evening frock. Then, histrionically, Bloom re-enacts the melodrama of losing her to another; and we see that other, Denis Breen, the shuffling half wit, as one of Hely's sandwich-board-men.

Mrs Breen is still playing the flirt she was at the party, but Bloom has become Molly's husband again, and when Mrs Breen coquettishly asks, 'Have you a little present for me there?', he answers the question as though it came from Molly. Mentally he has arrived home, must explain the meat in his pocket, and also what he was doing all evening. Hence 'I was at *Leah*.' The
576   surface Bloom takes over, the defensive Bloom who lies and covers truth with hackneyed jargon ('Trenchant exponent of Shakespeare').

365   Talk of the pig's feet recalls the meal in the Ormond, and Richie Goulding materializes, his heavy legal bag full of meat, fish, and pills. Pat the waiter adds himself. Richie, whose ill-health made a vivid impression on Bloom in the Ormond, cries with pain, 'Bright's' (his disease) and then, 'Lights!' (Claudius's cry in the play-scene of *Hamlet* as his conscience is probed: and see the false resurrection pictured by Bloom in *Hades* – 'every fellow mousing around for his liver and his lights', p. 87/*133*). Bloom, the victim of earlier violence at the citizen's hands, is fearful of a scene and becomes once more the apprehensive

apologist. Whereupon Mrs Breen resumes her first role of scolding critic. Bloom pleads ingratiatingly. He will tell her 'a little secret'; and she 'must never tell'. She softens into Josie 366 Powell again. The bawd, in the realm of reality, is unheeded. Leopold and Josie, sport-suited, recapture a day soon after Milly 577 was weaned when they 'all went together' to Leopardstown Races and Molly won seven shillings on a horse called Nevertell. (426) On the return journey, in a waggonette, some intimacy occurred whose recall we approach excitedly but which in fact we never 367 recapture. On the point of recall, Mrs Breen fades away, the 578 eager and expectant 'Yes, yes, yes . . .' on her lips.

We are back in night-town with Bloom walking on towards hellsgates. Amid a bunch of loiterers a pair of armless people flop in 'maimed sodden playfight'. The pissing woman and the maimed men are potent symbols of the absence of decency and health. The reader's expectation of hearing a secret from Bloom's past is now tardily and ironically satisfied in the broken-snouted gaffer's story of Bloom's emergency evacuation in Beaver Street into what he believed to be a plasterer's bucket, but in fact contained the men's porter (see p. 377/588). Through the dismal setting, among the armless, the legless, the broken-nosed, the cleft-palated, and the cheap whores calling obscenely from doors 368 and corners, Bloom 'plodges' towards a lighted street beyond. 579 Meanwhile the drunken navvy, seeking a brothel, staggers into Privates Carr and Compton.

Bloom begins to suspect that his pursuit of Stephen is a 'wild- 369 goose chase'. He has followed Stephen and Lynch in the train from Westland Row station; is not sure why, except that Stephen is 'the best of that lot'. The coincidence of their coming together at the hospital seems to have had a fatalistic touch. His narrow 580 escape from the sand-strewer recalls an earlier close shave when he was just minutes too soon to be hit by a bullet in the street. An obscene scrawl on the wall recalls Molly drawing on the carriage window at Kingstown. Wreaths of tobacco smoke from waiting whores in the doorways waft towards him the sickly flavour of his book *Sweets of Sin*.

Bloom's mood is uncertain, interrogative. Why is he here? Why has he bought the meat, wasting money? ('One and eight-pence too much' aptly recalls the Reuben J. Dodd 'redemption' story, pp. 78/118 and 125/192. Once more perhaps too high a price is being paid in the effort to save a 'son'.) When the

370   friendly retriever nuzzles against his hand, his apprehension transforms it into an obscenely wriggling Garryowen, and he feeds it the crubeen and trotter.

581   At this point we forsake the realm of externality until p. 387/599.

(430)   Two watching policemen materialize in response to Bloom's mood of furtive uncertainty and apprehension. Symbols of authority, they bring again the awesome power of past school-masters to bear upon him, declining his name as though it were a Latin noun. Their other phrases are standard slogans of the law, 'Caught in the act. Commit no nuisance.' Bloom's self-defence is that he is 'doing good to others', whereupon two earlier episodes of sentimentalism over animals are re-enacted in the return of the gulls he fed from O'Connell Bridge over the Liffey (p. 125/192–3), and of maudlin, drunken Bob Doran, swaying over Garryowen (p. 251/394). The voice of authority

371   records his plea as the prevention of cruelty of animals, and Bloom warms to his theme, even to the extent of condemning tales of circus life as 'highly demoralizing'. At this point 'the monster Maffei' materializes, a lion-tamer with whip and revolver. Bloom read of him this morning in Molly's novel, *Ruby:*

582   *the Pride of the Ring* (p. 52/77–8). Maffei expounds his beast-taming techniques in terms of knotted thongs, strangling pulley, and red-hot crowbar.

There is no escape for Bloom. From this point all his uncertainty, all the rebuffs and neglects, all that has served to make him an alien, an outsider, is brought to its culmination in an arrest and trial which match in power and relevance the 'trial' passages in *King Lear* and those in Kafka. Bloom's private guilts and the inescapable guilt of his very humanity are dragged remorselessly, not into the light of day, but into the dark of night and nightmare.

The Watch demand his name and address. Frightened, he pretends to be Dr Bloom, the dental surgeon (see p. 205/322), a relation of von Bloom Pasha, a millionaire with powerful connexions. Posing in red fez and with false Legion of Honour badge, he tenders his card and names his club and his solici-

372   tors. But the card, taken from his hatband, names him 'Henry Flower'. The Watch become more challenging, their phrases more relevant to the criminal, as a new vein of guilt is opened in Bloom. He struggles to explain away the name 'Flower' with

semi-nonsensical patter. The customary gambits of those caught red-handed are tried out, the plea for sympathy ('We are engaged you see, Sergeant'), the man-to-man approach ('It's a way we gallants have in the navy'), and sly bribery ('I'll introduce you, Inspector'). It would appear, by the way, that the sympathy line has to be tried on sergeants, the bribery line on inspectors.   583

Accusations gather round the subject of Bloom's confused identity. Martha appears (both Henry Flower's and Flotow's) crying for Henry–Leopold–Lionel to clear her name. The Watch becomes sterner. 'Come to the station.' Bloom tries out a Masonic sign and seeks in vain a relevant verbal channel of escape in confused chatter of mistaken identity, the Childs 'fratricide' (sic) case, wrongful accusation, and so on. But the accusing voice of a sobbing Martha speaks of 'breach of promise' and calls him a 'heartless flirt'. Bloom reproduces the judgement on others which has so often been relevant today, 'She's drunk.' Unfortunately, trying to articulate the test word 'Shibboleth' in proof of his own sobriety, he nervously mangles it into 'Shitbroleeth' and the Watch is tenderly horrified.   (433)   373

As the trial atmosphere closes in on him, Bloom pours out stock phrases of self-defence in a rhetorical speech to the jury, dwelling on his own integrity, his wife's military connexions, his father's public service as JP, his own imaginary military achievements. The Watch, less fantastically, asks his 'profession or trade'. Bloom dresses up his ad-cadging as 'a literary occupation. Author–journalist', and cites the Press for reference. Whereupon Myles Crawford strides into view, telephone in hand, still mouthing the kind of obscenity with which he brusquely rejected Bloom earlier in the day. Bloom's pretentious claim to be a writer calls up another challenger too, the Mr Philip Beaufoy who realized Bloom's own secret ambition by winning three and a half guineas with his prize tit-bit, 'Matcham's Masterstroke' (p. 56/83). Beaufoy accuses Bloom of plagiarism and proclaims the high quality of his own work. Bloom meekly quotes a questionable sentence in refutation, and Beaufoy's reply is a supercilious attempt to make Bloom look small and ridiculous and ignorant, a 'pressman johnny' who 'has not even been to a university'. Thus another of Bloom's private frustrations is aired (and one which must have been much in his mind during today's encounters with Stephen, the medical students, and literary or scholarly   584   374   585   375 men like A. E. and MacHugh); but he maintains the value of his own training in 'the university of life' and his right to pass judgement on bad art. Beaufoy's rejection of Bloom is hysterically *586* exaggerated, while Bloom's literary criticism of the short story with which he wiped himself is deliciously tempered. The piece is 'overdrawn'. Beaufoy, outraged, descends to crude abuse of Bloom's private life.

From this point the graver hidden guilts of Bloom begin to emerge. And the first concerns the servant-girl Mary Driscoll (see pp. 334/*535* and 609/*873*). Her cross-examination unfolds *376* a part comic, part pathetic episode in Bloom's past. At the time *(436)* when Mary worked for Molly and himself, Bloom gave her *587* presents and took her part when she was accused of pilfering. This gave him some power over her of which he took advantage one day when Molly was out. Bloom's reply is announced in advance by the clerk of the crown and peace as a 'bogus *377* statement'. In fact, it is a rich, compact anthology of tear-jerking *588* appeals to sentiment such as hard-pressed defendants have recourse to; but for all its tugging at the heart-strings, it produces only laughter in court and complaints from reporters that they cannot hear.

Another secret from Bloom's disreputable past is disinterred. Once, overcome in Beaver Street with sudden bowel trouble, he made use of what he took to be a plasterer's bucket (see p. 367/*578*). The episode returns to mind now as part of the unfolding of his hidden guilts. Bloom's apparently hopeless defence is take over by J. J. O'Molloy who, as the failed barrister *589* gone to seed (p. 103/*159*), is an appropriate apologist. His *378* speech exploits conventional phrases and modes of legal defence irrespective of logic and consequentiality. The effect is to bring Bloom's pathetic sense of guilt into sharp contrast with the uncomfortable farcicality, inadequacy, and artificiality of all excuses. The culmination of O'Molloy's first plea is that Bloom is an irresponsible Mongol; and Bloom is appropriately transformed into a dim, pigeon-breasted, oriental, lilting 'Chinese' English.

The audience in court howls Bloom down. O'Molloy is roused *590* to renewed illogicality on his client's behalf, and Bloom is pictured as the white man who treated Mary Driscoll as his own daughter and would never do anything to offend injured modesty. He is also down on his luck through the mortgaging

of his property at Agendath Netaim. Slides are shown of this   379
remote estate. The memory of the advertisement brings back
Dlugacz, in whose shop Bloom picked up the paper containing
it (p. 48/70). O'Molloy has now degenerated into the dying John
F. Taylor, whose famous speech Professor MacHugh quoted this
morning in the *Freeman* office (p. 116/*179*), but the identity does
not persist, and the rhetorical farrago he utters in fact echoes   591
Seymour Bushe's defence in the Childs murder case, as quoted
by O'Molloy himself (p. 115/*177*). (Did Joyce forget that Bloom
was no longer present in the *Freeman* office when these two
speeches were quoted?)

Bloom now gives references in support of his character,
and their recital brings into the open Bloom's secret social
pretensions and his hidden desire to be on speaking terms with
the great scientist, Sir Robert Ball. (See p. 126/*194*.) The social
pretensions call out challengers, a series of society ladies,   (441)
forceful, dominating personalities who seem to answer Bloom's
need to worship and to be mothered, and his intermittently
revealed desire to play the woman to a 'masculine' Amazon.
First, Mrs Yelverton Barry voices publicly Bloom's secret desire
for her stimulated by the sight of her 'peerless globes' in the
theatre box. Then Mrs Bellingham proclaims Bloom's secret wish   380
to enjoy proximity to her well-wrapped form, her silk-draped   592
legs and lace-decked thighs, and even to commit adultery with
her. Thirdly, the honourable Mrs Mervyn Talboys brings to light   381
Bloom's secret desire (a transient and unrealized one, we may   593
assume) to send her indecent photographs and obtain from her
the return of his letter obscenely soiled. (Thus we explore
submerged tendencies underlying some of the surface oddities
of Bloom's conscious thinking. Cf. pp. 131–2/*203*.) Finally, the
three ladies together proclaim Bloom's hidden desire to be
ridden and horse-whipped by them. This most hidden aberration from the depths of Bloom's consciousness, brought thus to
light, gives us a parallel to the conversion of Ulysses's followers
into swine. Mrs Talboys threatens to scourge Bloom. He has
now degenerated into the cringing bestial creature who would
love such treatment.

The women's threats gather. Bloom plays down his willing-   382
ness. 'I meant only the spanking idea. A warm tingling glow   594
without effusion.' The women's anger rises. Bloom becomes a
shrinking worshipper, praying for mercy. They proclaim him

cuckold and order him to lower his trousers for flogging. Davy
383 Stephens and other newsboys bring in the evening papers
with a special supplement containing the addresses of Dublin's
595 cuckolds. Canon O'Hanlon, Fr Conroy, and the Reverend John
Hughes, SJ, who were at Benediction when Bloom adored Gerty
MacDowell (p. 295/*468*), bring in the timepiece (cuckoo clock)
which announced Bloom's cuckoldom as he sat on the beach
(p. 313/*499*). The jingling quoits of Molly's bed complete the
cuckoldry symbols.

Bloom's trial now acquires a jury: they are men who today,
in one way or another, have made him feel an outsider.
As Bloom's offences are rehearsed they become associated with
384 the notorious crimes of the day: the Crier proclaims him 'dynam-
(445) itard, forger, bigamist, bawd ...', and the Dublin Recorder
596 condemns him to death. Thus Bloom's guilt, as indelible yet as
unidentifiable and, in a sense, unmerited as K's (in Kafka's *The
Trial*), has the quality of an inescapable human endowment.
It is the burden of Original Sin. It is also the burden of the
Sins of the World, man's burden and Christ's burden. Bloom is
at this moment proclaimed 'Judas Iscariot'; but we know how
far out that identification is.

H. Rumbold, master barber and executioner, mounts the block
ready to act. (See p. 253/*398–9*.) The church bell tolls. Bloom
385 desperately explains how kind-heartedly he fed the gulls (see
pp. 125/*192* and 370/*581*), tells how his sensitivities and his
tender heart led him astray, seeks help from Hynes. The Watch
597 accuse him of laying a time-bomb in the street; but Bloom
assures them it was only pig's feet he fed to a dog. He has
an alibi. He was at a funeral. The putrid carcass and mutilated
face of Paddy Dignam return to confirm the alibi. (His words
386 are the words of Hamlet's Ghost, but his voice is the voice of
Esau.)

It is clear now that Bloom's doings this day are being re-
enacted in a grotesque fantasy dominated by the themes of his
guilt and his isolation. The fantasy is compounded to a recipe
of farcical caricature, and flavoured with implausibility, yet the
logic of imaginative coherence is consistent and powerful.
Thus figures from the cemetery reappear, Fr Coffey reciting the
598 liturgy which, by confusion with events in Barney Kiernan's,
has become 'Namine Jacobs Vobiscuits', and John O'Connell,
387 the caretaker, assigning to Bloom his burial docket number,

field, and plot. Other images recall the rat in the graveyard (p. 94/*145*), Tom Rochford's machine (p. 191/*297*), and Reuben Dodd's two-shilling tip for the redemption of his son (p. 78/*118*).

Bloom 'plodges forward again', kisses cooing and warbling seductively around him, and we are back in the real world of *599* night-town from which Bloom took leave when feeding the dog (p. 370/*580–1*). It is notable that as the whores' wreaths of cigarette smoke heralded his departure from actuality, the cooing kisses herald his return. Zoe Higgins, a young whore, accosts Bloom and tells him that Stephen is inside Mrs Cohen's with his friend. And Bella Cohen is 'on the job herself tonight with *388* the vet' who pays for her son at Oxford. Zoe seductively slips her hand into Bloom's pocket, feels for his testicles, but brings out his talisman, his potato, which she puts 'greedily into a *600* pocket'. There is oriental music and, as Bloom looks into Zoe's *389* eyes, images associated with his dreams of the languorous, *(451)* seductive east materialize – gazelles, cedar-groves, wine-grapes, 'a fountain among damask roses'. The image of the 'womancity' under a sapphire sky derives from the book of *Revelation* where the new Jerusalem is the bride of Christ, but as Zoe bites Bloom's ear lovingly and her stale breath reaches him, the roses draw apart to disclose 'a sepulchre of the gold of kings and their mouldering bones'.

But Bloom is in the ascendant. No longer the outsider, he is wanted, admired. Caressed, Zoe asks for a cigarette, and Bloom condescendingly tells her that he rarely smokes. It's a 'childish *390* device'. 'Go on. Make a stump speech out of it,' Zoe says, and *601* Bloom, now in the full assurance of his dominating role, is mentally metamorphosed into a radical agitator denouncing the evils of tobacco. Midnight chimes acclaim his performance. A political career speedily opens up for him, escalates. Riding on the tide of his newly established authority, Bloom becomes an Alderman of Dublin and addresses the electors, advocating the construction of a tramline to convey cattle across the city to the docks (see p. 81/*122*). He is cheered, greeted, and congratulated by the burgesses and city magnates. The late Lord Mayor Harrington proposes the printing of Bloom's address at public *391* expense and other honours to commemorate him. Bloom replies *602* with an impassioned, exalted speech against ill-defined evils, which is too full of high rhetoric to have sense or logic. It is greeted by prolonged applause.

What follows now is a sequence which fully explores and expands the most secret desires of Bloom for recognition, acceptance, and approval. Everyman's day-dreams of success and triumph are realized in a glowing riot of ceremony and acclamation. Armed forces and watching crowds assemble in the streets.

603
392
A procession representative of the highest civic, ecclesiastical, and commercial authorities precedes the royal attendants and the mantled, sceptred figure of Bloom, who is seated on a richly

604
393
caparisoned milk-white horse. The poor and the rich, the humble and the noble, praise the great Bloom in appropriate idiom. To mark the moment of fulfilment the weather blooms archetypally with a 'sunburst in the north-west'. The Bishop of Down and Connor presents Bloom 'emperor president and king chairman', Leopold the first, and the crowd acclaims him. The Archbishop of Armagh administers the coronation oath and

605
394
(456)
anoints him. 'Bloom assumes a mantle of cloth of gold and puts on a ruby ring.' Bells and fireworks greet his coronation. Peers do homage. Bloom nominates his faithful charger Grand Vizier, repudiates his 'former spouse' (who is forthwith carried away in the Black Maria), and bestows his hand on the blue-robed Princess Selene.

Not content with the paraphernalia of a British coronation, Bloom receives too the heartfelt congratulation of John Howard Parnell as the successor to his famous brother. Thus Bloom's authority and popularity establish him in suprem-

606
395
acy over both nationalist circles, British and Irish, from which he has felt excluded. He is the man with the heroic revolutionary record ('There's the man that got away James Stephens', cf. pp. 56/83 and 134/207) as well as the establishment's epitome. Small wonder that he is in a position to proclaim 'a new era' and to announce the building of the golden city, the new Bloomusalem. The colossal edifice is erected forthwith, at some cost in the lives of interested spectators.

607
The first dissentient note in this triumph is struck by the man in the macintosh, who springs up to claim that Bloom is an impostor whose real name is Higgins (Bloom's mother's maiden

396
name). Bloom imperiously orders him to be shot. He is eliminated, and many other powerful enemies at a nod.

From Bloom the popular, Bloom the triumphant, Bloom the all-powerful, we move to Bloom the generous. He becomes

the dispenser of gifts – gifts which connect with many items that Bloom the businessman and advertising agent has dreamed of, trafficked in, or plugged; ready-made suits, season tickets, the World's Twelve Worst Books. Thus Bloom, the hem of his robe touched by pressing women, is now the loving and loved Father-Giver, tickling babies in the ribs, warmly embracing the afflicted and the aged, playfully joining in the games of boys and girls, wheeling twins in a pram, and doing conjuring tricks for the entertainment of his admirers. He is the great condescending fount of charity and sympathy, kissing the bed-sores of a palsied veteran ('Honourable wounds!'), tripping up a policeman, flirting with a blushing waitress, and even refusing Hynes's proffered repayment of the three-shilling loan.   608
397

Amidst new acclaim from the emotion-choked masses, Bloom proceeds to a new wish-fulfilment in the role of the great Jewish law-giver. The Court of Conscience is opened. Suppliants press for advice and judgement, which Bloom is able to deliver in brief sentences that cut through all complexities and represent the lucid, capsulated wisdom of a Daniel come to judgement. The range of subjects on which advice is sought is wide – fire insurance, bladder trouble, astral physics – but Bloom's omniscient wisdom is equal to the demand. Indeed, Bloom the law-giver quickly merges into Bloom the all-wise, capable of answering puzzle-corner riddles on the spur of the moment. No longer the wheedler or briber, he is now the bribed, or rather the magnanimous and upright rejector of bribes. And next moment, by a logical transference, he is the high-minded moralist and public reformer, proclaiming religious reunion, new and juster distribution of property, compulsory manual labour for all, the grant of electric dish-scrubbers and a general amnesty. He is virtually establishing a new creation. 'Free money, free rent, free love, and a free lay church in a free lay state.' His vast schemes of social regeneration are enthusiastically taken up, in spite of hostility from the conservative element represented by Fr Farley, Mrs Riordan, and Mother Grogan.   609
398
(460)
610
399
400
611

When Nosey Flynn calls for a tune, Bloom assumes another desired persona, that of successful entertainer, quick at throwing off a (secondhand) quip, and declared 'the funniest man on earth'. Finally, in this series of wish-fulfilments realized (each   401
612

one neatly related to the Bloom we already know), Bloom becomes the worshipped idol of women, who commit suicide out of devotion to him.

At this point the tide turns and Bloom begins to be put on the defensive again. Alexander J. Dowie ('Elijah is coming', p. 124/*190*) declares him a hypocrite and worshipper of the Scarlet Woman. The mob becomes hostile. Shopkeepers throw things at him. Bloom is the apologist once more. First he claims it is all a mistake: he is being confused with his brother Henry. Then he calls expert medical evidence. Responding, Buck Mulligan (now Dr Mulligan) pleads Bloom's dementia, epilepsy, elephantiasis, exhibitionism. Mulligan's zeal for the case adds less extenuating details. Dr Madden, Dr Crotthers, and Dr Punch Costello corroborate the medical report with further findings, while Dr Dixon cites him as a 'finished example of the new womanly man' . . . simple, lovable, dear, coy, . . . and, in culmination, about to have a baby.

Universal sympathy is generated by this news, and donations pour in for Bloom's benefit. Aided by the midwife, Mrs Thornton (p. 133/*205*), he realizes another of his most hidden desires, giving birth to eight male children, all handsome, well dressed, highly intelligent and cultured. Bloom is on top again. A voice proclaims him Messiah and Bloom mysteriously accepts the identification. A miracle is called for, and Bloom obliges with extravagant generosity, performing gymnastic wonders, marvellous healings, and brilliant impersonations. The papal Nuncio gives his official stamp to Bloom's Messiahship, tracing his descent from Moses and calling his name Emmanuel. On the wall a dead-hand writes 'Bloom is a cod' (God).

The tide turns again. Three witnesses of what are apparently Bloom's masturbations (A Crab, A Female Infant, and A Hollybush) question him incriminatingly. The hostility has a less menacing air this time. A stagey persecution begins, an armchair 'crucifixion', martyrdom on the cheap. First Bloom sits in the pillory, wearing asses' ears, while children dance around him. Hornblower (who heralded an 'incarnation', p. 70/*107*) announces that Bloom 'shall carry the sins of the people to Azazel' and that he shall be stoned and defiled. Whereupon 'soft pantomime stones' are thrown. Mastiansky and Citron approach (Jewish friends of Bloom in earlier days before his apostacy), wag their beards, and mock Bloom as the false

Messiah. Reuben J. Dodd, Iscariot to Bloom's Christ, comes in carrying the drowned corpse of his son. Brother Buzz places a bag of gunpowder round Bloom's neck and hands him over to the civil power. The Fire Brigade set fire to him. Bloom–Christ, in seamless robe marked IHS, suffers his 'crucifixion'. 'Weep not for me, O daughters of Erin,' he says. The daughters of Erin   *618* response with a litany which, clause by clause, rehearses the   *407* dominant themes of the previous episodes of *Ulysses* (Kidney, Flower, Mentor, Canvasser, etc., i.e. *Calypso*, *The Lotus-Eaters*, *Hades*, *Aeolus*, etc.). Then a choir renders the Alleluia chorus.

In a brief return to actuality we hear the voice of Zoe saying, 'Talk away till you're black in the face,' which follows immediately on the talk of smoking on p. 390/601. But fantasy takes over again. Bloom becomes the stage Irish peasant of a Synge play, pleading to be allowed to go home. Then he tries to enact an even more theatrical getaway, decked out with the hackneyed phrases of the drama ('Life's dream is o'er. End it peacefully').

Zoe brings him back to reality. When he tries the rhetoric in   *619* fact, instead of in fancy, she sees through it sulkily. ('I hate a   *408* rotter that's insincere. Give a bleeding whore a chance.') Bloom relaxes and begins to fondle her, but when he feels for her nipples she calls a halt, naming her price. Bloom is still being too sentimental to talk business. Zoe promises to 'peel off' if   *(471)* he will come in. Bloom goes through the traditional 'reluctances' of the whoring married man, pleading the burden that infidelity brings. Zoe remains unmoved. 'What the eye can't see the heart can't grieve for.' Bloom, beginning to yield, wallows in baby-talk while Zoe, the laughing witch (won by the *masterstroke* in   *409* Beaufoy's story, p. 56/*84*), draws him with the lure of odour,   *620* perfume, paint, and silk. The victims of the enchantress's past, the male brutes who have succumbed to her, are embodied in the drugging reek of proffered sex. There are many whose footing on the earth is unsure in this episode, and Bloom, tripping up on the steps into the brothel, is only just saved from falling. Within, the Circean situation of men transformed into brutes is reflected in many images: the ape's gait, goatee beard, and two-tailed braces of the purple-shirted stranger; 'the spaniel eyes of a running fox'; the lifted, sniffing head with which Bloom follows Zoe into the music room. There Kitty Ricketts sits on   *621* the edge of a table, swinging her leg, and Lynch sits on the   *410* hearthrug, his cap back to front. (For him Bloom's entry is that of 'a ghost'.)

Amidst the trivial chatter of the whores, Stephen stands at the pianola playing perfect fifths (his hat and stick on the pianola) and talking highfalutin drunken nonsense. His state of mind is expressed in the form of a brief dialogue with Lynch's cap,* which mocks his clever-clever generalizations and challenges him to bring his high-sounding chatter about the perfect fifth to some significant conclusion. He tries. The Dominant–Tonic interval is the greatest possible ellipse consistent with the ultimate return to the Tonic as its conclusion and fulfilment. Thus it reflects the journeying of God in making and entering a world intended to return to him, the daily journeying of the sun around the earth, the journeying of a Shakespeare from Stratford to London and back (with all that it produced), the journeying of a commercial traveller (a Bloom, presumably) from home (and Molly) and back to them. These correspondences corroborate those explored in *Scylla and Charybdis*. The earth is the dominant to God's tonic; noon the dominant to midnight's tonic; London the dominant to Stratford's tonic, and the plays he wrote the dominant to Shakespeare's tonic; Bloom's wandering in Dublin the dominant to Molly's tonic. A crucial correspondence, again implicit, is this: As God made His world, then entered it and suffered in it, so Shakespeare made his world, the plays, entering them and suffering in them. Likewise Joyce has made his world, *Ulysses*, entered it and suffered in it as Stephen the son. Here the gramophone outside in the street, blaring out 'The Holy City', keeps alive the theme of the New Jerusalem while reinforcing the theme of God's incarnation in His world and the artist's incarnation in his work. (Note that Bloom's one completely satisfying emotional fulfilment today came with the resolution of dominant into tonic at the end of 'M'appari', pp. 226–7/355–6.)

Florry Talbot, one of the whores, tries to rise to the level of Stephen's intellectual conversation. She has read in the papers that the last day is coming and Antichrist expected. The idea materializes in the mind of Stephen. Newsboys run past with

---

* 'Jewgreek is greekjew.' The coming together of artistic and intellectual Dedalus ('Your absurd name . . . Greek', p. 3/4) and emotional, commercial Bloom, represents a Hellenic–Hebraic synthesis necessary to health and balance in our civilization.

622
411
623
412
(475)

a stop-press edition announcing the safe arrival of Antichrist.
Reuben J. Dodd, Antichrist and Wandering Jew, stumps forward,   413
bearing a boat pole from which hangs the sodden body of his
son. Punch Costello, now a crook-backed hobgoblin, tumbles   624
and somersaults after him. While Florry crosses herself and the
gramophone sings 'Jerusalem', the End of the World materializes in the form of A. E.'s two-headed octopus (p. 135/*209*)
whirling along a tight-rope. Elijah appears. In the accents of   414
Alexander J. Dowie, the American hot-gospeller, he challenges   625
Florry Christ, Stephen Christ, Zoe Christ, and the rest to prepare
for the second advent, realizing their higher selves and taking
a 'buck joyride to heaven' in the strength of his vibration.
Passion turns him black in the face and his idiom changes
to that of the Negro evangelist pleading with 'Mr President' up   *626*
above for the soul of Miss Higgins (Zoe: she has the same name   415
as Bloom's mother) and Miss Ricketts (Kitty). The whores are
touched and, each in turn, Kitty, Zoe, Florry, confesses how
first she fell into sexual sin ('In a weak moment I did what
I did on Constitution hill') in a sequence oddly reminiscent of
the three 'confessions' in *The Waste Land* ('Trams and dusty trees
. . .', etc. – *The Fire Sermon*).

The fact that Zoe should have the surname, 'Higgins', which
was Bloom's mother's maiden name, is at first sight surprising:
but there is a bigger surprise to follow. For the duplication of
the three girls' Christian names here ('Kitty–Kate', 'Zoe–Fanny',
'Florry–Teresa'), just when the girls are coming clean about their   (479)
past, surely conveys that 'Kate', 'Fanny', and 'Teresa' are their
'true' original names. (That Kate should be called Kitty is
natural: that Teresa should choose to practise her profession as
Florry is explicable.) If then Zoe is really Fanny Higgins, she
has exactly the same full name as Bloom's grandmother, Fanny
(*née* Hegarty) who married Julius Higgins (p. 558/*797*–8).

That Bloom, in prostituting Zoe, would as it were be virtually sullying his own female ancestry is a neat moral and artistic
point. The 'Granny', throughout this episode, is the symbol of
Ireland. The prostitution of the nation's womanhood is another
aspect of the sale and betrayal of the nation's human resources
which has been at issue since the opening of the first episode
of the book, where Buck Mulligan offered up the cracked mirror
(Irish art) and the sharp razor (Irish intellect – Stephen or 'Kinch,
the knife-blade'. p. 4/*3*), and then tried to persuade Stephen to

trade his brains for Haines's cash. (For more light on this network of parallels see p. 456/*666*.)

Other encounters from Stephen's day recur, strangely transmuted, to play their part in his vision of the end of the world. His companions of the drinking bout, Dixon, Madden, Crotthers, and company, reappear as the eight Beatitudes. (To judge from their liturgy, 'Beer beef battledog' etc., are the 'B' attitudes.) From the meeting and discussion in the National Library there return Quaker-Lyster, discreetly seeking the light, Best, hymning

627   the divine as a 'thing of beauty', Eglinton, in pursuit of unaes-
416   thetic 'plain truth for a plain man', and A. E., in the shape of his own Mananaan MacLir, bearded, druid-robed, holding a bicycle-pump (p. 136/*210*), and moaning esoteric nonsense.

We return to reality as the 'whistling sea-wind' voice of A. E. becomes the whistling gas-jet in the brothel, which Zoe

628   promptly adjusts. Lynch throws her a fag and with his poker
417   'wand' lifts up her skirt. Bloom smiles 'desirously' at the sight of her bare flesh (she is not wearing knickers) and we leave

(481)   reality once more, this time firmly in the mind of Bloom, as his grandfather Lipoti Virag, 'sausaged into several overcoats' and a macintosh, chutes down through the chimney flue.

Of the three dominant mental interests of Bloom – the sensual-aesthetic, the commercial, and the scientific – Grandpa Lipoti appears to be the ancestral source of the third. He gives voice to that detached vein in Bloom's thinking which dissects analytically. Thus he here sums up the anatomical attractions and limitations of the three whores with a textbook pedantry. He notes the injection mark on Zoe's thigh. Number 2, Kitty, is dismissed as being too skinny under clothes vainly calculated

629   to give her shape; and Bloom is also warned against her bogus
418   mournfulness. Number 3, Florry, has her physical attributes
630   catalogued more relishingly, notably the 'natural pincushions'
419   which she carries before and behind. Bloom dislikes her stye, and Virag delivers a brief lecture on the treatment of styes and warts, ranging from old wives' superstitions ('Contact with a goldring') and herbal remedies ('Wheatenmeal with honey and nutmeg') to amputation. (Such is the incongruous mixture represented by Bloom's 'scientific' knowledge.) This disquisition, Virag's previous assessment of the whores, and the pages that follow, all have notable verbal echoes of pig and poultry

631   breeding ('injection', 'coop', 'fattening', 'stye', 'wart') that reflect

the Circean basis. A few of Bloom's dominant ambitions come together in Virag's reminder of his plans to study 'the religious problem', to square the circle, to win a million with an inspired competition entry, and in his detailed references to women's underwear.

The 'everflying moth' (see p. 409/620) still circles the light as Bloom's thoughts circle the opposite sex. In a 'pig's whisker' Virag comments on the phenomenon of reiterated coition in the animal world. (The quality of Grandpa Virag's English style may be guessed from the quotations from his sexological treatise – 'Some, to example, there are again whose movements are automatic'.) Obviously Bloom's mental assessment of the whores remains predominantly physical (anatomical and sexual) as Virag, gobbling like a turkey, recommends oysters and truffles (dug up by pigs) as aphrodisiacs. For Bloom the bi-valve oyster is a symbol of woman's bivalve construction which leaves her cloven and open underneath, and consequently fearful of creeping or crawling things that might enter her. The sexual and animal thinking is pressed farther in images of heavy-uddered women giving their teats to serpents and lizards. Meanwhile Virag is concerned for the safety of the moth (and of his grandson). He suggests that someone should drive it away from the light by waving a table-napkin. References to 'Gerald' touch two relevant themes – fascination by female clothes and interchange of identity between father and son (see p. 438/648–9). Hence for a brief moment Lipoti is identified with both the moth and Bloom as, reciting a jingle, he flaps against the lampshade, lured himself by the female light and the pretty petticoats.

The more detached, 'scientific' Bloom being thus temporarily out of action, another Bloom asserts himself – Henry, the romantic, mysterious lover with the Saviour's face and the legs of the tenor Mario (see p. 97/149). Then the three personae of the Bloom trinity are held for a moment in a single picture as Bloom the knowledgeable (Virag) stares at the lamp, Bloom the grave studies Zoe's neck, and Bloom the gallant (Henry) turns to the piano. Meantime Stephen, in his mocking way, sees himself as the Prodigal Son, filling his belly with husks of swine. He pictures a penitential return, then an ironically dignified clearing up of his position with Deasy. Florry asks him to sing. He refuses. Lacking voice, he is a 'most finished artist'.

420

632

421

633

(486)

634

422

635 And now an inner dialogue in Stephen's mind is made concrete
423 in the twin figures of Philip Sober, who urges him to take
Deasy's advice and watch his expenditure, and tries indeed to
recollect how much has been spent already, and Philip Drunk,
who pursues wild fancies – the nature of the octave, its reflection of the reduplication of personality (Stephen and the Philips,
the multiplied Blooms) – and tries to remember who it was who
was here before with him and talked about Swinburne. ('Mac
. . . Unmack . . .' It sounds like MacIntosh again.)

Florry wants to know if Stephen is 'out of Maynooth' (the
Roman Catholic Seminary). Out of it now, Stephen quibbles
to himself, and the inner voices mock his cleverness. Zoe tells
of a priest who came to her two nights ago. Virag, in the mind
of Bloom, sees the priest's use of the prostitute as logically
congruous with Catholic teaching about the fallen state of man.
Thoughts on the sex life of religous recall books of 'revelations'
by disillusioned ex-Catholics and the memory of Penrose who
636 had his eyes on Molly (pp. 128/196 and 149/231). From this
424 the mind moves to crude images of primitive sexual invitation
and indulgence. Meantime Zoe remarks that the priest did not
achieve a 'connection'. Virag, now bestialized, with scraggy
neck, moon-calf nozzle, and howling voice, rehearses various
anti-Christian theories – that Jesus had an earthly father, that
he had many fathers, that he never existed, was deformed, was
really Judas Iacchias, and so on.

(489)   The profanity is intensified. Kitty gossips of Mary Shortall
(the Virgin Mary) who got pox and had a child by Jimmy
Pidgeon (the Holy Ghost) that died of convulsions, and the
425 Philips Drunk and Sober press the above correspondences home,
adapting the quotation from Léo Taxil's book which Stephen
637 recalled on Sandymount shore (p. 34/51). Kitty takes off her
hat, and the description of her hair falling about her shoulders
brings back the tone of the *Nausicaa* episode and the picture of
Gerty. She describes the Shortall baby's convulsions as 'loco-
motor ataxy' (of which there is a good deal in this episode).
This 'learned' talk brings from Lynch the comment, 'Three wise
virgins,' and Virag returns to his objectionable theme in the
mind of Bloom. Our Lady was no virgin but a girl who sold
love-philtres. Panther, a Roman centurion, was the father of
Christ. Thus the correspondence between Bloom and the Black
Panther of Haines's nightmare gets a new edge. Bloom is to

emerge as the 'true' father of Stephen. After Stephen's 'cruci-fixion' it is Bloom who raises him up. (Hereabouts we seem to be involved in one of Joyce's perhaps overstretched symbolic networks. A single associative string seems to be threading together the desired whores, the desired Gerty, and the Virgin Mary, and also, through reference to 'wise virgins', the old dears of the Parable of the Plums and therefore Molly herself. See commentary on p. 561/802.)

By this point Virag has become a diabolical figure with a phos-phorescent tongue and the gibbering cries of a baboon. His cries call up a semi-animalized Ben Jumbo Dollard, hairy-nostrilled, shaggy-chested, shock-maned and with padded paws, singing again 'When love absorbs my ardent soul' and being mobbed by the virgin nurses Callan and Quigley (of *Oxen of the Sun*). The words of the 'Voice' ('Hold that fellow with the bad breeches')   426 and Ben Dollard's reply repeat the conversation between Simon and Ben in *The Wandering Rocks* (p. 201/314), already echoed in the counterpoint of *Sirens* (p. 220/344). The fact that neither Bloom nor Stephen was present when they were actually uttered might appear to raise a difficulty; but perhaps the words repre-sent a familiar bantering greeting used by Simon and Ben.

Henry Flower now caresses a severed female head and sings to the lute (as he woos by post the unbodied Martha). Then   638 Virag and Henry depart in bestial guise, Virag sloughing his plumage, cocking his tail, and butting a flybill; Henry giving a last cow's-lick to his hair. Virag unscrews his own head and it is carried out crying 'Quack' of Dr Hy Franks, the pox doctor advertised on the flybill (see p. 126/193).

In the sphere of the actual the talk between Stephen and the girls still runs on the clergy. Florry is sure Stephen is a 'spoiled   427 priest'. Lynch proclaims him a 'Cardinal's son', and immedi-   (491) ately, in his own mind, Stephen is metamorphosed into Cardinal Dedalus, attended by seven dwarf simian acolytes, cardinal sins. A rosary of corks, ending in a corkscrew, hangs round his neck.   639 (The corkscrew is appropriate because of the circumstances of Stephen's fall and 'crucifixion'. He is to share Christ's thirst on the cross. See p. 456/666. 'Thirsty fox.' All this is foreshadowed in *Proteus*. See p. 42/63, 'Come. I thirst, Clouding over. . . . Allbright he falls'., etc.) He sings a rollicking limerick. A multi-tude of midges swarms over him so that he suffers the agony   428 of the damned. He shuffles off, shrinking, into the distance.

640   Bloom is disturbed by the sound of the mystery man going downstairs and taking his waterproof hat from the rack. Hearing his voice, he wonders for a moment whether it might even be Boylan, either compensating for failure with Molly or indulging in a double. As Zoe divides up his chocolate, Bloom, still
429   obsessed by the mystery man, mentally conjures him masonic-
641   ally to depart, and he is heard to go. Bloom relaxes, accepts chocolate, tries to remember whether it is an aphrodisiac, recalls Zoe's account of the priest who failed to achieve satisfaction with her, and decides that he must try truffles to avert the same trouble himself.

Bella Cohen, the whore-mistress, comes in. (She has been letting 'MacIntosh' out.) As she studies Bloom, fanning herself,
430   Bloom's silent reaction is expressed in the form of a colloquy
642   between her fan and himself. The quicker movements of the fan seem like a challenge to him as a married man under a dominating wife. As the fan comes to rest, first against Bella's ear, then against her waist, it seems to offer a tender invitation. Tapping more closely, it asserts a possessive, irresistible claim ('It is fate').

The fan, like the earlier cigarette smoke (p. 369/*580*), wafts Bloom into the fantasy world, and some of the oddest desires and interests buried in the subconscious mind are disinterred. These often perverse appetites and concerns, which make but rare and fitful incursions into the full consciousness of healthy men and women, are here allowed to realize themselves and to acquire the stature of the articulate. By their very nature they cannot assume the coherence or cogency of the fully rational, but they utilize the utterance and imagery of ordinary life and literature in order to assert their own latent potency and buried extravagance. Thus, before the powerful figure of Bella, the
(*495*)   latent femininity and submissiveness of Bloom emerge. Before her exuberance he is a tired, lost, ageing creature, conscious of
431   having missed the bus (or the post) in life. Even now twinges remind him of his fading prime and of the end to which he must come – like his father, who came to rely on his dog Athos to keep his bed warm at night. Richie Goulding, associated today in Bloom's mind with ill-health and failing powers (pp. 224/*350* and 365/*576*), materializes to drive the point home.

The fan directs Bloom along the path of realized submission.
643   He bends down and ties Bella's bootlace, fulfilling a dream long

cherished in youth when he stared in shoe-shop windows.
As ever, the animal imagery recurs, to accumulate intensively   432
at points of crisis. Bella's foot has become a 'hoof', conscious
of its own weight, ready to kick if Bloom bungles. The action
of submission accelerates the metamorphosis. Bloom, with dull-   644
ing eyes and thickening nose, becomes a humble, infatuated
creature, while Bella fully takes over the masculine role, becomes
'Bello', and orders Bloom down on all fours. Bloom sinks down   433
grunting and snuffling at Bella's feet. (From this point Joyce
uses masculine pronouns for Bella, 'Bello', and feminine pronouns for Bloom. I have decided *not* to make use of this device
in the commentary.)

The masculine Bella pins the grovelling Bloom's neck with
her heel and threatens him mockingly. Bloom, enthralled and   645
lamb-like, creeps under the sofa to hide behind the girls' skirts.
The girls plead touchingly for him, and Bella coaxes him gently   434
back with tender talk, only to turn on him violently, threatening
to ride him, slaughter him, and cook him for breakfast. She   646
twists his arm till he screams, slaps his face while he whim-   435
pers, then gets the girls (assisted by Mrs Keogh, the brothel
cook) to hold him down while she sits on his face to smoke a
cigar and talk business. Bloom's ear she uses as an ashtray.   436
She rides him, digging her knees into him and squeezing his   647
testicles. Florry and Zoe clamour for a turn too, but Bella has
other indignities to inflict on him, till Bloom, breaking out in a
sweat, confesses he is now 'Not man . . . Woman.' 'What you
longed for has come to pass,' Bella says, and orders him to shed
his male clothes and don women's. She details his feminine   437
toilette and wardrobe. Bloom ('Martha and Mary') will find the   648
frillies a bit chilly at first, but they bring their consolations.

The recall of Bloom's more specific sexual aberrations,
whether actually realized in the past, whether merely contemplated, or whether indeed only hinted at in the vaguer dormant   (502)
urges within, begins here with what seems to be a literal
memory. Bloom once tried on his wife's clothes as a prank; and
he washed her things to save laundry bills when they were
hard up. Now Bella holds up the picture of Bloom posturing
femininely in the second-hand black undies he bought from
Mrs Miriam Dandrade in the Shelbourne Hotel (p. 132/*203*).
He clipped his rectal hairs and swooned on the bed in an imaginary feminine surrender to imaginary male dominators – the

military, the man of government, the romantic tenor, the
438 youthful lift-boy, and so on. Bloom protests that his friend
649 Gerald gave him his taste for corsets when he took a female
part in a school production of *Vice Versa* (a dramatic version of
Anstey's novel whose theme is interchange of identity between
father and son, see p. 421/*633*). Bella accuses Bloom of assuming
the female even in his mode of sitting on the lavatory. Bloom's
excuse is that this posture was prompted by scientific curiosity
and by a desire not to wet his clothes; whereupon Bella turns
upon him as though he were a dirty animal.

The succeeding clamour from 'The Sins of the Past' recalls
the most outrageous of Bloom's momentarily contemplated
indecencies and his suppressed inclinations rather than his
actual history. The acts recounted are the aberrations of the
650 sexual exhibitionist, the voyeur, and the coprophilist. The culmi-
439 nation is a confession by Bloom which proves to be literally
unspeakable. In response Bella imposes a series of appropriate
penalties on him. They include the performance of menial
651 sanitary duties as a servant-girl during the day, and at night
440 the duties of a well-perfumed whore. Whereupon offers are
invited for the services of Bloom the harlot. The first bid is two
shillings. The auctioneer's lacquey from Dillon's rings for the
offer (p. 195/*304*) and a voice repeats Simon Dedalus's joke,
'One and eightpence too much' (p. 78/*118*). Bella, the auctioneer,
asks for a higher bid, pointing out in detail the high quality of
the stock on offer in terms of soft muscles, tender flesh, and
652 high milk-yield. A mystery bidder, apparently stocking up a
441 Caliph's harem, offers a hundred pounds. Bella welcomes all-
comers and trains Bloom in the techniques of feminine lure.

The next moment she is taunting Bloom for his lack of virility
and for the fact that Boylan, 'a man of brawn', has now taken
over Bloom's marital duties at his home in Eccles Street, and is
making a thoroughly manly job of it. (On brawn see p. 561/*802*.
(507) The anal 'shock of red hair' is the usurping adulterer's dia-
653 bolical tail. See p. 489/*696*.) Thus Bloom's latent feminine
442 inclinations coalesce with his sense of failure as a husband,
and he cries to Molly for forgiveness. But Bella reminds him
that the years have passed since the time when he could re-
establish himself with Molly as easily as that. He has slept away
twenty years like a Rip van Winkle. Seeking to go back and
recapture the Molly of his youth, he finds only the Milly of

today, telling him how old he has grown. Bella remorselessly goes on revealing him to himself. He has followed other women *654* while other men have romped with Molly, desecrating his home. *443* He is a castaway from it, could only go back as 'a paying guest or kept man'. Thus Bloom's sense of being rejected from his own home reaches a peak of intensity in Bella's command that he should sign his will, die, and be buried in the shrubbery jakes. (In view of correspondences that emerge later, pp. 565–7/ *808–11*, it is relevant that the boy murdered by the Jews in Chaucer's *Prioress's Tale* is thrown into a privvy, and that this story has been earlier in Bloom's mind, p. 89/*137*.) *655*

The image is realized. Wailing Jews lament the passing of *444* Bloom. The 'dead' Bloom wakes in the presence of the immortals, in particular of the Nymph who figures in the picture, the 'Bath of the Nymph', which hangs over his bed in Eccles Street (p. 53/*78*). The picture was given away with the Easter number of *Photo Bits*, and the Nymph reminds Bloom here that he found *656* her in evil company, among the crude photographs and the *445* vulgar advertisements of this journal, then framed her and set her above his bed. She recalls how he has studied her naked- *657* ness; worse, what she has heard him say; and worse still, what *446* she has seen, in the Bloom bedroom. Bloom apolgizes for what her sensitive eyes and ears have had to put up with; for the soiled linen, the cracked commode, the one-handled chamber pot.

The bedroom noise of flowing urine materializes in the form of the waterfall at Poulaphouca, near Dublin, over which the yews whisper. And the yews recall a day when Bloom, a boy of sixteen, came to Poulaphouca on a high school excursion. His classmates appear, and Bloom, rejuvenated, remembers *447* how little in those days sufficed to excite him sexually. The *658* yews, the nymph, and the waterfall hint at an unmentionable *448* accusation. Bloom pleads the provocation of youth, the spring, *659* the sight of Lotty Clarke getting ready for bed (seen through papa's opera glasses), and claims that no one saw him. Plainly *(513)* he is guiltily remembering a masturbation. His last excuse is that girls wouldn't satisfy his needs when he was a boy. They thought him too ugly.

The mind moves quickly at this point – to Howth Hill, the sheer drop from cliff to water, the act of throwing the 'Elijah' throwaway off O'Connell Bridge (p. 125/*192*), and the act of

449   suicide as a dramatized fulfilment of the young Elijah Bloom's
      rejection by others. The rejection theme brings back Councillor
      Nannetti who this morning snubbed Bloom (p. 100/154) and is
660   now sailing to England, 'alone on deck' (p. 259/408), but quoting
      Robert Emmet's last words, as studied by Bloom in Lionel
      Marks's antique shop window (p. 238/375).

The Nymph now speaks as one of the sculptured goddesses
Bloom examined in the museum (p. 165/257), pure, sexless,
ashamed of Bloom's prying curiosity. The image of the stone-
450   cold female buttocks clashes with what we hear now from
      remote voices still in the world of reality, Kitty, Florry, Lynch,
      and Zoe, joking about a cushion hot from Florry's behind. Bloom
661   balances the reality, the heat from women's 'divaricated thighs',
      with the unreal notion of stone-cold chastity, this time repre-
      sented by remembered nuns. He moves. A button bursts on the
451   back of his trousers, and reality is victorious over unreality in
662   more ways than one. The pure, idealized nymph acquires a
      large moist stain upon her robe, and Bloom asserts his proper
      masculinity in response to this evidence of her fleshly frailty.
      She flees and, in the form of the sculptured statue from the
      museum, cracks wide open to emit the stench of living flesh.
452   Bloom's full virility is recovered, and more. He scoffs at the
      departing nymph, then turns on Bella to mock her worn flesh
663   and double chin and superfluous hairs. He is not a screw
      propeller and cannot serve her turn. Thus the imaginary
      colloquy between Bloom and Bella ends in an equality of mutual
      recrimination.

The full return to reality is marked by Bella's question, 'Which
of you was playing the dead march from Saul?' which follows
almost immediately on her entry line, 'My word! I'm all of a
mucksweat' (p. 430/641).

453   Bloom recovers his potato from Zoe, who hid it in the top of
664   her stocking. Bella Cohen asks for payment and Stephen puts
454   down money for the three of them. Zoe and Kitty get their half-
665   sovereigns. Bloom pays for himself and gives back to Stephen
455   the excess money he has paid. Meantime Stephen's drunken
(520) ramblings revive the riddle of the fox burying its grandmother
      from this morning's lesson (p. 22/32), the French title of *Hamlet*
      from the talk in the library (p. 153/239), and the theme of the
      fallen Lucifer from the *Portrait* and from *Proteus* (p. 42/63).
456   Bloom takes over the care of Stephen's money which he is in

danger of losing. Stephen, identified with the fox because he is   *666*
hunted (the Shakespearean 'Christfox', p. 159/247), guesses that
the fox killed its own grandmother as he 'killed' his mother.
Georgina Johnson, his favourite whore, is likewise 'dead and
married'. (The broken glasses theme returns, as it does on p.
111/171, taking us back to the *Portrait*.) She, too, is unfaithful
to her bard, making the 'beast with two backs' at midnight.

The clustering of strong symbolic themes on these last few
pages inevitably suggests new parallels. Lynx-eyed (panther-
eyed) Stephen strikes a lucifer match. The striking of a match,
weighted with significance in *Aeolus* (pp. 107/165 and 115/177),
becomes momentous (another lucifer match) in *Ithaca* (p. 547/
781), indeed a veritable masterstroke by Match'em Bloom
('As God made them He matched them', p. 306/487). At the
same time the direct transition in Stephen's mind from the fox
burying its grandmother, which it probably killed, to the fact
that Georgina Johnson, his favourite whore, is 'dead and
married', suggests a correspondence between Georgina Johnson
and Stephen's grandmother which would match the correspondence, already firmly established, between Zoe Higgins and
Bloom's grandmother (p. 415/626), though Stephen's grandmother was Christina Goulding (*née* Grier) (p. 558/798). To fill
out the pattern we need to recall the feminized 'christine' of
Mulligan's mock offering in episode I (p. 3/1). The betrayal of
the nation's womanhood represented by prostitution (often to
British customers like Privates Compton and Carr) is on a par
with the trading of its art and its brain-power. Mulligan's words,
in offering up 'the genuine christine: body and soul and blood
and ouns', are seed and summary of much that has followed
them. Indeed the fourfold offering may well represent the main
characters, Boylan, Stephen, Molly and Bloom. Georgina herself,
it should be noted, has escaped betrayal and burial at the
eleventh hour. She has been redeemed by Mr Lambe from   *457*
London, who has taken away the sins of the world.

Zoe takes Stephen's hand to read his palm, and sees courage   *667*
there. Stephen denies it, Lynch too. Stephen has only 'sheet
lightning courage' (see p. 323/515–6). When Lynch slaps Kitty's   *458*
behind, using the words 'Pandy bat', Stephen's thoughts go back
again to the memorable episode in the *Portrait* when Fr Dolan   *(523)*
punished him for breaking his glasses and he appealed success-
fully to Fr Conmee for justice. Zoe pronounces Stephen's hand

459 a 'woman's hand', thereby adding to his links with Bloom.
668 Bloom has his hand read next and one of Zoe's readings strikes home. 'Henpecked husband. That wrong?' Black Liz, the hen, reappears from *The Cyclops* (p. 259/*408*) to take her place amid the abundant pig and poultry imagery of the stye and coop. The weal on Bloom's palm recalls an accident of twenty-two years ago when he was sixteen – as Stephen, now twenty-two, has been reminded of an accident sixteen years ago. Thus history 'moves to one great goal'.

Zoe, it seems, has enchanted Bloom again. As she whispers
460 and giggles with Florry, leaving him once more outside the
669 circle, he is carried away into a fantasy of exclusions in which his grossest fears of what Molly and Boylan have today been up to are realized in concrete form. A hackney car passes with Boylan and Lenehan sprawling on the side-seats (while Zoe and Florry, whispering and giggling together, become Lydia Douce and Mina Kennedy gazing over the cross-blind of the Ormond: their giggles, too, excluded Bloom). Boylan is boasting of his afternoon's fun to Lenehan. He has been 'plucking a turkey', and offers his finger, still smelling of Molly's
461 vagina, to Lenehan's nose. Bloom, meanwhile, is reduced to the level of a footman, and worse, in his own home. Boylan, entering, 'hangs his hat smartly on a peg of Bloom's antlered head'. Bloom's role as hat-holder to home-breakers Menton (p. 95/*146*) and Parnell (pp. 531/*754* and 535/*761*) achieves here its most comic and humiliating expression, as he is metamorphosed into a hat-stand and his cuckold's horns into hanging pegs. Boylan's entry into his home, so frequently imaged in Bloom's mind today (pp. 55/*81*; 225/*353*; and 232/*364*), is a focal moment around which cluster other experiences of exclu-
670 sion. Humbly Bloom shows Boylan up to Madam Tweedy, who receives her visitor in her bath. Marion and Boylan give Bloom
462 permission to watch through the keyhole while Boylan 'goes through her a few times'. The coition is described by Misses Kennedy and Douce, who wallow in its extravagances. That Molly rides a cock horse (cf. p. 436/*646*) is Breadwinner Bloom's Banbury cross. (He fed Banbury cakes to the gulls, p. 125/*192*.)
671 Above the 'real' laughter of the whores we hear the voices of Molly and Boylan at the moment of orgasm. Bloom, wildly
(528) excited, both wants to see and wants not to see. His 'Show! Hide! Show!' brings together two Shakespearean moments – the

Weird Sisters' 'Show! Show! Show!' when the full irony of destiny is revealed to sonless Macbeth in the vision of the royal lineage of Banquo (Act IV, scene i) and Macbeth's earlier couplet,

'Away and mock the time with fairest show;
False face must hide what the false heart doth know.'

(Act II, scene ii)

The fusion of associations from numerous experiences of exclusion and treachery give a characteristic power and inten- 463 sity to the text. Lynch quotes Hamlet's words about holding 'the mirror up to nature', and both Stephen and Bloom, gazing into the mirror, are identified with a cuckolded Shakespeare, who adapts Goldsmith and crows, caponlike, another betrayal (Othello choking his Desdemona, 'Oldfellow' his 'Thursday-momun').

Bloom returns to reality to ask the girls what they are laughing at. Zoe tells him that he will learn 'before you're twice married and once a widower', and forthwith Bloom mentally sees Mrs Dignam, widowed, with her orphan children like a 'brood of cygnets', and Shakespeare raging, almost incoherently, that 'None wed the second but who killed the first' ('Weda 672 seca . . .' See *Hamlet*). Shakespeare's face becomes Martin 464 Cunningham's (for in the funeral cab this morning Bloom thought how Martin's sympathetic and intelligent look was 'like Shakespeare's face', p. 79/120). Then, logically enough, Mrs Cunningham, whose drunken behaviour Bloom likewise pondered this morning (p. 80/120), becomes the Merry Widow who has managed to finish off her husband at last.

Stephen claims that the horns of the righteous shall be exalted ('*Et exaltabuntur . . .*'), and moves mentally from cuckold's horse to bull's horns, recalling how his 'grandoldgrossfather' Dedalus equipped Pasiphae with a metal shell in the shape of a cow so that, sitting in it, she could indulge her perverted lust for the bull.* His talk of perversions brings a rebuke from Bella, (530) whose traffic is respectably orthodox, and Lynch explains that Stephen is fresh from Paris and perhaps not mentally acclimatized yet. Zoe begs him to play the Frenchman, and he obliges, 465

---

* In the Joycean canon generally the metal cow made by Dedalus to serve the lusts of Pasiphae and the bull is the artificial Ireland created by Irish artists to prostitute their country for the pleasure of the English.

673   advertising Parisian sexual entertainments in English with a
French syntactical flavour. The ingenious perversions he describes reduce Bella to hysterical laughter and the girls to a
466   demand for more. Whereupon Stephen recalls his dream of last
674   night – the water-melon, the street of harlots, the red carpet
spread (p. 39/58–9). Bloom, the promised inviting stranger,
approaches Stephen to fulfil the dream; but Stephen runs away
from his destiny. He flees the *Pater*, whether God, fatherland,
Simon, home, Bloom, in his pursuit of freedom. Hunted, he
gives the hunting cry, and Simon Dedalus swoops down on him
467   like a buzzard.
   The image of the hunt materializes. The fox, the hunted
Christfox, the fox who has killed and buried his grandmother,
is chased by the staghounds, the huntsmen, and the hunts-
women. There is clamour from bookies and touts in a noisy
675   crowd and the chase merges into the Ascot Gold Cup race in
which a riderless dark horse (Bloom) leaves the bucking horses
well behind, not only Boylan's *Sceptre* but also the favourite
Cock of the North, ridden by Garrett Deasy, a figure symbolizing
468   both the absurdity ('plastered with postage stamps') and the
physical benefits (in cash and food, 'coins of carrots') of pedantry
(534) and conformity.
676   Privates Compton and Carr, with Cissy Caffrey, pass by in
the street below, singing '*My Girl's a Yorkshire Girl*'. For Stephen
the noise in the street recalls how he identified God with a
'shout in the street' in his discussion with Mr Deasy (p. 28/42).
Zoe puts twopence in the pianola. Its lights go on and it begins
469   to purr a waltz rhythm. (Professor Goodwin is recalled, by
Stephen presumably, tottering to the piano as he did at the
concert remembered by Simon Dedalus and Ben Dollard in the
677   Ormond, p. 220/345.) The pianola launches into '*My Girl's a
Yorkshire Girl*'. Stephen seizes Zoe and they waltz round the
room. (Zoe told Bloom she was 'Yorkshire born', p. 408/619.)
Florry and Bella push the table back. (In Stephen's mind
Professor Maginni makes an impressive dancer's entrance, beautifully attired for an exhibition performance of professional
agility. See pp. 181/282 and 194/382.) Appropriately, in view of
what is to come, the pianola sings of the two young fellows
'talking about their girls, sweethearts they'd left behind'.
678   Under the direction of Maginni a Dance of the Hours is
470   performed by the Hours themselves, and Stephen is swept into

a delirious series of gyrations with Zoe, Florry, and Kitty in   471
turn. There is a general exchange of partners. Stephen takes   679
up his ashplant and performs solo in the midst. The voice of   472
Simon warns him of the wild ways of his mother's ancestry,   680
the Gouldings, but Stephen continues his 'dance of death'.
As his performance reaches its climax, images whirl around
him, merging one into another in a compressed, scarcely disen-
tanglable linguistic swirl in which animals and lameness play
a conspicuous part. (Many of the images, and the mode of their
assembly here, relate back to episode 10, *The Wandering Rocks*
– the calmer, slower, noonday 'dance' about the centre of   473
Dublin.) Finally, Stephen totters to a standstill to see the emaci-   (539)
ated figure of his dead mother rising through the floor, while   681
Buck Mulligan, fully metamorphosed into a clown, repeats his
mocking remark that she is 'beastly dead'.

Mulligan's mockery is intensified into extremes of contempt
and farcicality. The Mother, recalling how on her deathbed   474
Stephen sang for her the song '*Who goes with Fergus*?' (see
pp. 8/9 and 497/702), is transformed into an epitome of   682
reproachful womanhood, exuding pathos, sentimentality, and
piety. Stephen's latent remorse, guilt, and defensiveness are
realized and rendered articulate. The weight of the Mother's
love, possessiveness, and piety proves too heavy for Stephen's
rebellious spirit. Panting with the tension of inner conflict,
he turns on his mother with crude abuse as she begs him to
repent from fear of hell. And when she threatens him with the   475
vengeance of God, his assaulted spirit, raging with resistance,
screams out an obscenity. The scream enters the world of reality,
disturbing Bloom at the window, and Stephen sums up his
creed, '*Non serviam*', a phrase from Fr Arnall's sermon in the
Portrait touching Lucifer's fall through the sin of pride – 'the
single thought conceived in an instant: *non serviam: I will not
serve*. That instant was his ruin.'

All is not over yet. The Mother prays desperately to the Sacred
Heart, while Stephen shrieks out his rejection. In the agony of   683
death she prays for the divine mercy on him, and he lifts his
ashplant and smashes the chandelier, crying *Nothung*. At this
moment of supreme crisis in the pattern of Stephen's day,
the Wagnerian cry, echoing Siegfried's shout as he forges the
sword of deliverance, and the 'stage-direction' about 'ruin of all
space, shattered glass and toppling masonry' (see pp. 20/28 and

36/54), together hint at a cosmic cataclysm in which the heroic
476   individuality of the artist is asserted even against the light.

Lynch tries to restrain Stephen; Bella calls for the police;
(542)   Stephen flees from the room, and a general stampede ensues.
Bella holds Bloom back and demands payment for the broken
477   lamp. Bloom, with his usual presence of mind, assesses the
684   damage coolly and moderately. He is a calming influence and
reminds Bella that it would not be good business to involve the
police and create a scandal over a Trinity student – since
students are good customers. He also makes a masonic sign,
hints at Stephen's influential connexions, and reminds Bella that
she, too, has a student son. Thus Bloom the diplomatist tries
478   every weapon in the smoothing-over armoury, and then puts
down a shilling to cover the damage.

Bloom leaves, passing through the cluster of whores on the
685   doorstep. A hackney car arrives, bringing custom in the shape
of Corny Kelleher and two companions, and the girls prepare
to ply their trade. Bloom's desire not to be recognized and his
consequent furtive getaway are fantastically inflated, so that
686   Bloom becomes the quarry of a hunting pack which seems to
479   include almost everyone who today has in any way made him
feel alien, unwanted, insecure, unsure of himself.

At the corner of Beaver Street, beneath the scaffolding (the
very site of Bloom's disgraceful blunder with the plasterers'
bucket, p. 367/578), Bloom catches up with Stephen to find him
in the centre of a quarrelling knot of people, and a brawl seems
imminent. In his chase Stephen has somehow got involved with
Cissy Caffrey, loitering along because her two escorts, Privates
Carr and Compton, have lingered behind her to relieve themselves. Catching up with Cissy again, the soldiers are spoiling
for a fight with the interfering student. Stephen, still drunk,
seems unaware of danger, and parries all questions with high-
687   falutin intellectual mockery.
480   The reader not only hears the actual dialogue, he also sees,
through the mind of Stephen, the various absurd attitudes that
the speakers adopt exaggerated and rendered concrete. Thus,
when the soldiers' irrational aggressiveness asserts itself, Lord
Tennyson appears in Union Jack blazer and cricket flannels to
proclaim 'Theirs not to reason why'.
481   Bloom pushes his way through the crowd and, his wits about
688   him as usual, addresses Stephen as 'professor' for the benefit

of the onlookers. The whores are so impressed that, in Stephen's ears at lest, they exchange the idiom of the street for that of the lecture-room. Meantime Stephen has used an unfortunate metaphor to express the urgent need within his brain to rebel against all authoritarianism that seems to fetter him ('But in here it is I must kill the priest and the king'). The soldiers' hackles rise against what seems like an insult to the king and, in Stephen's mind, Edward VII makes his appearance, complete with masonic regalia and plasterer's bucket, and mouthing hackneyed slogans. (Thus an 'Edward King', if not exactly that of Milton's *Lycidas*, has risen again. See p. 21/30.) Stephen, challenged, tries to be clever-clever about patriotism, and the soldiers are correspondingly more irritated. Bloom does his best to appease their anger, apologizing for Stephen's drunkenness, pleading that he is a gentleman and a poet. The soldiers are not impressed. Stephen seems to be content to annoy them. He is a green (Irish) rag to a bull (John Bull). (Kevin Egan comes to mind, in the role of matador, repeating his abuse of Queen Victoria referred to on p. 36/53.) (548) 482 689 483 690 (550)

The word 'green' has given a direction to the quarrel. A bawd shouts for red and the king, and the citizen materializes to revile in verse the English dogs. Stephen (and Bloom) sees the absurdity of the nationalistic and revolutionary poses as well as of the British *imperium*. Hence the martyred Croppy Boy is burlesqued alongside the demon barber–executioner Rumbold, who hangs him. 'Horhot ho hray hor hother's hest' is the Croppy Boy's tongueless attempt to quote the second line of – 484 691 485

'I went through the churchyard one day in haste
'And forgot to pray for my mother's rest.'

This is part of the boy's confession in the ballad (see p. 233/367). The failure to pray for Mother is, of course, Stephen's archetypal sin. The protruding tongue links the Croppy Boy with the crucified Sambo of p. 269/426, as the violent erection links him with the executed martyr of p. 250/393. Rumbold disembowels the martyr and cries, 'God save the king,' while the king himself, rattling his bucket, dances and sings contentedly. 692

The soldiers continue their angry cross-examination. Stephen cannot take them seriously – nor anything they stand for. The spirit of oppressed and injured Ireland materializes in the form

of 'Old Gummy Granny' (see p. 12/15) to show that he cannot
486 take their opponents seriously either. Private Carr begins to tug
693 at his belt menacingly; Private Compton encourages him. The
threatening atmosphere is concretized in the mutually hostile
487 figures of Major Tweedy (see p. 46/67) and the citizen. Bloom
(554) tries to make peace, recalling occasions when the Irish fought
alongside the English. But the soldiers prepare for action;
massed bands play rival patriotic tunes; Cissy Caffrey is overjoyed to be the cause of a fight; whereupon (in Stephen's mind)
694 the fracas assumes the quality of a burlesque knightly jousting
488 before the ladies. Bloom is still desperately trying to prevent a
blow from being struck by urging Cissy Caffrey to come clean.
(Mentally he sees her as woman the sacred life-giver, for she
has Stephen's safety in her hands.) But Cissy plays out the
drama of the injured woman in need of protection.

Stephen's imagination takes its cue from Cissy and theatrically inflates the situation at the moment of imminent impact
by focusing upon it the traditional imagery and literary paraphernalia of tragedy and cataclysm; brimstone fires, clashing
695 armies, darkness, earthquake, and, in farcical contrast, the
hysterical fright of society ladies who lift their skirts above their
heads. Thus the flavour of epic conflict, of personal embarrassment, even of cosmic disaster is added to the crisis moment.
Most significant of all are the Crucifixion parallels: the sun is
darkened, the earth trembles, the dead 'arise and appear to
489 many'. Finally a Black Mass is celebrated on the naked belly of
Ireland's poor but fertile body, Mina Purefoy ('pure faith') by
Fr Malachi O'Flynne (usurper Mulligan priestified) and the
696 Reverend Hugh. C. Haines Love, a composite of the sexual,
cultural, and property-owning usurpers – Boylan, Haines, and
the Rev. Hugh C. Love (p. 201/315). The betrayer's carrotty
diabolical tail (pp. 3/1 and 441/652) is here again. ('Htengier
490 Tnetopinmo . . .' Liturgy in reverse.)

Old Gummy Granny, a pantomime exponent of Irish patriotism, and a caricature of the old woman who brought the milk
this morning to the Martello tower (p. 12/15), urges Stephen to
resist the soldiers to the point of martyrdom, while in the realm
of actuality Bloom and Lynch try to drag Stephen away. There
is another explicit parallel with the Crucifixion at this point
for when Lynch forsakes him Stephen identifies him as Judas,
underlining the correspondence between himself and Christ.

(The correspondence is reinforced similarly on p. 503/707.) Stephen stays, for the conflict with the soldiers has assumed the comic status of a dialectical contest, 'a feast of pure reason'.   491 Accordingly Private Carr knocks him down, and immediately   697 the phantom of Major Tweedy calls the firing squad to salute, the execution accomplished. The crowd, divided in their sym-   (558) pathies between Stephen and the soldiers, begin to argue, claw at each other, and spit. Bloom pushes them back. Two policemen   492 appear and ask questions. Bloom boldly puts the blame on the   698 soldiers.

Corny Kelleher arrives, 'a death wreath in his hand', appar-   493 ently ready to offer his professional services as an undertaker. Bloom appeals to him, identifying Stephen; Kelleher squares   699 the police with a we've-all-been-young-once approach, and they go. Kelleher and Bloom lie to each other in order to explain   494 each his presence in the brothel area. Their explanations very   700 properly provoke a horse-laugh from the horse standing with   495 Kelleher's car. Having inspected Stephen's condition and found   701 'no bones broken' (Christ's condition on the Cross), Kelleher   496 mounts the car and is driven away.

Bloom returns to Stephen and tries to waken him, calling his name. In response Stephen groans and mutters incoherently. In his words the 'Black Panther' of Haines's nightmare, already associated with the saving and intruding 'divine' Bloom (see pp. 4/3; 337/539; and 425/637), merges with the 'vampire' of his poem composed on the beach this morning (see pp. 40/60 and 109/168). The succeeding broken phrases of verse come   702 from Yeats's 'Who goes with Fergus?' Mulligan quoted this poem in the song this morning and it stirred Stephen because it was the song he sang to his mother, at her request, when she lay on her deathbed (see pp. 8/9 and 474/681). Bloom's paternal   497 solicitude is stirred by what he sees and hears. He bends down and unbuttons Stephen's waistcoat to help him to breathe. Stephen stretches, sighs, and curls up. Bloom stands watching tenderly over him and gripping the ashplant. (The ashplant is a symbol of the Cross. Stephen took it up when left alone by the others in the dance of death, p. 472/679. Later, when we learn that Bloom's second name is Paula, p. 594/852, another strand is added to the symbolism here, for St Paul was the apostle to the gentiles and he was present, looking on, at the stoning of the first martyr, Stephen. In *The Cyclops* episode the citizen mocked Bloom specifically as a 'new apostle to the gentiles', p. 273/432.) Stephen's face reminds Bloom of Mrs Dedalus. He muses on the broken phrases which seem to him to hint at love for some girl, a Miss Ferguson, he wrongly conjectures. The best thing that could happen to him, Bloom thinks. The phrases of the masonic ritual come to his murmuring lips.

(565)   Paternal longing rises within him and the figure of his lost son, Rudy, appears before him, eleven years old as he would have been had he lived, and highly idealized in delicacy of
703   feature, studiousness, cheerfulness, and charm. The 'white lambkin' establishes him as the paschal victim. The home-rule Son will yet arise in the north-west.

Part III

Chapter 16

Eumaeus

Returning at last to Ithaca, Homer's Odysseus comes in the disguise of a beggar to the hut of the swineherd Eumaeus. He fabricates a complex false story to account for his coming, but when Telemachus arrives, Ulysses reveals himself, and father and son are united. Together they plan to destroy the suitors who have so long plagued Penelope.

Though the shelter near Butt Bridge plainly corresponds to Eumaeus's hut and Skin-the-Goat roughly parallels Eumaeus, there is again no exact person-for-person and event-for-event correspondence between this episode and Homer. The parallel to the false account of his voyage which Odysseus invents is the boasting reminiscence of the sailor, Murphy, whom Stephen and Bloom encounter in the shelter. But the self-revealing of Bloom to Stephen and Stephen to Bloom (ill-understood as it is by Bloom in many respects) echoes the reunion between Odysseus and Telemachus.

Eumaeus, the first episode of Part III, parallels *Telemachus*, the first episode of Part I. The technique of presentation here is what Stuart Gilbert calls 'Narrative (old)', whereas the technique of *Telemachus* is called 'Narrative (young)'. *Telemachus* is concerned with the three young men, this episode much more with older men. *Telemachus* takes place in the early morning light, this episode in the hour after midnight. *Telemachus* has a vigorous, alert, concise style: this episode has a flabby, weary, rambling style, aptly suggestive of the vague, sleepy, inert mood of the early hours. Syntax and sentences trail on inconclusively, lose themselves, or feebly recover. The discipline of alert sobriety is withdrawn.

Bloom helps Stephen to compose himself. Stephen asks for a (569) drink, and Bloom suggests that they go to the cabman's shelter

705   near Butt Bridge. They walk into Amiens Street, but there is no
       sign of a taxi-cab except for one waiting outside the North Star
       Hotel, which ignores Bloom's attempts to hail it. They saunter
502   on, Bloom slightly incommoded by the loss of a back button
       from his trousers. A Tramways sand-strewer passes, and Bloom
       recounts his narrow escape from one earlier in the evening
706   (p. 355/567). Where Stephen's thoughts turn towards such
       subjects as Ibsen, Bloom's are more concerned with the smell
       from Rourke's city bakery and their jingling advertisements.
           Though the companionship is thus a union between artist–
       intellectual and the more sensual man of commerce, neverthe-
       less Bloom takes the opportunity to give sensible moral advice
707   to his young protégé on the subject of drink and whoring, and
503   the dangers thereof. Bloom observes that the police tend to look
       after the respectable middle-class areas and neglect the more
       dangerous slums. He dislikes the practice of equipping soldiers
       with small arms. Quite apart from the dangers of physical
       violence, he dwells on the financial disasters that debauchery
       brings, and notes that Stephen's roistering companions deserted
       him – all but one. And that one Judas, Stephen observes of
       Lynch (cf. p. 490/696).
708   Passing a watchman's brazier and sentry-box, Stephen recog-
       nizes the watchman as a one-time friend of his father's, Gumley
       (one of the 'Invincibles' – see pp. 112/172 and 264/418), but he
       avoids a meeting. Someone else, in the distance, calls out to
       Stephen and for a moment Bloom is apprehensive of a night
504   hold-up; but it turns out to be 'Lord' John Corley, the dissolute
709   son of Inspector Corley. He claims to be down on his luck and
       begs help. (Corley appears in Dubliners: 'Two Gallants'.) Stephen
       tells him that tomorrow or the next day there will be a job
710   going at Dalkey in Mr Deasy's school. Corley thinks Stephen is
505   well-off and presses for more tangible help. Stephen digs into
711   his pockets and is about to give Corley what he thinks are
       pennies. Corley himself points out that they are half-crowns and
(574) Stephen, more generous than he had intended to be, lends
       him one.
           Bloom meanwhile observes the interview critically from a
712   distance, hanging about near the watchman's brazier. Gumley
506   himself is asleep. Stephen rejoins Bloom, hands on Corley's
       request that Bloom should ask Billsticker Boylan to give him a
       job as a sandwich-board-man, admits that he has been touched

for half a crown, and suffers a cross-examination from Bloom   713
on where he is going to spend the night and why he left his
father's house. 'To seek misfortune,' Stephen replies.

Bloom, who has been with Simon Dedalus at the funeral
today, remarks on Simon's pride in his son. Having observed   507
how Mulligan and Haines seemed determined to get Stephen
off their hands at Westland Row station, he sees no future
in Stephen's going back to Sandycove, and thinks he would be
better advised to return home: but the image of home as he   714
last knew it, which this suggestion brings to life in Stephen's
mind, is both sordid and unattractive. Bloom, however, points
out that Mulligan is doing no good to him, though looking
after himself pretty well, and indeed may well be suspected of
having dropped some drug into Stephen's drink earlier in the
evening. Determined as ever to be fair, Bloom adds a word
about Mulligan's versatility, his medical prospects, and his
bravery in rescuing the drowning man. He is nevertheless   715
baffled by Mulligan's behaviour, and suspects him of trying to
pick Stephen's brains. Stephen's expression does not make clear
whether he has been duped by his companion or is fully aware
what Mulligan is about.   508

They pass a group of Italians chattering round an ice-cream   (577)
car, and then enter the cabman's shelter. The keeper of it is
reputed to be Fitzharris, one of the former 'Invincibles' known
as 'Skin-the-Goat' (see p. 112/172). They sit down under the   716
curious stares of the other customers and Bloom prevails upon
Stephen to have a coffee and a bun. Bloom discourses on the
beauty of the Italian language, heard outside the hut. Stephen
deflates this theme. The Italians in question were haggling over   509
money: sounds are impostures, names meaningless.   717

A red-haired, somewhat drunken individual, probably a
sailor, who has already betrayed special interest in Stephen and
Bloom, breaks into their conversation to ask what Stephen's
name is. Hearing it, he asks whether Stephen knows Simon
Dedalus. 'I've heard of him,' Stephen says. Encouraged by this   718
apparent ignorance, the sailor, who is an inveterate liar, em-
barks on reminiscences of Simon Dedalus's achievements as a
marksman, dramatizing one of them impressively – a feat the   510
sailor claims to have seen him perform in Stockholm when   719
touring with Hengler's Royal Circus. This is a tissue of false-
hoods. In spite of Simon Dedalus's rumoured marksmanship

and wanderings, *he* is not the Ulyssean father of Telemachus–
Stephen.

(580)   The sailor identifies himself as D. (W.) B. Murphy of Carrigaloe,
Queenstown Harbour, where his wife is waiting for him – and
he has not seen her for seven years. Bloom images the traditional
sentimental sailor's return after long voyaging, to find his wife
720   before the fire with a new 'husband' and baby. (The dream, as
amusingly presented here, seems to owe most to the story of
Tennyson's *Enoch Arden*. It is one more fanciful projection of his
511   own dilemma. The theme of the Wanderer's Return recurs frequently in this episode. See pp. 520/736 and 530/753.) The sailor
also announces that he came up this morning at eleven o'clock
on the three-master *Rosevean* from Bridgwater. This is the ship
Stephen stared at when walking the beach this morning (p.
42/64). It has brought a cargo of bricks.

Urged on by the cabin-keeper and his customers, the sailor
721   tells several tall stories of his travels, touching eventually on
the man-eaters of Peru, and exhibiting a postcard which pictures
512   Bolivian Indians. Bloom ponders the Chilean name and address
722   on the back of the card and mentally queries Mr Murphy's
identity. Then the talk of travel excites his modest *wanderlust* to
dreams of voyaging to London by sea for the benefit of health
723   and for the pleasure of calling in at South coast ports *en route*,
and then renewing his acquaintance with the metropolis.
Dreams rove over the possibility of a concert tour of English
seaside resorts, with Molly heading an all-star Irish cast ('the
513   Tweedy–Flower grand opera company'). The difficulty would
be to find someone to handle the necessary publicity.

Next moment Bloom the businessman is wondering why new
routes between England and Ireland are not being opened up
to meet the travelling needs of the public. It seems to him that
724   there must be a vast latent demand for holiday travel if only
it could be provided at an economic rate – travel within Ireland
as well as without. The tourist industry is in its infancy, he
believes, wondering whether traffic creates routes, or vice-versa,
or both.

725   The seaman recalls the sight of oriental paper pellets which,
514   when dropped in water, would burgeon into ships and houses,
and of a knifing in a Trieste brothel. The mention of cold steel
726   leads to an accidental conversational reference to the Phoenix
Park murders which both Stephen and Bloom regard as rash in

the present company. (See p. 112/172.) But the indiscretion is swallowed up in general silence and in Skin-the-Goat's total inscrutability.

Bloom, his mind drawn back as ever to its pole, asks the seaman if he has been to Gibraltar. It appears not, for he answers evasively, refusing to be drawn further. 727
515

Bloom falls to wool-gathering about the sea, its immensity (585) and its strange appeal. As he gets wearier, his ruminations assume an ever looser, less consequential, less compact form. His thought drifts, flounders – from the notion that because the sea is there some people have just *got* to seek it again and again, to the notion that in many respects people manage to reserve 728 the difficult or unpleasant things for others (hell, for example), and thence to the notion that lifeboatmen, harbourmasters, and their like, do a thoroughly worthy job, and funds for them ought to be supported.

Meanwhile the seaman tells of his son, Danny, who left a comfortable job in a draper's shop in Cork to run off to sea. Then, having cause to open his shirt and scratch himself, he 516 displays his chest, elaborately tattooed with representations of 729 an anchor, a figure 16 (the number of this episode?), and a young man's face. And so to the story of Antonio, the tattooer (and Greek), whose portrait it is, and whose skill was such that the frowning face changes to a smiling face when Seaman Murphy pulls the skin in a special way. This party trick excites general admiration. 730

A street-walker peers in round the door of the shelter. Bloom, 517 in some embarrassment, recognizes the half-mad whore of the lane whom he saw this afternoon on Ormond Quay (p. 238/374) and who, when he formerly made use of her professional services, revealed a dangerous knowledge of Molly, and also incidentally asked to do his washing for him. So (not for the first time) to the theme of washing one's beloved's dirty 731 linen.

To Stephen Bloom remarks how astonishing it is that any man will risk his health by commerce with a woman so diseased: but Stephen has not noticed her and refuses to moralize on this subject. The trading of bodies is less evil in his eyes than trading in souls – as the Church does (for that, presumably, is his implication). Bloom, who is all for the licensing and compulsory medical inspection of brothels, takes up Stephen's point 732

518   about souls. He believes in the brain, for its physical nature has
been established and its existence evidenced in human inventions, but the soul? Stephen tries to concentrate, and quotes
the scholastic definition of the soul as simple, incorruptible, and
immortal provided that God does not annihilate it. Bloom,
operating mentally on a different level from Stephen and ignorant of the metaphysical terminology of the scholastics, cannot
concede that the soul is 'simple' and has difficulty in accepting
733   the existence of a supernatural God. While Stephen argues for
(589)   arguing's sake on the technical philosophical level, Bloom trots
out the stock 'new' thought of nineteenth-century progressive
liberalism (and modernism), questioning the authenticity of the
gospels, as of Shakespeare's authorship of the plays.

   Bloom stirs the unappetizing coffee, reflecting on the conveniently lucrative philanthropy of the Coffee Palace in running
519   shelters such as this and regaling the poor with lectures, drama,
and concerts, while paying precious little to their performers.
734   (Molly has been one.) The coffee also stirs Bloom's hygienic
mind to reflect on the need for inspection of cheap eating-
houses. Nevertheless, he prevails upon Stephen to try it, while
Stephen prevails upon him to remove a horn-headed knife
that reminds him of Roman history. Talking of knives, Bloom
confidentially questions the authenticity of the seaman's yarns.
735   Meanwhile he studies the seaman and finds it possible to believe
520   him either an ex-convict with a murderous past or a mere bluffer
making the most of the credulity of the Dublin jarvies.
(Correspondences between Murphy and Sinbad and the Flying
Dutchman build up the Odyssean-Wanderer theme. We have
already had Enoch Arden and Rip van Winkle. See p. 510/719.)
736   Bloom admits to Stephen that he has himself seen human physical freaks on display and the seaman's yarns need not be false.
Even his knifing yarn was compatible with the temperament of
the Italian who figured in it. Spaniards, too, have passionate
temperaments, Bloom adds, happily bringing round mind and
737   talk to the lodestar subject, Molly. Citing his own wry instances
521   of Italian passion, Stephen keeps Bloom going on the subject of
the fiery Latins who are 'washed in the blood of the sun'. Hence
to praise of Mediterranean contours as evidenced in the statues
he examined in the museum today. Such bosoms and hips one
doesn't readily knock against in Ireland. Moreover, Irish taste
in dress is careless.

The others are talking about shipwrecks and accidents at sea, the sailor claiming a special security due to a pious medal he *738* wears, and various notorious wreckings are mentioned. Then the sailor goes out, heavy-footed, to have a drink of rum from *739* one of the two bottles he carries and to relieve himself noisily *522* in the street. Meanwhile watchman Gumley wakes, stirs, and sleeps again. He is a man of decent home background who was left £100 a year and managed nevertheless to drink himself into penury. *740*

In the shelter they talk of the falling-off of Irish shipping, and Skin-the-Goat sees the conspiratorial hand of the British *(594)* Government at work when a ship hit a rock in Galway bay and spoiled the scheme (involving Captain Lever) to develop the harbour. As Murphy returns, Skin-the-Goat seeks his corroboration of the rumour, but the drunken sailor, missing the point, *523* chants an obscene limerick about 'Johnny Lever' (which should *741* be 'Leave her, Johnny, leave her'), then returns to his seat.

Skin-the-Goat warms to his theme. Ireland is by virtue of its natural resources the richest country in the world, but England drains its wealth away. England's days of supremacy are numbered. Germans and Japanese will see to that; and Ireland will be England's Achilles' heel. Rising to the praise of the *742* Irish, the sailor maintains that Irish troops and sailors are *524* the 'backbone of our empire'. The use of this phrase naturally annoys Skin-the-Goat. In his eyes no Irishman worth his salt would serve any empire, whoever it is supposed to belong to. An altercation ensues. Bloom, as ever, regrets it. He refuses *743* to underestimate either the strength or the good sense of the English. The intelligent policy is to make the most of both countries, and he has no intention of being drawn into the argument either on the side of the sailor, whom he thinks bogus, or of Skin-the-Goat, whose former violence he disapproves of *744* (though with a secret admiration for the courage of conviction which it expresses). Then Bloom remembers that Skin-the-Goat's *525* part in the Phoenix Park murders was that of car-driver, and this was what saved him at the trial. Anyway it is all ancient history. In Bloom's eyes Skin-the-Goat is a man who has outlived his career; like an actress who keeps returning for another 'positively last performance'.

Bloom tells Stephen of his experience with the fanatical nation- *745* alist in Barney Kiernan's, and how he made the point that Christ was a Jew. Stephen underlines the correspondence between Christ and Bloom. Bloom, the twentieth-century Messiah, thereupon sums up the religion of tolerant, liberal, pacific, twentieth-century man. Violence achieves nothing. Goodwill, tolerance and equality are the ideals. Political and nationalistic

526   dissension are often mere cloaks for economic rivalries. The
746   Jews, being practical, give strength to a nation. Religion, especially Roman Catholicism, weakens nations by setting
747   people's hearts on a future life. Finally, Bloom advocates an egalitarian society embracing all creeds and classes, and dispensing secure, tidy-sized incomes all round. 'I call that patriotism.' This is indeed the twentieth-century prophet. In the New

(599)   Bloomusalem all can live well who are prepared to work.

'Count me out,' Stephen says cryptically of Bloom's insistence

527   on the need to work; and Bloom hastens to assure him that literary as well as manual work is allowed for in his scheme. The intellectual and the peasant are both needed. Both 'belong

748   to Ireland, the brain and the brawn. Each is equally important.' (Bread completes the trinity – brain, bread, brawn – needed by Molly. See commentary on p. 561/*802*.)

Stephen, artist, individualist, will not have his importance measured by his contribution to the community. His own system of values reverses this principle. Ireland is important, he suspects, 'because it belongs to me'. Bloom is baffled. Stephen cannot make him understand. They therefore drop the subject. In short, there is no coming together here; no meeting of minds; only a collision between the socialistic, materialistic, liberal, twentieth-century mind, pinning its faith to the collective and to the assumed capacity of man to build his own Bloomusalem – and the rebellious, guilt-ridden, individualist inheritor of Christian culture who has lost his illusions along with his faith.

Pondering Stephen's peculiar remark, Bloom wonders whether to attribute his asperity to the 'fumes of his recent orgy' or whether the inadequacies of Stephen's home life have embittered him. He reflects that brilliant young men sometimes go

749   off the rails mentally or morally, recalling one O'Callaghan who exhibited his eccentricities and eventually had to be spirited away by his friends to prevent his being charged with a homosexual offence. Memories recur of known scandals and

528   hushed-up scandals touching the aberrations, homosexual and heterosexual, of those high in society, and even of royalty.

Thence to the thought that differences in dress, emphasized by   750
advertisers, heighten heterosexual desires in a way unknown to
primitive savages.

Bloom's meandering sequence of thought then comes back to
the theme of brilliant young men without advantageous
family backgrounds, not all of whom fail. Some climb to the
top in society by the force of their own efforts. There are, therefore, good prudential reasons for taking a continued interest
in Stephen, even though it is costing money. If nothing else,
Stephen repays the outlay by providing intellectual stimulation.
Moreover, to see life as Bloom is today seeing it, making contact   (601)
with life's oddities and outcasts, is in the spirit of the age, and
might even be turned to profitable account if he could write an
article about it.

As Bloom broods on the mysteries of Stephen's odd statement about Ireland and of the sailor's identity, his eyes fall on
the headlines of the evening *Telegraph*, pink sporting edition,   751
which is lying beside his elbow. He takes it up and reads   529
Hynes's report of the Dignam funeral. The report includes a
line of nonsensical misprint which Bloom imagines must have
crept in when Nannetti called for Monks, the day-father, thereby
distracting him (p. 100/7:190). Bloom's idea that Nannetti called
Monks 'about Keyes's ad' is surely pathetically off the mark.
Nannetti's interest in the Keyes's ad was much slighter than
Bloom would wishfully think it to have been. Another misprint,
annoying to Bloom, is the loss of an 'l' from his own name,
which is printed 'Boom' in the list of mourners. (The reader
must decide for himself whether the lost 'l' is compensated for
by the superfluous 'l' which crept into Martha's typewritten
letter – 'I do not like that other wor*l*d' on p. 63/95.) Bloom is
amused by the inclusion among the mourners of C. P. M'Coy   752
and Stephen Dedalus, neither of whom was present. He draws
Stephen's attention to it.

Stephen, smothering a yawn, asks whether the 'first epistle
to the Hebrews' is in the paper. 'Text: open thy mouth and put
thy foot in it.' This query relates to Mr Garrett Deasy's letter
on foot-and-mouth disease. Bloom finds it on p. 2, and while
Stephen reads it, he himself looks at the account of the Ascot
Gold Cup race on p. 3, noting the victory of *Throwaway*, the
rank outsider, and the failure of *Maximum II* which Bantam   530
Lyons backed.   753

Talk has by this time drifted to the inevitable topic, Parnell.
('There was every indication they would arrive at that,' Bloom
observes to Stephen.) Legends foretelling the return of the
lost leader are aired. Bloom is highly sceptical of rumours that
Parnell still lives. He attributes them to the mystery surrounding
Parnell's movements in his later days and to the incongruously
754   undramatic nature of the hero's death. He muses on the great
531   man's downfall, and recalls an occasion when, during a fracas,
he rescued Parnell's hat, returned it to him, and was rewarded
by a personal 'Thank you'. (See pp. 461/669 and 535/761.)
He reflects that returns after long absence by men whose places
755   have been usurped are rarely popular or successful. He has
already dwelt on this Odyssean theme in picturing the
sailor's return on p. 510/719, citing Enoch Arden and Rip van
Winkle. (See also p. 520/736 for Sinbad and the Flying
Dutchman.) Here the lot of the false claimant in the Tichborne
(604)   case is alluded to. All these cases have a pathetic relevance to
Bloom's personal situation. It is not unnatural that they should
come to his mind.

While the others enjoy crude humour on the subject of Kitty
O'Shea's charms and her husband's ineffectiveness, Bloom
surveys the main events of the story as they emerged in court
756   and in the Press at the time of the trial. His view is that of
532   conventionalized bourgeois romanticism which regards the
husband as a supernumerary and the gifted lover and yielding
wife as the victims of their own heroic stature and inflammable
757   nature. The ingratitude of priests, adherents, and former beneficiaries of the fallen hero is scathingly mentioned. But Bloom's
romanticism is a controlled, rationalized product. It is a mistake
to go back after a long time, he thinks. You cannot expect things
to be the same. Parts of Dublin's south side have changed a
good deal since he came to live on the north side. And, on the
subject of north and south, Kitty O'Shea's southern blood had
something to do with the tragedy.

The lodestar draws again. Bloom dwells on the subject of
758   the warm-blooded Spanish; then proudly displays to Stephen a
533   photograph of Molly, standing near a piano and wearing an
evening dress that reveals her lavish embonpoint. He boasts to
Stephen of her beauty and her accomplishments, dwelling
759   especially, with an artist's interest, on the opulent curves.
He resists the temptation to go out and relieve himself so that

Stephen can relish Molly's beauty undisturbed. The sudden 534
thought that Molly might not be there when he gets back drags
to mind Moore's *'Song of O'Ruark'* on the Prince of Breffni's
return to his wifeless home (*'I look'd for the lamp which, she told
me,/Should shine when her pilgrim return'd'*); but the memory of 760
this morning's routine scene of normality in the bedroom reassures him.

Bloom relishes the company of the educated Stephen and
appreciates Stephen's approval of Molly's photograph. Indeed,
their shared appreciation of Molly leads him to meander through
a series of reflections on matrimonial triangles and how they
are handled in the Press and in the divorce court. The Parnell
case is cited once more, and we get a more detailed recall of
the incident of the hat (cf. p. 531/754). Parnell's followers broke 761
up the type-cases in the offices of the *United Ireland* which had
been printing scandalous comment about Parnell's private
morals. In the ensuing fracas Bloom rescued and returned the 535
leader's hat, receiving a polite *'Thank you, sir'*, much more 762
cordial than Menton's frigid recognition of the comparable (609)
service Bloom performed at Glasnevin Cemetery this morning
(p. 95/146). (Bloom's role as hat-holder to home-breakers was
comically concretized in the *Circe* episode, p. 461/669.)

Bloom dislikes the frank, knowing tone with which the cabmen laugh off the Parnell story. His own view, framed in the
stale, cliché-packed style of contemporary journalism, is
shot through with the flavour of a weary twentieth-century trite-
ness, half sentimental, half cynical, which is the perfect
expression of inert decadence. He will not forego the stilted
Victorian romanticism which the cabmen would scoff at, but,
as a twentieth-century sceptic, he has rationally outgrown it. 763

Bloom regrets that Stephen should waste his time in brothels
and run the risk of getting venereal disease. Inspired by his
mistaken interpretation of Stephen's broken phrases, uttered 536
when recovering consciousness (p. 496/702), he entertains the
idea of a blissful romance for Stephen and the union with
'Miss Ferguson' or some other, though he admits to himself that
the conventional procedures of formal engagement are rather
out of character for Stephen. Pitying his present homelessness,
and thereby feeling fatherly towards him, he asks when Stephen
last ate, and is horrified to discover that it was over twenty-
four hours ago. 764

In spite of the difference between them, Bloom sees similarities too, and, studying Stephen, recalls the impulsive unconventionalities of his own young manhood, twenty years ago, when he took a prudently half-committed interest in revolutionary politics (the memory makes the citizen's attacks on him in Barney Kiernan's seem even more unjust), though violence and
765 extremism were never in his line.
537 It is time to retire. Bloom thinks of taking Stephen home with him, though the last time he took a lame dog home for the night, in the Ontario Terrace days, Molly was angry. However, Stephen cannot go back to Sandycove. The situation is delicate. Bloom is anxious to help Stephen materially without embarrassing him, and thinks the gift of a cup of cocoa and 'a shakedown for the night plus the use of a rug or two' could scarcely be resented. He notes, meanwhile, that the other
766 wandering Odyssean hero, seaman Murphy, seems disinclined to make his way home to his Penelope in Queenstown and is more likely to spend the next few days imprisoned by the charms of the sirens in some brothel off Sheriff Street Lower. Bloom is still indulging silent self-satisfaction about his repartee
(612) to the fanatical nationalist: the fact that God was a Jew is the Achilles' heel of the Irish patriot.
Bloom takes back his photograph of Molly and casually suggests that Stephen should come with him to talk things over.
538 He is privately indulging extravagant dreams of what might be
767 achieved by a friendly commercial exploitation of Stephen's talents as a writer and a singer. Bloom the agent (How dead right Joyce was in defining his twentieth-century Everyman) comes into his own as middleman turning culture into cash. Meantime we see twentieth-century mass culture already in action as, first, the cabby reads London gossip in the evening
768 paper and, then, the sailor takes his turn, poring over the meaningless sensations and sports reports. The style here reaches an appropriate peak of literary prostitution that matches the theme. Cheap puns ('pawed' – 'pored', 'Iremonger' – 'ire'), vulgar artifice ('King Willow' for cricket) press home upon the reader what the commercial exploitation of art in the long run amounts to. The harmless, well-meaning, twentieth-century progressive could be the death of it.
539 Bloom pays the keeper fourpence for the coffee and confec-
769 tionery, and the two of them leave the shelter. Stephen is still

'weak on his pins' (lameness again) and Bloom goes to his right-hand side to support him. The watchman, Gumley, is asleep in his sentry-box by the pile of stones. Gumley, former revolutionary, and the stones remind Bloom of the legend referred to in the shelter (p. 530/753) that Parnell is not dead and that his coffin was filled with stones. The legend has an ironical implication: those of Parnell's followers who turned on him at the crisis virtually stoned him. They were his beneficiaries, tenants whose holdings were his gift, but they took up stones to cast at him. Parnell, like Christ, like Bloom, was a rejected Messiah. (NB The vessel which brought back Murphy, the bogus Wanderer, is itself full of bricks.)

Bloom and Stephen discuss music. Bloom's taste is what might   770
be called middlebrow: he likes the easily assimilated, melodically attractive composers. Wagner is too heavy. But Mercadante,   540
Meyerbeer, and Mozart are among his favourites. The level of his not-contemptible but insufficiently discriminating musical culture is evidenced by the way he classes Mozart's *Don Giovanni* with Flotow's *Martha* as 'light opera' and speaks somewhat awesomely of Mendelssohn as representing the 'severe classical   (615)
school'. His cultural judgements are unreliable. His knowledge is half assimilated. He is too ready to think that he understands. And therefore he can commit the howler of citing Herrick's love lyric, 'Bid me to live and I will live – Thy protestant to be' as Protestant Church music – alongside Moody and Sankey hymns.

Talking of *Martha*, Bloom praises Simon Dedalus's rendering of 'M'appari', heard this afternoon in the Ormond. Stephen's reply is to launch out in praise of the altogether severer, less   771
sentimental, more disciplined music of the English Elizabethan and Jacobean composers such as Dowland, Byrd, Tomkins, and John Bull. Stephen, chattering now of purchasing a lute from the Dolmetsch establishment, is playing the highbrow in a big way.

They have to stop in the roadway for a poor old horse which is dragging a sweeper. This rather pathetic creature, doomed to   541
sweep up filth from the roads, is a 'big foolish nervous noodly   772
kind of a horse' in Bloom's eyes and he wishes he had a lump of sugar for him. Plainly this incident is based on Odysseus's touching recognition of his old dog Argus who lies abandoned on the dung-heaps.

Bloom talks of the pleasure his wife will surely take in making Stephen's acquaintance, meantime studying Stephen's face, noting his resemblance to his mother, and hoping that he has

773 his father's vocal gift. Stephen sings an old German song, and Bloom at once pours out his enthusiastic plans for having Stephen's voice trained and establishing him as a much-sought-

542 after society singer. Not that money need be the only aim.
774 Stephen would have the chance to lift Dublin's musical life from its conventional rut by his distinctive taste. Indeed, all that is required to make a brilliantly successful career for Stephen is that he should put himself in the hands of an agent who would provide the impetus to compensate for the natural inertia that tends to accompany youthful brilliance like Stephen's. Bloom even argues that Stephen will have plenty of spare time in which

775 to practise literature. In fact, Stephen has 'the ball at his feet'. Bloom knows when he is on to a good thing. Hence his present interest in Stephen.

As a last piece of advice, Bloom urges that Stephen should cut away from Buck Mulligan ('a certain budding practitioner'),

543 who does not hesitate to run Stephen down in his absence.

Stephen has dealt with this temptation before – the tempta-

(618) tion to betray his artistic conscience and calling, and to sell his talents for cash (p. 111/171). He does not reply here. He does not need to reply. For the horse replies on his behalf, steamily depositing three turds in the road.

776 So Bloom and Stephen go their way, linked in friendliness, but severed from each other mentally.

Chapter 17

Ithaca

In Homer Odysseus and Telemachus destroy the suitors who
have so long plagued Penelope. In Joyce the victory of Bloom
over his rivals is a moral one. There is no violence. Thus the
Homeric parallel, though providing a useful framework for the
construction of this, as of other episodes, has little to tell us
of its deeper meaning. Psychological interpretations abound.
Theological interpretation is also valid, and has been neglected.
For instance, though Stephen's act at the climax of the *Circe*
episode is a rebellious one and carries its Luciferian overtones
('*non serviam*') from as far back as the retreat sermon in the
Portrait, it is an artificial light that he extinguishes, and a sordid
scene that he obliterates and forsakes. Moreover his flight leads
to an act of martyrdom at the hands of Privates Carr and
Compton which parallels the Crucifixion. Images and allusions
mark Stephen as the crucified one (cf. p. 488/*694–5*). Thus the
development of a Father–Son relationship between Bloom and
Stephen establishes the crucified one as the Son of Man. Stephen
comes down to Bloom's level in episodes 16 and 17, taking his
nature to himself in all its pedestrian twentieth-century vulgarity
and, in exchange, helping Bloom to bear his wrongs and live
in charity with his Earth-goddess and corrupted partner in
the flesh.

The risen Stephen–Christ, with his wounded hand (p. 537/
765), shaking legs and bruised side (p. 539/*769*), is taken into
Everyman–Bloom's home. There he brings a light to shine that
transfigures everything it touches. It is the light of a lucid, sharpened intellect which submits all it encounters to a rigorous
catechistical analysis. Once more the comic spirit asserts itself
in what is a profoundly significant experiment in literary form

and style. The techniques of formal logic, scholastic deduction, and scientific analysis are all exploited so as to show the whole world transfigured in the light of a new revelation. The artist and the intellectual meet the twentieth-century Everyman with his strong physical and material interests, his half-education, his smattering of culture, his scepticism and credulity, his half-baked notions, his indigestible mixture of idealism and disillusionment. Symbolically Godhead and manhood are joined, their respective natures mutually shared, Stephen and Bloom becoming 'Blephen' and 'Stoom'.

Ithaca then gives us a new revelation; environment and experience transfigured in the light of an intellectual clarity bred of the communion between Stephen–Christ and Everyman–Bloom. It is a twentieth-century revelation, a transfiguration achieved through modes of presentation characteristic of the scientific and philosophical approaches that mark the high peak of our secular civilization. All is illuminated in the light of a humour, a clarity, a charity, and above all an omniscience, which give this episode something of the quality of a climactic vision.

The exact route followed by Stephen and Bloom is recorded and the topics touched on in their conversation. In Bloom's 777 eyes they have a common enthusiasm for music, a common resistance to religious and political orthodoxies, a common in-(619) terest in sex. (But, of course, the two are much less akin than Bloom's limited intelligence recognizes. Stephen treats Bloom less seriously than Bloom treats Stephen.) They differ plainly in that Stephen has little interest in Bloom's socio-political 545 philosophy and Bloom little understanding of Stephen's artistic creed – or of his abstruse intellectual theories. Again, while Bloom attributes Stephen's collapse to its obvious causes, Stephen blames the 'reapparition of a matutinal cloud'. This is the cloud which in episode 1 (p. 8/9) covers the sun as Stephen reflects in the Martello tower on Fergus's Song, his mother's death, and 'love's bitter mystery' (themes which, of course, recur at the time of the collapse in *Circe*), and the cloud which is seen likewise by Bloom walking back from the pork-butcher's in episode 4 (p. 50/73) and which there brings to him a momentary chill of desolation – a sense of horror, barrenness, and death. 778   Mention of the effect of street-lighting on the leaves of trees brings back a detailed record of previous occasions in Bloom's life on which conversation has touched the same subject. Thus

Bloom's past suddenly takes shape around a new point of reference, and Bloom senses that as one gathers age and experience the range of personal contacts seems to get more limited. On this basis the pattern of life is glimpsed: one comes into existence as an individual, treated as such by the many who surround (621) one; gradually one's individuality is submerged as one becomes a part of the vague many known vaguely by the many; and 779 eventually one's individuality is lost as one's death deprives everyone of any chance of realizing it.

As they reach Bloom's house at 7 Eccles Street, Bloom finds 546 that he has forgotten his latch-key which is in his other trousers (see p. 46/67). The alternatives before the 'keyless couple' are 'to enter or not to enter. To knock or not to knock'. (They are both shut out from their 'homes' – Ireland, orthodoxy, faith. 'Knock and it shall be opened unto you'; but neither is prepared to knock on the door of Molly, the mystical Bride, founded upon the 'Rock'.) Bloom therefore climbs over the railings, drops into the basement yard, and gets into the house through the scullery 780 door. He goes into the kitchen, lights the gas, then a candle, 547 and Stephen soon after sees its glimmer through the window over the hall door. Bloom opens the door and leads Stephen 781 along the hallway and down some steps into the kitchen. Here Bloom kneels on the hearth and lights a fire 'with one ignited lucifer match'. The act becomes for Stephen (like the talk of the effect of street-lights on trees earlier for Bloom) a point of reference around which his past life takes shape afresh. It came to his mind in the *Aeolus* episode that the striking of a match might determine 'the whole aftercourse of both our lives' (p. 115/177), and here he images past occasions on which he has watched a kneeling figure kindle a fire. Three of these instances take us back to memorable moments in the *Portrait*: in the Clongowes infirmary, in the parlour after the removal into Dublin, and in 782 the physics theatre at University College. For the image of Dilly 548 see p. 200/312. (In Homer it is immediately after the slaughter of the suitors that Odysseus gives his order, 'The first thing I want is a fire in this hall'.) Stephen's range of vision (he is sitting with his back to the window) also takes in the house-bells on the wall opposite and some laundry hanging across a recess.

Bloom takes a kettle to the sink and turns the tap to fill it. Straightaway we are given a divinely omniscient, all-embracing

783 (God's eye) view of the course of the water from Roundwood reservoir and the detailed workings of the Dublin water system.
549 This, in turn, leads to an even more comprehensive survey of water, its nature, properties, and uses, in the form of a packed
784 scientific catalogue, encyclopaedic in its fullness, cosmic in its
785 range.
550 Having put the kettle on the fire, Bloom returns to the sink and
(625) washes his hands, using the lemon-scented soap he bought this morning (p. 69/105). Stephen refuses to wash. His dislike of contact with water is related explicitly to his distrust of 'aquacities of thought and language', implicitly (by the words *partial*, *total*,
786 *immersion*) to his rejection of his own baptism. Bloom accepts Stephen's unhygienic habits as the eccentricity of genius, marvelling at his self-confidence and his powers of recuperation.

The heating of the kettle and the boiling of the water are
551 scientifically described with the usual extensive range of refer-
787 ence. It is suggested that Bloom might have used the boiling water for shaving. There are advantages in shaving at night – in the softer skin at night, in the opportunity it provides for quiet reflection on the past day, and in the fact that one feels fresher on waking. Besides morning shaving is apt to be hurried, tends to be interrupted by morning noises, and one is thus more likely to cut oneself. At night, though the light is poor, Bloom
788 can shave undisturbed, for his hand has the sureness and sensitivity of a surgeon's. (But he does not like shedding blood, and prefers nature treatment to orthodox surgery.)

Bloom opens the kitchen dresser and the contents of the
552 shelves are revealed and catalogued. Meanwhile two torn betting
789 tickets on the dresser apron catch his eyes. For a moment his brow is furrowed as he recollects the day's coincidences touching the victory of *Throwaway* in the Ascot Gold Cup race. He recalls hearing news of the race from Lenehan in Barney Kiernan's (p. 267/422) and an inquiry about prospects from Flynn in Davy Byrne's (p. 142/220). More intriguingly, he remembers how a young YMCA man gave him a throwaway in O'Connell Street, announcing that 'Elijah is coming' (p. 124/190), and how he had been about to throw away his newspaper when Bantam Lyons borrowed it this morning in Lincoln Place to check up on a horse running in the race (p. 70/106). *Throwaway*, the dark horse, the outsider, has obvious correspondences with Bloom, with Elijah (who is coming), and with Christ. (The Gold Cup is chalice as

well as female vessel, cf. the implicit parallel in *Nausicaa*.) Bloom
here recalls that after the strange tip had been vouchsafed to him
in episode 5, he went on his way to the Baths (like Moses in John
F. Taylor's speech, p. 117/*181*) 'with the light of inspiration shin-
ing in his countenance and bearing in his arms the secret of the   790
race, graven in the language of prediction'. Thus a correspon-   (629)
dence with the Annunciation is intended on pp. 70–1/*106*–7,
in the racing tip and the greeting of Mr Hornblower in the
'heavenly weather', and Incarnation is hinted at in the bath scene
on p. 71/107.

Bloom consoles himself by weighing the risk of misinter-   553
preting a prophetic tip such as that granted him and by
congratulating himself that he has lost nothing. Then he makes
two cups of Epps's cocoa and shows his courtesy and generosity
as a host, firstly by choosing for himself a cup exactly like his
guest's (instead of using his favourite moustache cup) and,
secondly, by adding most of Molly's breakfast cream to   791
Stephen's cocoa and only a little of it to his own. (The frequent
use of the word 'host', the words 'mass-product' and 'creature
cocoa' seem to turn the drinking into a jocoserious act of
communion.)

Bloom decides to reserve for Molly later the privilege of mend-
ing Stephen's torn jacket (see p. 309/*492*) and for himself later
the pleasure of presenting Stephen with a handkerchief.

As they drink cocoa, Bloom thinks that Stephen's silence is a   554
sign that he is mentally composing poetry. The thought puts
Bloom into a distinctly 'literary' frame of mind, and he recalls
how he has tried to solve difficult problems by consulting the
works of Shakespeare, though without complete success. Then   792
his mind turns to his own creative efforts in the field of literature – the verses he wrote at the age of eleven for a newspaper
competition, the anagrams he made in youth on his own
name, and the amatory acrostic which he addressed to Molly   555
on St Valentine's Day, 1888. The peak of Bloom's literary aspira-   793
tion seems to have been reached when he considered writing
topical verses required for a song in the pantomime *Sinbad the
Sailor* at the Gaiety Theatre in 1893. Various complications of a
political, prudential, technical, and even erotic kind prevented
the fulfilment of this ambition.

The relationship between the ages of Stephen (twenty–two)   794
and Bloom (thirty-eight) is stated and explored mathematically. 556

795   Previous meetings between the two are recorded. The first was in the lilac-garden of Matt Dillon's house, Roundtown, in 1887 – the occasion already referred to three times when Menton danced with Molly (p. 87/*134*), when Menton and Bloom disagreed over a game of bowls (p. 94/*146*), and when Bloom watched Stephen ('a lad of four or five in linsey woolsey') standing on the urn and staring at his mother a little reproach-
(632)   fully (p. 344/*553*). The second meeting was in the coffee room of Breslin's Hotel on a rainy Sunday in January 1892. Stephen (now aged 9–10) was with his father and grand-uncle. Stephen asked Bloom to dinner and the childish invitation was seconded by Simon, presumably in the embarrassment of inescapable courtesy. Bloom naturally declined the invitation.

Bloom and Stephen find another past link between them. Mrs Riordan (Dante of the *Portrait*) lived with the Dedaluses from 1888 to 1891, when Stephen was 6 to 9 years old. (This does not appear to fit the chronology of the *Portrait*.) Later, from 1892–4, she lived in the City Arms Hotel, where the Blooms also stayed during 1893–4 while Bloom was employed as a clerk in the Cattle Market by Joseph Cuffe. We have already heard through the narrator of *The Cyclops* (p. 258/*408*) how Bloom got the sack from Cuffe's for being a 'know-all'. We have also heard from the same source of the fuss Bloom and Molly made in the
557   City Arms before little Rudy's birth, and after (pp. 275/*435* and
796   277/*439*). Bloom's present memories of Mrs Riordan are of the weaknesses and eccentricities of her senility. Stephen's chief memories of her remain those of his infancy, and include the green and red brushes mentioned in the *Portrait*.

The difference in age between Bloom and Stephen, highlighted
797   in these contrasting memories, is of course regretted by Bloom, who looks back to his early physical prowess and his own abandoned attempt to prolong youthful fitness into middle age by physical exercises. The difference in race between them is
558   understood but not discussed. Their respective parentages
798   are recorded in precise detail. Their respective baptisms are recounted. Bloom has three to Stephen's one (as he drank his cocoa in three sips to Stephen's one, p. 554/*791*). The first, by the Rev. Gilmer Johnston, was into the Irish Protestant Church to whose faith Bloom's father had been converted in 1865 by the Society for Promoting Christianity among the Jews (see p. 588/*843*). The second was a ducking during some

youthful rag. The third, into the Roman Catholic Church by the Rev. Charles Malone, CC, was presumably in 1888, when Bloom formally abjured Protestantism with a view to marrying Molly (see p. 588/*843*).

In comparing the educational careers of Bloom and Stephen the composite names 'Stoom' and 'Blephen' are used, suggesting a consubstantiality, or a unity of two natures, with obvious theological implications. Bloom, whose favourite observation is that he has studied in the 'university of life', refrains from saying (635) it here out of uncertainty whether he may not have said it to Stephen already. Thus half-educated Bloom reveals a restless blend of insecurity and embarrassment with assertiveness and self-confidence in the presence of the academically educated Stephen.

The temperaments of the two are distinguished as scientific   559
and artistic. Bloom illustrates the practical nature of his   799
scientific interests by mentioning some of the inventions he has dreamed of making. These turn out to be toys for children designed to educate scientifically and to replace the popular children's weapons and games of chance. He dreams also of commercial success comparable to that achieved by Ephraim Marks's penny bazaar and Charles James's waxworks show.

More expertly perhaps Bloom dwells on the enormous possibilities, as yet unexplored, of modern advertising, when force, clarity, and simplicity of impact are combined. These qualities are illustrated in the Kino's 11*s*. trousers advertisement and the   *800*
Alexander J. Keyes advertisement. Their defective contraries – advertisements suffering from vagueness and over-complexity – are also illustrated. The depth of advertising ineptitude is represented by the Plumtree's Potted Meat jingle, so often in   560
Bloom's mind today (see pp. 61/*91* and 140/*218*), as inserted with farcical incongruity under the obituary notices in the paper. The peak of imaginative ingenuity in advertising is represented by Bloom's own idea for advertising stationery on an illuminated mobile show-cart containing attractive girls who are writing (an idea which he submitted in vain to Hely, as we learned on p. 127/*195*).

This idea suggests to Stephen a mysterious and romantic   *801*
episode in a highland hotel, in which a silent, moody young woman writes her address on a piece of notepaper. (It appears that this dramatic fragment carries heavy symbolic overtones.)

To Bloom the idea brings back memories of his father's death from an overdose of drugs on 27 June 1886 in The Queen's Hotel, Ennis. A coincidental meeting of minds occurs in that both Stephen and Bloom think of scenes in a 'Queen's Hotel'.

561   After his description of the hotel scene, Stephen narrates again
802   his 'Parable of the Plums' (pp. 119–23/183–9). The fact that this narration is described as constituting a 'second coincidence' invites symbolic interpretation of both narratives – as of the Plumtree advertisement from which they arise. (The Plumtree
(638)   is phallic, the meat a symbol of male sexuality, and the pot a symbol of the female vessel that receives and contains it.) If the Queen's Hotel ('Queen's Ho') is Molly's house, the young woman Molly, and the young man Stephen, we see prophetically Molly's restless half invitation to Stephen, and Stephen's silent detached response. He preserves his solitariness. (The thematic thread linking queenliness with the yearned-for woman is strong throughout. Even Seaman Murphy's Penelope is waiting back in Queenstown, Cork, see p. 510/719. On p. 61/91, Molly is associated with the Queen 'in her bedroom eating bread'.) If the two vestal virgins of the 'Parable of the Plums' together form a composite Molly, then the brawn they consume is presumably Boylan (see p. 441/652, where Boylan is 'a man of brawn'), the bread Bloom, and the four-and-twenty plums whose stones they spit out, are the rejected suitors listed on pp. 601–2/863. ('He gets the plums and I the plumstones' Bloom mused wryly of Boylan in the Nausicaa episode, p. 308/491.) We may note in the original version of the parable (p. 121/187) that the old dears, having eaten the brawn and the bread, wipe their twenty fingers in the paper the bread was wrapped in. This underlines the correspondence between bread and Bloom (Molly's breadwinner) already established by the Rip van Winkle charade ('breadvan delivering', p. 309/492) and the feeding of the gulls (p. 125/192). If it is argued that Bloom is thought of as a meat-eater rather than a bread-eater, we must remember that Christ's flesh is the Bread of Life, and correspondences with the Mass are frequent. (Brain, bread, brawn – Stephen, Bloom, Boylan – answer Ireland's and Molly's three needs. See p. 527/748.) The 'four and twenty ripe plums' (p. 119/184), symbolically inseparable from the suitors, inevitably recall the four and twenty blackbirds ('baked in a pie') of 'Sing a song of sixpence', earlier quoted in snatches: 'The king

was in his countinghouse' (p. 56/*83*), 'Queen was in her bedroom (*sic*) eating bread and' (p. 61/*91*), 'The maid was in the garden' (p. 55/*82*).

Bloom's response to the 'Parable of the Plums' is to dwell on the possibilities of exploiting Stephen's literary gifts to commercial, social, and sexual advantage.

The *Ithaca* episode illuminates universally, and further light is now thrown on Bloom's relationship with Molly. He has frequently pondered how best to keep wives occupied, weighing the merits of such pastimes as parlour games, sewing, music, *803* theatre-going, suitable paid employment, visits to hygienically controlled masculine brothels, and educative evening classes. *562* He has favoured the last-named especially in view of Molly's intellectual deficiencies in the way of literacy, computation, and general knowledge. Some of Bloom's methods of trying to *(639)* improve Molly's education – leaving open books about, trying *804* to stretch her mentally in conversation, and ridiculing to her the ignorance of others – are somewhat patronizing and suggest on his part deficiencies of sympathy and imagination which help to account for Molly's irritation and dissatisfaction with him. (The partial enlightenments which Bloom manages to give his wife are followed by consequent confusions and forgetful renewals of error which may be considered characteristic of her sex.) But Bloom can play the psychologist too, buying Molly a *563* new hat so that she will use an umbrella, an article which she dislikes and he likes. (We learned, on p. 331/*530*, for 'umbrella' to read 'contraceptive'. And the 'wise virgins' took theirs with them to the Nelson monument; see p. 119/*184*.)

Stephen's 'Pisgah' parable leads to some discussion of great *805* Jewish leaders, the Moses who led the children of Israel out of bondage, Moses Maimonides, the twelfth-century philosopher whose 'Guide to the Perplexed' was an attempt to reconcile reason and faith (for Maimonides's aim was to achieve a synthesis between Jewish revelation and Aristotle – Bloom and Stephen), and Moses Mendelssohn, the German philosopher who has been called 'the foremost champion of Jewish emancipation in the eighteenth century'. Other eminent men of Jewish race are mentioned, comparisons are made between the ancient Hebrew and ancient Irish languages, and thus the correspondence *564* between the two rejected peoples (clearly made in Professor MacHugh's quotations from the speech by John F. Taylor in the

806 *Aeolus* episode, p. 116/*180*) is pressed home. Mention is made of what the two nations have suffered from dispersal, persecution, and oppression, and also of the prospects of national
807 revival.
565   There is a curious moment of mutual recognition between Stephen and Bloom, Stephen sensing in Bloom's voice the deep
808 wealth of the past, and Bloom sensing in Stephen's alertness and youth the promise of the future. Superimposed on this mutual recognition is another, for Stephen senses in Bloom's appearance the figure of the Christ, the logos personalized with white skin, dark hair, and a touch of pedantry, as He is in the works of the staunch defenders of orthodoxy such as St John
(642) of Damascus (*c.* 675–749) and St Epiphanius (*c.* 315–403). Bloom senses in Stephen's voice the ecstatic note of coming catastrophe.

The mention of St John of Damascus is alone enough to lend corroboration to attempts to probe more deeply into Joyce's theological symbolism. According to the *Oxford Dictionary of the Christian Church*, St John's Trinitarian theology 'develops the conception of "circumincession" in order to express the Inner-Trinitarian relations'. (And 'circumincession' means 'the reciprocal existence of the persons of the Trinity in one another', OED) Further, we are told that St John 'saw in the interpenetration of the two natures in Christ the formation of "Theandric Activities"' – that is, of activities characteristic of the God–man. Finally, St John held a high doctrine of the Blessed Virgin Mary, teaching her 'Divine maternity', her 'exemption from all stain of sin, and her assumption into heaven' (ODCC).

Now we have at this point in the book an apparent instance of circumincession, in that father and son exist reciprocally in one another. We may argue, too, that the episode as a whole reflects Theandric Activity by analogy in that much of it seems to express the composite nature and will of a 'Stoom' or a 'Blephen' rather than to convey a dialogue. Moreover, Molly, the 'Queen', is present by influence throughout, extending her divine maternity over both.

Bloom, looking back to his own youth, recalls some of his unrealized ('Pisgah') dreams of success in the Church, at the Bar, and on the stage. With Bloom's encouragement Stephen sings a ballad telling the story of a little boy who goes to
809 play with a Jew's daughter and is murdered by her. The ballad

is based on the old legend of St Hugh of Lincoln, cited in   566
Chaucer's *Prioress's Tale*. (See pp. 89/*137* and 443/*654*.) The
image of the Jew's daughter 'all dressed in green' is too near
the bone and disturbs Bloom. (For 'green-vested' Milly Bloom,   810
see p. 442/*653*.) Stephen's own reflections on the ballad present   567
himself as the 'victim predestined' led to an 'infidel apartment'
and there destroyed. Joyce uses the word *host* ambiguously here,
of Bloom entertaining his guest, and of Stephen as 'host' (victim
and sacrificial offering) in the theological sense.

From thoughts of murder, Bloom moves to thoughts on the   811
abnormal states of mind which sometimes cause murder, thence
to instances of the paranormal in his experience, in particular   568
of susceptibility to hypnotic suggestion and of sleep-walking.   (645)
His daughter Milly in childhood also suffered on two occasions
from night-time hallucinations. The thought of Milly introduces
memories of her infancy; how she shook her money-box (mini-   812
aturing the Dublin vestals, p. 119/*183*–4); how she threw away
her sailor doll (as Molly her Sinbad–Odysseus, as the vestals
turned their backs on Nelson?). Bloom also recalls how Milly's
blonde hair (he and Molly are both dark) reminded him of a
remote Austrian strain in her ancestry, and sometimes frightened him with recollections of Molly's affair with Lieutenant
Mulvey. (Fortunately, Milly's Jewish nose appeased his apprehension.) Later memories of Milly's childhood and adolescence   569
succeed till Bloom's attention is caught by the departure of his   813
cat. He broods on similarities and dissimilarities between
Milly and the cat. Both have gone out on the prowl; but only
the cat will return. Milly used to hold her head for him to
ribbon it as the cat holds its neck to be stroked. She would stare
at a fish in a lake as the cat will watch a mouse. She would
tug at her own hair as the cat at its own ear. She would day-
dream. He recalls how he attempted to interest her in practical   814
and scientific matters. and how she bought him the birthday
moustache-cup, how she proved notably attentive to him when-   570
ever pay day came round, and how she flattered his knowledge
when it was not being aired for her benefit.

Bloom offers Stephen a room for the night, for he finds his
presence stimulating, and thinks it might take Molly's mind off   815
Boylan. Stephen could also help Molly with her Italian pronun-
ciation. Bloom even dreams of a possible union between Stephen
and Milly. Then he asks Stephen if he knew Mrs Sinico who

was killed a year ago: Mrs Sinico was naturally in Bloom's mind this morning because her funeral was the last he attended before Dignam's (p. 94/*145*). The question carries significant overtones based on the full Sinico story told in *Dubliners*: 'A Painful Case'. Captain Sinico welcomed Mr Duffy into his home under the delusion that Mr Duffy was interested in his daughter, when in fact Mr Duffy was deeply involved in a (at first purely intellectual) companionship with his wife. The affection, on Mrs Sinico's part, became love: she and Duffy agreed not to meet again. As a result she faded, took to drink, and committed suicide. So the drift of Bloom's subconscious 'thinking' here is fascinating.

Stephen declines Bloom's invitation. (Bloom returns Stephen's 27s. which he took into safe keeping in the brothel; see p. 456/*665–6*.) Other possibilities for continuing their acquaintance are canvassed. They are that Stephen should instruct Molly in Italian and she him in singing at Bloom's house, and that Bloom and Stephen should meet there and elsewhere from time to time for intellectual discussion. Bloom feels it is unlikely that these proposals will lead to anything. He is sceptical about ever finding a 'son' or experiencing a long-wished 'return', remembering how a clown at Hengler's circus once claimed him for a 'father' as a riotous joke, and how he once marked a florin in the vain hope that it might one day come back to him. (It was at Hengler's Royal Circus that Murphy claimed to have seen Stephen's father, Simon Dedalus, exhibiting his skill in marksmanship; see p. 510/*719*.)

At the conclusion of the 'discussion' between Bloom and Stephen, Bloom, though full of humanitarian zeal for the improvement of social conditions, is depressed at the thought of the many natural obstacles that stand in the way of human happiness and prosperity – carnivorism, pain, disease, death, insanity, etc. – and baffle the human brain. (He is Everyman lamenting man's natural condition.) Stephen's reply is to affirm the significance of man as a rational being, but the affirmation is not received 'verbally'; rather it is received 'substantially' through the very presence of Stephen, through the entry of Stephen into a share of Bloom's own nature. Here is the analogy with the Incarnation. Stephen is the Christ who has taken Everyman Bloom's nature upon himself. Thus Bloom, the 'competent' but 'keyless citizen' goes out of the house in procession with his saviour. Bloom carries the candle, the light to lighten the gentiles; Stephen raises his ashplant (the Cross) aloft, and the 573 113th psalm is chanted 'secreto'.

The 113th psalm, celebrating the escape of the children of Israel from Egypt , the house of bondage, is in Christendom universally interpreted as a celebration of the Redemption of man by Christ. Thus Stephen–Christ leads man out of bondage to sin and error. Incarnation, Crucifixion, and Redemption have been variously represented in the text throughout the day, and the moment is right now for Christ's departure from the world of men. Thus the scene is set for the Ascension into Heaven. 819 'The heaventree of stars hung with humid nightblue fruit.'

It is a suitable moment to survey the vastness of the stellar universe by comparison with whose age and immensity man's threescore years and ten seem 'a parenthesis of infinitesimal brevity'. Bloom follows this god's-eye view of the stellar (651) universe with a god's-eye view of the ages of geological history and the infinitely minute complexity of matter. Thus to reflec- 820 tions on the wonder and magnitude of the mathematical world, 574 on the possibility that life exists on other planets, on the discov- 821 eries of astronomy, and finally, on the astrological theory that celestial bodies influence terrestrial ones. In this connexion we 575 hear of the appearance of stars marking the respective births of William Shakespeare, Leopold Bloom, and Stephen Dedalus 822 respectively.

In conclusion Bloom, the twentieth-century Everyman, re- 823 mains sceptical of the existence of a heaven beyond the earth. There is no method of proceeding from the known earth to the unknown heaven. He rejoices in the aesthetic splendour of the 576 universe and remains open-minded about certain astrological theories connecting the celestial and the sublunary. For instance, he is ready to admit that woman's nature reflects that of the moon in many respects. Thus thoughts return to Molly, with her 'nocturnal predominance', her constancy and her incon- 824 stancies, her power to enamour, mortify, invest with beauty, or lure to insanity; her light, her splendour, and her attraction. The light from her window is seen and noted. In the affection and admiration it stirs in Bloom, in the unity of common 577 masculinity which the sensed mystery and illumination of womanhood plants in the two of them, both are silent, abashed, knowing each other, and ashamed. Casting their eyes up to the 825

'luminous and semiluminous shadow' on the blind, they make
water together, Bloom's mind on the physical aspects of the
male organ, Stephen's on the intellectual questions surrounding
826   Christ's circumcision. A star (Molly) shoots across from Vega in
the Lyre (Boylan) towards the sign of Leo as Bloom unlocks the
garden gate. The insertion of male key in 'unstable' female lock
also prefigures sexual reunion. Moreover overtones hint at the
climactic drawing of the Ulyssean bow ('obtaining a purchase
578   on the bow . . . withdrawing a bolt') to bring about the revealing
of an 'aperture for free egress and free ingress'. In every sense
the 'key' to sexual return is here. The two men shake hands,
and at the moment of Stephen's departure the bells of St
George's church bring back to Stephen the memory of his
mother's deathbed ('*Liliata rutilantium*', see p. 19/27). Indeed,
827   the moment of parting is, as ever, a reminder and rehearsal of
death, recalling to Bloom the Dubliners who attended Dignam's
(657)   funeral today, chilling him with a sudden sense of desolation,
579   reminding him of many lost friends.
828   The approach of dawn tempts Bloom to linger in the garden
as he lingered that night of the charades at Luke Doyle's, but
instead he takes a deep breath and returns inside. Going into
the front room, he bumps his head on the sideboard, for
Molly has changed the furniture around during his absence.
829   Through Bloom's eyes we see the contents of the room. Some
580   of the articles, like the feminine easy-chair and the masculine
cane-chair opposite it, carry 'significances of similitude, of
posture, of symbolism . . .'. Thus on the piano the ashtray,
830   the fag-ends, and the music of '*Love's Old Sweet Song*', with its
final eloquent indications, '*ad libitum . . . animato . . .*' and
so on, tell their own story of Molly's afternoon encounter with
Boylan.
    Bloom lights a cone of incense, using the prospectus for
581   Agendath Netaim to convey the flame from the candle, then
831   looks at himself in the mirror above the mantelpiece. Wedding
gifts from Matt Dillon, the Doyles, and Alderman John Hooper
832   decorate the mantelpiece. The mirror reflects these. It also
582   reflects the contents of Bloom's book-case – whose titles, too,
carry the accustomed 'significances . . . of symbolism, of circum-
stantial evidence . . .' relating to Bloom's character and career
833   (and to Joyce's total plan). Thus *The Hidden Life of Christ* (black
boards), *In the Track of the Sun* (Son), and *Physical Strength and*

How to Obtain It all carry overtones relevant to Bloom and his   583
activities today. Bloom rearranges the volumes disturbed by   834
Molly's efforts (some are upside down), then sits down and
contemplates with pleasure a nude statue of Narcissus which
stands on the table.

Relaxing, Bloom removes his collar and tie, unbuttons his   835
waistcoat, shirt, and trousers. Involuntarily he fingers the   584
bee-sting on his abdomen and scratches himself. Then he makes
a survey of the day's expenditure in the form of a mental   836
balance-sheet which summarizes the day's activities. He takes   837
off his boots and his right sock, picks off a piece of toe-nail,   585
and smells it. The odour takes him back mentally to childhood,
and in particular to evening prayer and the 'ambitious medi-
tation' of boyhood. The smell has something of the function of
one of Proust's moments of 'involuntary memory': for it sets
him re-dreaming his favourite vision of earthly blessedness,
which constitutes a neat summary of the ideals of twentieth-
century middle-class suburban man.

The dream-house is a two-storeyed villa in five or six acres   838
of ground in a Dublin suburb, furnished with the antique pick-   (665)
ings of a confirmed auction-sale purchaser's career, as well as   586
all the best in contemporary items and fittings. The plan for   839
this domestic New Bloomusalem includes details of humane
salary scales and pension schemes for employees. It also includes
the ideal garden and the dream-equipment of the aspiring   840
bourgeois with a taste for fishing, gardening, and refined do-   587
it-yourselfery. The name of the perfect home is to be 'Bloom   841
Cottage' or 'St Leopold's' or 'Flowerville', and the owner will
move with dignity among his flowers and fir trees, 'achieving
longevity' in homespun tweeds.

The dream expands under contemplation. Bloom pictures his
indoor pursuits – photography and the study of comparative
religion, erotica, and astronomy. The details of the lighter recre-
ations conjured up meet the secret longings of those frustrated
by life's minor difficulties – cycling, minus the steep hills;
boating on 'unmolested' rivers; and carpentry at the hammer-
nails-and-screws level. The possibility of becoming a gentleman   588
farmer is added to the rising demands of Bloom's aspirations,   842
and in culmination he sees himself as a landed JP, Member of
Parliament, Privy Councillor, and the recipient of an honorary
degree, whose movements are recorded among the society

843 intelligence, and whose dispensation of justice fulfils the highest ideals of equity, patriotism, and legality. In this connexion images recur of Bloom's firmness in the past on behalf of truth and rectitude. The first of these is a boyish rejection of the Irish Church of his baptism. (As an instance of 'rectitude' it is rather tarnished by the information that Bloom later became a Roman

589 Catholic 'with a view to his matrimony'.) The other instances show Bloom disinterestedly espousing progressive views and radical causes in the economic, scientific, and political spheres.

844 The ways in which the cost of the dream-house might be defrayed are now considered. A sane and balanced calculation of hypothetical financial arrangements to cover the mortgage is followed by a series of day-dreams in which great wealth is suddenly forthcoming from invention of a private telegraph system that would enable one to make a bet after hearing the

845 result of a race, from discovery of a rare postage stamp or some other object of great value, from a mysterious bequest,

590 a brilliant business deal, a scientifically worked-out gambling system, or the solution of the problem of how to square the circle.

Once stimulated, Bloom's survey of his money-spinning

(670) inventions and schemes runs its full course, touching the

846 reclamation of waste soil, the utilization of waste materials, the harnessing of tidal power, the development of the peninsular delta of the North Bull, the exploitation of dogs and goats as traction animals, and various transport schemes designed to

591 benefit tourist trade and Irish industry.

847 The fact that the realization of any one of these dreams must depend either on the support of one of the world's wealthiest financiers or on the discovery of an inexhaustible gold seam makes fulfilment seem remote. But Bloom is pragmatist as well

848 as idealist. He justifies his indulgence in these day-dreams on the grounds that they tranquillize the mind before sleep and help to ensure a good night's rest – all the more important to

592 him because one of his secret fears is that he may commit homicide or suicide during sleep through some violent cerebral aberration. His last 'dream' does at least bring him back to the level of daily avocation: it is the devising of the uniquely perfect advertisement.

Bloom unlocks one of his private drawers. It contains sou-

849 venirs (like one of Milly's earliest copy-books and a brooch belonging to Bloom's mother), odds and ends, three letters from Martha Clifford, and Martha's name and address in code. (To decipher the code, a reversed alphabet should be super-imposed on the ordinary alphabet. Vowels are replaced by stops, and the surname CLIFFORD is reversed.) The drawer   *850* also contains such private objects as two obscenely erotic post-   *593* cards and a leaflet about *Wonderworker*, a suppository for rectal complaints whose virtues are testified to by various grateful   *851* users. Bloom adds today's letter from Martha to his collection, reflecting on the day's welcome evidence that he can still make   *594* a favourable impression on the opposite sex (Mrs Breen, Miss Callan, and Gerty MacDowell), and indulging a momentary image of himself, well-dined and wined, fascinating a cultivated and elegant courtesan.

Bloom unlocks the second drawer. It contains his birth certifi-   *852* cate (with his second name, 'Paula'; see pp. 273/432 and 497/702), financial documents and the deed-poll recording his father's change of name from Virag to Bloom. There are other relics of Rudolph Bloom too – his hagadah book, his spectacles, a photocard of the Queen's Hotel, Ennis (of which he was   *853* proprietor), and his last letter to Leopold, found after his death.   *595* The jumbled phrases of this letter run through Bloom's mind   *(676)* alongside memories of the old man in his latest days, drugged against the pains of neuralgia, and then on his deathbed.

Bloom feels remorse that he treated his father's Jewish beliefs and practices with disrespect, for now they appear neither more nor less absurd than other religious beliefs and practices. (There appears to be an inconsistency here, in that Bloom senior became a Christian in 1865, before Leopold was one year old. See p. 588/843.) Bloom's earliest memories of his father come to   *854* mind. The account of his European wanderings which he gave to Leopold at the age of six is submerged under later recollec-tions of the old man's idiosyncrasies when under the influence   *596* of drugs – eating without removing his hat, drinking fruit juice straight from a plate, wiping his lips at table with a torn envelope, short-sightedly counting coins, and belching after meals.

To compensate for these memories, which accord so ill with   *855* Leopold's fastidious tastes, there remain the insurance policy, the bank account, and the investments bequeathed by father to son. Bloom dwells for a moment on the frightful possibilities

of poverty which might have lain in store for him had these
safeguards not existed for him to fall back on in the event of
failure in business. Thus he sees himself reduced to street-
door hawking, then to begging, bankruptcy, oddjobbing, public
597   destitution, and the workhouse. He sees, too, that the indigni-
856   ties of such poverty could be escaped only by death or by
disappearance from the district, and of the two the latter seems
the more satisfactory way out. Indeed, Bloom reflects, there
would be much to be said for getting away completely. He
and Molly, so long familiar, are less tolerant of each other's
defects than they used to be. Molly is in the habit of spending
money independently. The two of them have now brought up
their family. In this mood Bloom is lured mentally by dream-
pictures of other regions to which he might escape – within
857   Ireland and abroad. The claims of Ceylon, Jerusalem, Greece,
598   and so on, are pressed in the stock phrases of the tourist travel
brochure.

Thus Bloom sets out in imagination, by night a star his guide,
by day a pillar of cloud, leaving behind him the unsolved mys-
858   tery of his disappearance. (Legends attribute further journeys
to Ulysses after his return to Ithaca.) Everyman and Noman,
Bloom would explore the farthest limits of space and time, eventually to make the great archetypal Return of the 'estranged
(680)   avenger' and 'sleeper awakened'.
599   Homelier and more mundane considerations bring him down
859   to earth. It is too late to set out. It is dangerous to leave the
beaten path. He is tired; and bed calls him with its warmth and
cosiness. As a last reflection before retiring, Bloom recapitulates
the events of the day in terms of Jewish ritual, thereby once
more illustrating the many-sidedness of Joyce's symbolism.
But for all the tidiness of this new synthesis, the untidiness of
860   our world remains, with its loose ends of problems unsolved
and mysteries that defy the understanding. Thus at this moment
600   the wooden table cracks noisily and Bloom is taxed by the recurring question, 'Who was M'Intosh?'

As well as its mysteries, the day has had its frustrations and
disappointments too; for Bloom failed to get a firm renewal of
the Keyes advertisement, to obtain some tea from Thomas
861   Kernan's, to find out whether the nude female statues in the
museum have holes in their behinds, and to get a ticket to see
Mrs Bandmann Palmer in *Leah*.

Entering the bedroom, Molly's face suddenly reminds him of her father's as he watched him once leaving by train and once again returning by train at Amiens Street Station. He sees   601
Molly's clothes lying on what was her father's trunk and her hat on the commode. He puts his own clothes on a chair, fully   862
undresses, puts on his nightshirt, and gets into bed. He is aware of the imprint left by the usurper, Boylan, and he has to remove some crumbs and flakes of potted meat remaining from the   863
afternoon encounter. But the god's-eye view asserts itself: each of Molly's admirers may have thought himself unique in that role, but each was but a unit in an infinite series. The suitors are listed, from Lieutenant Mulvey to Blazes Boylan, like a   602
procession of men doing homage to the Great Mother. For Molly is Eve and Everywoman. she is also the Mystical Bride, the Church, in whom is personified, perhaps too readily, Donne's daring image of the divine spouse –

'Who is most true, and pleasing to Thee, then
When she'is embraced and open to most men.'

Thus Bloom is able to see Boylan, not only as the vigorous, tough, go-ahead rival but also as one more in a series of impressionable victims of Molly's repetitive allure. He envies Boylan's   864
physical and sexual advantages, and he is jealous of the rhythm of mutual attraction between Boylan and Molly: but he suppresses hostile emotion because Boylan and he are friends,   603
because Boylan is young and impulsive, because of the psycho-   (684)
logical complications that arise between Jew and Gentile, and   865
because the coming musical tour will profit them both. Moreover, Bloom's equanimity is re-established by his characteristic reflections that the liaison is neither criminal nor greatly damaging, but natural to the human species and by its nature 'irreparable'.

Bloom therefore rejects all violent or drastic action against   866
Molly and Boylan, while reserving the possibility of some kind of pacific action in the future calculated to win legal damages, or to supersede Boylan by another, or to bring about a separation. Various common-sense considerations combine to   604
strengthen Bloom in passive acceptance; notably the fact that to achieve anything by way of action requires a disproportionate outlay of effort, the fact that it takes two to make an adultery and the woman is not in all respects the weaker, the fact that   867

the supply of virile adulterers is inexhaustible ('the continued
product of seminators by generation'), the fact that to win a
case is futile, and the fact that it is easier to do nothing.

In this mood of acceptance Bloom's pilgrimage ends. He
resigns himself contentedly to the human situation. He accepts
the world, the two hemispheres, eastern and western, here
represented by the two cheeks of Molly's behind, warm, ample,
full of promise and comfort. They express the silent, unchangeable animal reality underlying our changing moods and restless
cerebration. They are 'redolent of milk and honey' like the
Promised Land. They are the symbol of abundant Nature in all
her sureness and rest. Odysseus was so happy at returning to
his own homeland that 'he kissed the generous soil': Bloom,
stirred with desire, shifts himself and accepts the revelation
given by Molly's plump melon-sweet rump in silent contemplation. He kisses each cheek in turn, and the kisses represent
his decisive and final Yes.

605   Molly responds, sleepily at first, and wants to know what he
868   has been doing all day. Bloom recapitulates his adventures, omit-
ting the reference to such delicate matters as the letter from
Martha Clifford, the row in Barney Kiernan's, and the episode
with Gerty MacDowell. He lays most emphasis on his encounter
with Stephen Dedalus, 'professor and author'.

869   Amid their snatches of conversation, Molly is conscious of
the long gap of ten years since Bloom and she last enjoyed full
coition (27 November 1893), some five weeks before little Rudy's
(688)   birth. Meantime Bloom is conscious of the breakdown of full
606   mental intercourse between them during the nine months that
have elapsed since the onset of Milly's puberty. This event has
brought wife and daughter together in a combined campaign
of what can only be called 'nagging' at Bloom over his doings
generally.

870   Thus we leave husband and wife in this complex archetypal
relationship, he lying oddly with his head at the bed-foot, in
foetal posture, and both swinging forward through space by the
607   rotation of the earth. The wanderer has returned, the child–man
871   back to the Great Mother, Sinbad the Sailor home from sea.

Chapter 18

Penelope

To enter the mind of Molly Bloom after so much time spent in the minds of Stephen and Leopold is to plunge into a flowing river. If we have hitherto been exploring the waste land, here are the refreshing, life-giving waters that alone can renew it. The flow is the flow of Nature that runs thought Eliot's *Dry Salvages*, the river within us whose 'rhythm was present in the nursery bedroom', the untamed, intractable god, 'reminder of what men choose to forget'. But the waters are also the waters of Baptism, for Molly is the Mystical Body, born on the Rock, and before the end of the episode blood as well as water flows from her, reminding us of our double inheritance, as natural men born into the order of nature and as Christians saved by the redeeming Blood.

To enter the mind of Molly Bloom is also to be lifted bodily on to a great revolving sphere, swinging about its axis and about its centre with a sure system and symmetry yet to be fully explored. That the sphere has its macrocosmic significance in terms of the female body we know from Joyce himself, who noted that 'it begins and ends with the female word *Yes* . . . . It turns like the huge earthball slowly surely and evenly round and round spinning. Its four cardinal points being the female breasts, arse, womb and . . . expressed by the words *because*, *bottom . . . woman*, yes.' (*Letters*, 170.)

SENTENCE 1

Apparently Bloom has asked Molly to bring him his breakfast to bed in the morning and the request takes Molly back mentally to the City Arms days when Leopold played the sick man as

part of his campaign to get round Mrs Riordan – an unsuc-
cessful campaign as Mrs Riordan's will proved, for she left her
money for masses for her own soul. Molly is critical of her
872   husband's tendency to dramatize his ailments, and doubts
(690) whether he could remain for long in a hospital without putting
a nurse or a nun in the family way. Critical as she can be of
her husband, it is soon clear that she is even more critical
of other *women*. Mrs Riordan's disapproval of bathing-suits and
low-necks is hypocritical in her eyes, Miss Stack's visit to
Bloom's sick-bed an old maid's ruse to get inside the male
sanctum. (NB 'never see thy face again'. Molly's thoughts
are naturally larded with phrases from the songs she is always
practising.)

Molly senses that Bloom must have 'come' somewhere,
because he is hungry; but it can't be 'love' – also because he is
609   hungry. She suspects that he has been with a prostitute. In fact,
she has sensed the falsity of his story ('Hynes kept me . . . Who
did I meet? Ah yes, I met . . . do you remember . . . Menton').
873   This sort of thing has not taken Molly in. She remembers Menton
all right, with his 'boiled eyes' and his flirtatiousness; but she
is more interested in who Bloom has been with – some whore,
or some 'little bitch' – recalling how the day before yesterday,
she caught him covering a letter with blotting paper. (The letter
was to Martha Clifford of course, p. 88/*136*.)

And so to the memory of the last servant-girl the Blooms
kept in the house, when they were living in Ontario Terrace –
Mary Driscoll (whose story we heard at the nightmare trial of
Bloom in *Circe*, pp. 375–6/*586–7*; see also p. 334/*535*). Molly
was quick in sensing that Bloom was making up to her, and
874   got rid of her, ostensibly for stealing some oysters. From Mary
Driscoll Molly's thought drifts to the night Boylan and she
squeezed hands as they walked home by the Tolka, side by side
with Bloom, singing their duet ('*The young May moon, she's beam-
610   ing, love*'; see p. 137/*212*). She knows Leopold suspects what is
happening, but she is not going to give him 'the satisfaction'
of open proof. The idea of seducing a young boy asserts itself
875   momentarily, and then she is back to the recollection that full
coition with her husband is over and done with for good.

And why not? The sex act is exciting the first time, and afterwards there's nothing to it. But the feminine desire to be kissed
makes nonsense of this thought almost before it is framed. And

so to the embarrassments of having to confess one's sexual lapses to a priest, to specific memories of the confessional, especially of Fr Corrigan (who is listed among the suitors on p. 602/863), and then back to Boylan. Molly resents his rudeness in smacking her behind as he left, yet can't help wondering – Did she satisfy him? Is he dreaming of her now? Who gave him that flower in his buttonhole? We learn more of this afternoon's debauch with him, laced as it was with port and potted meat. She fell asleep, to be awakened by the clap of thunder which so distressed Stephen at the Maternity Hospital (p. 323/515). To Molly, as to Stephen, the thunder seemed like the divine voice announcing punishment. Unlike Stephen, Molly replied with a hurried 'Hail Mary'. What else but an act of contrition can avail in such circumstances, Molly asks, with a side glance at her husband's scepticism. Then to more lurid details of Boylan's crude performance this afternoon, with his enormous penis, his brash self-advertisement, his 'vicious' roughness; and to the disadvantages of being a female, constructed with a big hole in the middle, destined to give pleasure while paying the price in childbearing. Mina Purefoy's annual gestation is quoted in evidence.

876
(693)
611

877

Which raises the question, Why not have another child? Not by Boylan, in spite of the size of his organ. Bloom has more 'spunk' in him; witness the emission he seems to have had, presumably the result of his meeting with Mrs Breen (Josie Powell, his old flame) and his having to think today about Boylan and herself. Josie is the link that takes the mind back to a party at Georgina Simpson's before the Blooms married, memorable because Molly seems to have had to regard Josie as a rival at this stage, and because she and Bloom had a quarrel over Bloom's progressive politics. (The party was recalled by Bloom in the *Circe* episode, p. 363/574.) She admires her husband's odd stock of knowledge nevertheless. She wistfully reflects that she could easily make up the physical break between them. There are times when one kiss 'would send them all spinning'. An imaginary Josie–Leopold–Molly triangle is briefly toyed with, and then Molly recalls Bloom's tentativeness at the wooing stage, her own technique of leading him on, Josie's continued interest in Bloom, and her disappointment on Molly's engagement. Which brings Molly to some rather smug reflections on Josie's bad fortune in marrying a man who has become a lunatic, a man who would come to bed in his muddy boots.

878
612

879

613
880

Bloom has at least the advantages of cleanliness and respectability in his habits. Not that Molly can forget that Bloom got a pretty good bargain in the marriage market too: especially when compared with the dreadful wives some people find themselves tied to. Mrs Maybrick, husband-poisoner, is cited, and thus the (696)   first 'sentence' of this monologue ends.

SENTENCE 2

Molly recalls her first meeting with Boylan, who eyed her unmistakably when she and Bloom were having tea in the Dublin 881   Bakery Company tea-room – an occasion memorable also for Molly's urgent visit to the Ladies' lavatory where she left, and lost, her suede gloves. Boylan's special interest then, and since, in her feet, links this memory with that of certain occasions 614   when Bloom evinced a somewhat perverse interest in her feet. From Bloom, via a man in the Lucan dairy, thought moves to the tenor, Bartell d'Arcy, who raved about Molly's low notes, who kissed her on the choir-stairs after she sang 'Ave Maria' 882   (sic), then said wasn't it 'terrible' to do such a thing in such a place. Molly disagrees. It wasn't. She feels capable momentarily of taking Bloom along and pointing out the exact location of the act – just to shock him and show him that he doesn't know everything.

Bloom's behaviour in the courting days comes back to mind – his devotion to her gloves, to her drawers, indeed to any woman's drawers, his smartness as a young man, the way he 883   pestered her to lift her petticoat in the street by threatening to 615   kneel down publicly in the rain if she refused. For her part, meantime, Molly, responding with delicate touches of her hand, was wondering whether he was circumcized. Bloom wrote her a lover's letter containing words she had to pretend not to 884   understand. Soon he was writing daily, sometimes even twice a day, with delicious tact sending her eight poppies on her birthday (8 September), kissing her heart at Dolphin's Barn, though he never embraced as well as Lieutenant Gardner, a young man who keeps revisiting her mind.

From the excitement of Gardner's embrace, thought moves naturally to the hope that Boylan will come again at four next Monday as he has promised. So to people who call unexpectedly at an awkward time and find you unprepared, as Professor

Goodwin did once when she was boiling stew. Today Boylan's
advance present made her wonder whether it was a 'put off',
until his firm knock on the door reassured her. (She was still
dressing, we hear, when she threw the penny to the lame sailor.
See p. 185/*289*.) A week hence she and Boylan go to Belfast for
the start of their concert tour, and Bloom will conveniently be
obliged to go to Ennis for the anniversary of his father's death,   (699)
so she will be spared the embarrassment of sleeping with Bloom   616
in a hotel room, knowing that Boylan is sleeping with his ear   *885*
cocked in the next one. She will also be spared the kind of
embarrassment created by Bloom when their train came in once
as they had just had hot soup served in the refreshment room.
Bloom insisted on his rights, carried the soup to the train, and
wouldn't pay the waiter until the soup was finished, thereby
holding up the train and causing a disturbance. The guard
evidently locked them in their compartment for revenge, but
Bloom dealt with the lock by means of his knife. If he hadn't,
they would have been taken on to Cork.

Hopes of privacy with Boylan on the train to Belfast, and a
momentary thought that she could achieve useful notoriety by
eloping with him, lead to reflections on the 'little chits' like
Kathleen Kearney now holding the Dublin concert platform.
(See *Dubliners*: 'A mother'; though Kathleen is piano accompa-
nist there.) And so to the astonishing story that Bloom got Molly   *886*
her part in the performance of *Stabat Mater* (p. 67/*101*) by
making up to the Churchmen, pretending he was setting '*Lead
kindly Light*' to music, and thumping out his version (plagia-
rized from an old opera) on the piano. The Jesuits' discovery
that Bloom is a Freemason has now put him outside the circle.
Molly thinks that Bloom is also thick with some of the nationalists, but she has no use for politics or for war. The Boer War
and enteric fever killed her young admirer Lieutenant Gardner
(who seems to have been the subject of the remembered confession to Fr Corrigan – 'he touched me father ... where and I
said on the canal bank like a fool', p. 610/*875*).

From soldiers to the thought that Boylan's father made his   617
money by selling horses to the Government during the Boer
War (p. 262/*414*), that Boylan can buy her a nice present on a
shopping spree in Belfast, and that she had better leave off her   *887*
wedding ring for the tour, that she and Boylan might become
the objects of a public scandal, then that she doesn't care

anyway. Boylan has money: she might as well have some of it. But does he really like her? Memory of his sexual performance returns, of his anger this afternoon when he came back with a paper and news of the Gold Cup race. For Boylan betted on *Sceptre*, acting on Lenehan's tip. Molly recalls Lenehan's advances to her in the carriage after the Glencree dinner (see Lenehan's own account of this, p. 192/*300*), then Val Dillon's

888 interest in her and the dinner itself (remembered by Bloom, p. 127/*196*), the food, the silver, all contrasting with the irritating domestic economies which Bloom's limited income imposes on

618 them. She would like more clothes, and new corsets to control her figure. She needs to slim a bit: perhaps she could cut out

(701) stout for dinner. Larry O'Rourke (p. 47/*69*) supplied some poor stuff in the last delivery.

889 So back to Bloom's pathetic attempts to indulge his wife's tastes with the new garters and the face lotion bought out of his last monthly cheque. Molly would like to be able to spend freely; she laments the need to measure out every spoonful of tea carefully, the smallness of her wardrobe, the need to remake old hats, the passing of her youth. (And she underestimates her own age by a year here. She will be thirty-four, not thirty-three, in September. See p. 605/*869*.) She takes comfort in thoughts of women who have remained beautiful and attractive at a later age – Mrs Galbraith, Kitty O'Shea (whom she lived opposite in

890 Grantham Street), and Lily Langtry, Edward VII's mistress. From
619 legends about this royal romance thought moves to other matters that strain Molly's credulity, including Rabelais, the flagellation in *Ruby: the Pride of the Ring*, and statues of the Virgin with a disproportionately large baby Jesus.

The contrast between the lot of a Lily Langtry, with her wealthy lover, and her own lot produces reflections on Bloom's failure to get or keep a steady job. And thus, intermingled with a rigmarole about buying dresses and hats with the help or

891 hindrance of her husband, we hear how Molly paid a visit to Mr Cuffe after he sacked Leopold for his obstinate rudeness (pp. 258/*408* and 334/*535*). Cuffe was all stiff formality with her at first, but very soon she made an impression on him. Plainly he appreciated her chest, and she believes she could have got Bloom promoted to a managership under Cuffe if only

620 he hadn't been so pig-headed.

SENTENCE 3

Reflections on her own ample breasts introduce the third sen-   *892*
tence. Molly can appreciate their appeal for the opposite sex
when she considers the ugliness of the sexual apparatus that
a man carries before him. She remembers various occasions on
which male exhibitionists have tried to attract her attention by
display of their organs, and also an occasion when she was
driven by the cold to relieve herself in a gentlemen's urinal.   *893*
It's a wonder that men do not get their remarkable sexual equip-
ment damaged as they walk about. Female exposure is beautiful   *(705)*
by comparison of course. Indeed, after he lost his job at Hely's,
Bloom once suggested that she should capitalize her own charms
in nude photography. And so to Bloom's habit of answering her
questions wordily and unintelligibly, and to his failure over
such simple matters as cooking kidneys without burning the
pan. Then back to the breasts (one of them bitten by Boylan, it
appears), to the pain she had over feeding and weaning Milly,
and to Bloom's help in sucking off surplus milk. 'He wanted to   *621*
milk me into the tea,' she recalls. 'He's beyond everything. I
declare, somebody ought to put him in the budget. If I only could
remember the one half of the things and write a book out of it.
. . .' Restless desire moves in her again with the memory of
Boylan's virile performance this afternoon. She counts the days   *894*
impatiently till next Monday when he is due to come again.

SENTENCE 4

A train whistles, turning Molly's thoughts to the power of the
engine, the lot of train-drivers in their roasting cabs, today's
burning of old newspapers, the heat of the late afternoon, and
then to memories of Gibraltar, especially of a frock she received
there from a Mrs Stanhope who had left Gibraltar for Paris.   *895*
Hester Stanhope's present was accompanied by a letter (to her
'dearest Doggerina'). Phrases from it thread their way though   *622*
recollection of their happy times together. Hester and her (much
older) husband 'Wogger' took Molly to a bull-fight at La Linea.
The two girls became very intimate and Hester lent Molly books,   *896*
including one called *Molly Bawn*. But Molly doesn't care for
books featuring a 'Molly', and Bloom seems to have made a
mistake in trying to interest her in Defoe's *Moll Flanders*.

897   The last parting from the Stanhopes is recalled, when their
623   ship left the dock; but Mrs Stanhope ceased to write, and Molly
      suggests that she may have noted Wogger's interest in herself.
      Things became dull for Molly in Gibraltar after they left, and
(708) she recalls the dreary monotony of seeing the Rock's military
      routine and listening to her father, Major Tweedy, sharing
      campaign reminiscences with Captain Grove. There were no
898   longer any letters, except those Molly wrote to herself through
      sheer boredom. It was as dull as life is now, when there isn't
      even a young man living opposite for her to attract, as there
      was in Holles Street. The young man in question, a medical
      student, refused to take the hint when she put on gloves and
      hat at the window to show she was going out, and he proved
      equally insensitive when she met him later outside Westland
624   Row chapel. Students are not quick on the uptake, she decides.
      Nor were the country farmers she used to meet in the City
      Arms days.
         And so back to the general dullness of things, particularly
      the lack of mail other than business mail, and to a letter some
899   time ago from Floey Dillon, announcing her marriage to a rich
      architect. This memory leads to that of old Mr Dillon, of his
      death, the death of Nancy Blake, and the difficulty of writing
      letters of condolence to the bereaved. Molly hopes Boylan will
      write her a longer letter next time. She is bursting with grati-
      tude for his bringing new heart to her, new excitement to life.
      She pictures an exchange of romantic correspondence with him
      in which she would answer from her bed, but briefly, for she
      has no taste for the wordy formalities in which Atty Dillon
      indulged when writing to the man 'in the four courts' who jilted
      her.

SENTENCE 5

900   This sentence is largely Lieutenant Mulvey's. He is the first of
      the twenty-five suitors listed on pp. 601–2/863. (NB The fact
      that Mulvey and Molly never got as far as coition makes clear
      that we are *not* to regard the twenty-five suitors as lovers with
      whom Molly has had sexual intercourse. Rather they are men
      in whom Molly aroused 'the same concupiscence, inflammably
      transmitted . . .'. See p. 602/864.) Molly recalls how Mrs Rubio,
      the Tweedys' housekeeper in Gibraltar, brought a letter from

Mulvey into her bedroom with the morning coffee (thus beginning the series that was to lead up to this morning's receipt of
a letter from Boylan).

Mrs Rubio's Spanish patriotism, her religious and moral
strictness, together with her age and ugliness, are remembered
without pleasure. But Molly revels in recalling the first assig-   625
nation with Mulvey, the first kiss, and the fun she had   901
pretending to be engaged to a Spanish nobleman, Don Miguel
de la Flora ('Flower'!). Most touching of all, she recalls their
last meeting, the day before Mulvey sailed. They were together
in a fir-tree cove up on the rocks, Molly in a seductive white
blouse, her breasts just beginning to be plump, the sea and the
sky around them and the Malta boat passing in the distance.
Molly prudently limited the young lieutenant's exploration of   902
her own body, but she unbuttoned him and caught his sperm   626
in her handkerchief. They promised to give themselves to each   903
other when he came back, even if Molly should be married in   (712)
the meantime, and the permissive password was to be 'fir-tree
cove'.

But all this, though it seems like yesterday, was twenty
years ago. Mulvey may be dead, promoted admiral, or married
to someone who little guesses what Molly Bloom once did to
her beloved husband. Molly brings back a few more memories
of this day – bursting a biscuit bag and scattering the birds,
pretending to read out Hebrew inscriptions in the parish graveyard, wanting to fire Mulvey's pistol, and adjusting his naval
cap (significantly labelled 'HMS *Calypso*'). Thence to memories
of a bishop's sermon against the free ways of modern girls who
ride bicycles and wear bloomers. And so, via Bloomers, back
to Bloom, the advantage of being a 'Mrs Bloom' rather than a
Mrs Breen, Briggs, Ramsbottom, and so on, the possibility   627
(lightly touched on) of becoming Mrs Boylan, and the lovely   904
name of her mother, Lunita Laredo.

Mulvey comes back again. She recalls running with him, her
young breasts jumping as Milly's do now. Mulvey went to India
and talked of writing a book of Voyages. From a hilltop Molly
watched his boat sail away through Captain Rubio's spy-glass.
He lingered afterwards in her mind for weeks and she kept her
handkerchief under her pillow. He gave her a ring as a memento,
and she later gave it to Lieutenant Gardner who died in the
Boer War.

The train whistles again. *'Love's Old Sweet Song'* threads its
905 way through Molly's thoughts, its phrases mingling with those
mental rubrics which guide her during performance ('Breath.
Lips forward. Sad look. Eyes open') and with thoughts of rival
singers and their pretensions. Kathleen Kearney (cf. p. 616/*885*)
and her like may be well in with the nationalist political circles,
but they haven't had Molly's triumphs with the opposite sex –
'walking down the Alameda on an officer's arm'. She knew
more about men at fifteen than they will all know at fifty.
628 Witness the devotion of Lieutenant Gardner. Witness, too, the
passion of Boylan. So, with the powerful image of Boylan as
its impetus, *'Love's Old Sweet Song'* continues its course, performance rubrics again added ('Deep down ... Chin back'), and
possible encores are considered. *'My Lady's Bower'* is too long.
She decides on *'Winds that blow from the south'*, the song Bartell
d'Arcy gave her (p. 128/*197*) and the song which echoes
Stephen's poem written on the beach this morning (pp. 40/*60*
and 109/*168*). She also makes plans to change the lace on her
black dress so as to show off her bosom to better advantage.
906 And so, with mention of a little vaginal discomfort that presages
what is to come, and with the release of a little wind, Molly
(714) ends her sentence to the fading out of *'Love's Old Sweet Song'*
and to the train's whistle, now distant.

SENTENCE 6

We move through thoughts of digestion, pork-chop, and the
bedroom lamp, to memories of childhood, to worries whether
Bloom may be getting too much mixed up with drunken
medical students, coming in at 4 a.m. and ordering his break-
907 fast, then to pictures of the more usual morning routine,
Bloom himself bringing the tray up and the cat rubbing
629 around his legs. So to the subject of tomorrow's food – cod as
a change from meat – to a plan for a group picnic involving
908 Boylan, and to the fright and discomfort she once suffered when
Bloom took her out in a boat, pretending he was a skilled
oarsman. The subsequent allusion to Pisser Burke ('there was
no love lost between us'), who is numbered among the suitors
on p. 602/*863*, again makes clear that the list is not a list
of accepted lovers. Evidently it includes rejected aspirants to
Molly's friendship.

More memories of the boating episode lead the mind back momentarily to Gibraltar, but we return quickly to the loneliness of their 'big barracks' of a house at night when Bloom is out late, to Bloom's earlier plans to exploit the place as a musical *909* academy or a private hotel, thence to the variety of Bloom's *630* unfulfilled plans, including his promise of a romantic honeymoon in Italy. Instead of which Molly finds herself in Eccles Street all day, afraid that a begging tramp at the door will turn out to be a criminal like the one whose murder of an old woman has just been recorded in *Lloyds Weekly News*. Mingled reflections on being married to a murderer, on the discomforts of life imprisonment, on the need for corporal punishment, lead to a memory of Bloom going timidly downstairs one night, armed with a poker, when Molly thought she heard burglars in the kitchen.

And so to Milly. Molly manages to have it both ways. The *910* house is lonely without Milly – and why ever did Bloom send her away to learn photography? But Milly's ubiquity about the house was becoming a nuisance, and Bloom cunningly got her out of the way of the Boylan relationship. That Milly broke the hand of the statue before she left would seem to have some significance in the complex symbolism linking this article with Bloom's and Molly's joint interest in the young artist, Stephen. But the main sequence of thought here reveals Molly's jealousy *(717)* of her maturing daughter, touching Milly's friendship with her father, her new flirtatiousness, her taste for cigarettes, and her *631* claims to adult treatment when dressed for the theatre. (They *911* went to see Martin Harvey in *The Only Way*, an adaptation by Freeman Wills of Dickens's *A Tale of Two Cities*.)

Milly's fastidiousness about having her skirt crushed in the theatre sets off a brief train of memories in Molly of furtive sexual contacts made under the cover of the press in theatre queues. But thought returns quickly to Milly the rival, needing attention when ill with mumps, having her girlish love-affairs, and being overcome with admiration for Martin Harvey. Molly, too, is touched by Sydney Carton's self-sacrifice in the stage version of Dickens ('it must be real love if a man gives up his life for her that way'), wonders whether such devotion exists *912* nowadays, and then recollects that people who throw away their lives are 'usually a bit foolish in the head', like Bloom's father, lost after his wife's death.

Thought returns to the challenge of Milly, her red lips, her
632 way of answering back, the slaps on the face Molly gave her
for it once in a fit of temper. The next movement of thought
puts the blame for mother–daughter troubles on Bloom for
having them 'slaving here instead of getting in a woman long
ago' (but Molly herself got rid of the last one, p. 609/874).
Mrs Fleming, the daily help, is so aged that Molly has to follow
913 her around helping her. Now Molly turns back in mind to her
husband's foolish ways, in bringing Stephen Dedalus back with
him, climbing over the railings, taking him into the kitchen; and
then, after the kitchen has provoked further reflections on Mrs
Fleming's inadequacies, what with her paralysed husband,
Nature intervenes in the monologue. Molly's monthly period
comes on.

The first reaction is that the period won't be over in time for
Boylan's next visit, on Monday ('unless he likes it. Some men
do'). Reflections on the inconvenience of the female curse lead
914 to recall of the night in the box at the Gaiety when it suddenly
came on when Bloom was talking about Spinoza. (See pp.
633 223/349 and 233/367 for Bloom's memories of the same
(720) evening.) The flow increases. Molly gets out of bed, lamenting
woman's lot and the jingling of the bed quoits. (Apparently she
and Boylan were driven by sheer noise to use the floor this
afternoon.) A few personal thoughts about the possibility of
cutting off her pubic hair, and about Boylan's reaction to her
915 weight and her breath this afternoon pass lightly by, and soon
she is seated on the chamber pot with water as well as blood
flowing from her.

SENTENCE 7

It's only about three weeks since her last monthly. Is there something wrong? Ought she to visit the doctor? Molly is a little
cynical about the rich ladies who visit Dr Collins and the gilt
('gold maybe') mirrors he purchases out of their custom.
She recalls her last visit to Dr Collins to check on a feminine
ailment, when he overwhelmed her with technical talk of her
'vagina' and questions about 'omissions' (emissions, obviously).
634 This was before her marriage, when Bloom was writing romantic
916 letters ('my Precious one everything connected with your glorious Body everything underlined that comes from it is a thing

of beauty and a joy for ever') and exciting her to frequent
masturbation.

So to memories of her first meeting with Bloom while she
was living in Rehoboth Terrace, when they stared at each other
as if they had met before. The Doyles boosted Bloom with her
as a future MP. Bloom came the highbrow, pressing her to   917
sing a classy French song (from Meyerbeer's *The Huguenots*),
and trying to interest her in his religious and political theories.
But soon he found an excuse, when she was living in Brighton
Square, to run into her bedroom.

The discomforts of the chamber pot direct her thoughts to
her husband's kneeling posture when using it, and to his present
odd position in bed, head to foot, hand on nose. She gets up,
takes a sanitary towel from the press, fixes on her harness, then   635
climbs into bed again, lamenting to herself the lack of worldly   918
progress in sixteen years of married life with Bloom – years of
moving from house to house (Raymond Terrace, Ontario Terrace,   (722)
Lombard Street, Holles Street), on the run from landlords. Whenever things seem to be picking up, and Bloom has a regular
job, he puts his foot in it and gets the sack. Thus he lost his
successive jobs at Thom's, Hely's, Mr Cuffe's, and Drimmies'.
Molly is afraid that he may lose his job with the *Freeman* too,
either through getting mixed up with the Irish nationalists or
through his Freemasonry.

St George's Church bells strike two o'clock. Molly feels new
irritation with Bloom for coming in so late, and wonders what
he has been up to. His foetal posture reminds her of the illus-
tration in Aristotle's ('Aristrocrat's') 'Masterpiece'. His request
for breakfast in bed recalls other instances of demands he has   919
made on her, of his sulks and odd habits. Still wondering what
woman, if any, he has been with, she decides it can't have been   636
Josie Breen because 'he'd never have the courage with a married
woman' – if you can call poor Denis Breen a husband. Molly's
thoughts travel quickly here, touching on her husband's prompt-
ness to make eyes at the opposite sex, on the Dignam funeral
as recorded in the evening paper, on the mourners named there,
on Tom Kernan (see *Dubliners*: 'Grace', for the story of how he   920
'bit his tongue off falling down the Men's WC drunk'), on Fanny
M'Coy's pretensions as a singer (see Bloom on this, p. 62/92),
on Jack Power and his barmaid (p. 77/116), on her own determination to keep Bloom out of the clutches of these thriftless

roisterers, on the unfortunate position of the Dignam widow and orphans, and on Paddy Dignam.

Thus we come once again to the Glencree Dinner, which Paddy Dignam attended (pp. 127/*196* and 617/*887*), to Ben Dollard and the night he borrowed the overtight evening suit from her (recalled by Bloom in the Ormond, p. 222/*348*), to
921 Simon Dedalus duetting and 'flirtyfying' with her at Freddy Mayers' private opera, to Bartell d'Arcy, back again to Simon
637 Dedalus, and thence to his son Stephen, around whom a more sustained sequence of thought develops.

Bloom has given Stephen the exalted status of author and university professor-to-be, and has suggested that she should have Italian lessons from him. Molly knows, too, that Bloom has displayed her photograph to Stephen. She recalls seeing Stephen and his parents driving to the station when she was in mourning for little Rudy 'eleven years ago' (ten actually; Rudy would be ten now, had he lived, not eleven until 29 December; see p. 605/*869*). Then she remembers the earlier meeting at Matt Dillon's house (already recalled by Bloom, pp. 344/*552*–3 and 556/*795*; see also pp. 87/*134* and 94/*146*). A touch of fatalism is added in Molly's recollection that reading the cards this morning brought promise of a 'young stranger'
922 and a 'rise in society', and that a dream last night had 'something about poetry in it'. Rapidly she calculates Stephen's present age, decides that she is not too old for him, that he
(725) can't be 'stuck up' since he came into the kitchen for cocoa with Bloom, that as a poet needing a female subject to write about he is unlikely to find anyone more suitable for the role than herself.

638 The imagined Stephen appeals largely to that side of her
923 which Boylan has trampled on and which Bloom has left unsatisfied. He offers intelligence combined with sensitivity, glamour, and youth; satisfaction to the desires stirred by the little statue of the male nude, the hunger for a sexual partner who is clean, boyish – and as *ideal* as Bloom's Gerty MacDowell. But Molly is too fully a woman to leave it at that. A moment later she sees herself receiving the poet's homage, and in turn drenching him with her irresistible sexuality, till their relationship is a public scandal. Thence back to the question, What about Boylan? On which the seventh sentence ends.

SENTENCE 8

By comparison with the 'ideal' Stephen, Boylan is crude. He slapped her familiarly on the bottom for not calling him Hugh. (We recall the breeders in the cattle market more fittingly 'slapping a palm on a ripemeated hindquarter', p. 48/71, and Ned Lambert slapping 'a piebald haunch', p. 190/297.) He undressed 924
before her without ceremony. He has nothing to talk about. Of course, he's right in a way to make no fuss about coition. And, anyway, his haste could be accounted for by her own irresistible plumpness. Sensitive on this point, she can almost envy a man's pleasure in a woman's body, and consequently wonders what it is like to be the possessor of a penis. She recalls a riddle she heard in the streets about Uncle John putting his long thing into Aunt Mary's hairy thing – and it turned out to be a handle 639
and a sweeping brush. Next she envies the freedom of men to choose their women compared with the jealous possessiveness with which women are watched. She sees herself unappreciated by Bloom, who never embraces her except in his sleep and then 925
at the wrong end, who kisses her most expressionless part, her bottom.

So back to Bloom's oddities, to her own hungry desire to be embraced and loved, to her wayward dreams of picking up strange men in the streets – a sailor, or a gipsy, or even a murderer. She has seen men pick up girls in the same casual 926
way; and then they go home to their wives. She becomes conscious of Bloom's 'big carcass' and his noisy breathing, and recalls what she read on the cards this morning about a meeting 640
with a dark man in some perplexity. There he is, rolled up like a mummy, insensitive to her, and she is supposed to rush around getting his breakfast. Men treat you like dirt, and it would be better for the world to be governed by women. Men kill and (728)
gamble and know nothing of what women go through, yet they are all dependent on their mothers.

Thus thought moves to Stephen, who seems to be running wild, away from home. Those who have a fine son like Stephen don't appreciate him, while she and Bloom have failed to get and keep a son. She remembers the occasion of little Rudy's conception, then the woolly jacket she knitted for his 927
burial, but pushes off the gloom and returns to Stephen and his nocturnal wanderings. Thought moves quickly again; to the

mutual friendliness of men, the mutual bitchiness of women, the wish that Stephen could have stayed overnight, his queer surname, the elaborate names of streets and people in Gibraltar.
641 Mentally Molly tries out her Spanish accent again and pictures
928 herself instructing Stephen in Spanish while he instructs her in Italian. So to another wayward dream in which she plays woman and wife to Stephen. Stephen could stay in the house, read in bed in the mornings while Bloom makes breakfast for the two of them. The appropriate new garments for this *ménage à trois* are touched on – red slippers, semi-transparent morning gown or peach-blossom dressing-jacket.

Next moment Molly is planning to give Bloom one more chance to re-establish full sexual relations. She will get up early,
929 fetch something fresh from the market, take up Bloom's breakfast, then dress herself in front of him in her best new underwear. And if that doesn't work she'll let him know what a cuckold he is, make him witness and assistant at his further cuckolding. All this expresses her repression and resentment at Bloom's sexual neglect of her. 'It's all his own fault.' If all her
642 efforts stir Bloom only to his perverse desire to kiss her bottom, then he shall have that sort of satisfaction in full measure and she'll get some money out of him in exchange. (She flatters
930 herself that she has never soaked her husband by signing his cheques.)

The further build-up of this prospect is halted: Molly remembers her period. Another quick picture of satisfying Bloom in an off-hand way, then leaving him to wonder what she is up to, is broken by a clock striking the quarter hour, and there is a swift sequence of thought – people getting up in China, nuns ringing the morning angelus, attempt to dose off, the flowers on the wallpaper, the stars on the Lombard Street wallpaper, the apron Bloom gave her in the Lombard Street days. Then the plan to go out early tomorrow to order flowers introduces
(731) a new series of plans in preparation for a possible visit by
931 Stephen: these include cleaning the piano keys, wearing a white rose, buying cakes at Lipton's, and perhaps getting a nice plant for the middle of the table as being cheaper than flowers.

But she loves flowers, would like to have the 'whole place swimming in roses', for there's nothing like nature, and a
643 *Benedicite* in its praise sets the tone for the book's conclusion. For the sea, fields, crops, cattle, rivers, lakes, flowers, all speak

of a God, and Molly has no time for the sceptics who deny
this, and then cry out for a priest on their deathbeds. Of course,
there is a great mystery — 'Who was the first person in
the universe ... they don't know neither do I so there you are
...'. But the sun rises daily and you can't stop it.

And from this image memory moves to the day of her first
full self-giving to Bloom when they lay together on Howth Hill
(pp. 144/224 and 308/491, *et passim*) among the rhododendrons
and he told her the sun shone for her. They kissed, and he
called her a flower of the mountain. That was what won her;
Bloom knew how a woman thought and what she wanted to   *932*
hear. So she responded by giving him all the pleasure she could,
leading him on till he asked her to say the final Yes.

At first she wouldn't reply. She stared out to sea, remembering all the things in her past which Bloom knew nothing of
— Mulvey, Stanhope, the Gibraltar days and nights with all their
colour and richness, when she was indeed a flower of the mountain. But then she decided that it might as well be Bloom as   *933*
any other. She put her arms round him and pulled him down   644
on her breasts, asking him with her eyes to ask her again, and
this time saying Yes.

Index